TOEIC® L&R TEST
990点獲得
最強 Part 7 模試

MediaBeacon
メディアビーコン

無料音声
ダウンロード付

ベレ出版

はじめに

本書はTOEIC L&R TESTで990点獲得を目指す方のためのPart 7対策書です。もしあなたが、「小手先のテクニックだけでラクして990点をとろう」とお考えなら、本書を使って勉強する必要はないかもしれません。

しかし、「990点獲得を目指すためには労力を惜しまない」とお考えでしたら、きっと本書がお役に立てると思います。

TOEIC L&R TESTが現在の新形式に変更されて以降、Part 7の問題は難化傾向にあります。新形式以前ではテスト本番で15分以上時間が余っていた990点獲得者でも、新形式では5分程度しか見直す時間がとれないということが起きています。つまり、小手先のテクニックではなく、限られた時間で英文をしっかりと読んで理解する、本物の力が求められるようになったということです。

我々は職業柄、ほぼ毎日TOEICの問題を作成し、リスニング教材の音声を聴き、TOEIC関連の英文・問題を読んでいます。また、毎回公開テストを受験して、テスト傾向の分析・研究を行っております。同時に900点超えや990点を目指す方々の指導もさせていただいております。これらの経験を通じて、990点を獲得するには、質の高い問題を「繰り返し」解いて、「大量に読む」ことが欠かせないという結論にいたりました。

本書は我々の経験を踏まえ、990点を狙う方に必要なトレーニングを効果的に積めるよう作成しました。本書を徹底的に使い倒して、あなたの目標スコア実現の一助となれば、これほど嬉しいことはありません。

心から応援しています。
あなたの人生の新たな一歩を踏み出す力となれますように。

メディアビーコン

TEST 1　解答・解説　正解一覧　13

TEST 2　解答・解説　正解一覧　61

本書の構成と使い方

本書の構成

［本冊］
- Part 7模試（TEST 1 / TEST 2 / TEST 3 / TEST 4）の解答・解説
- 正解一覧
- 学習記録
- Part 7 攻略アドバイス
- 問題のタイプ分けとそれぞれの解き方
- マークシート

［別冊］
- Part 7模試（TEST 1 / TEST 2 / TEST 3 / TEST 4）の問題

無料音声ダウンロードについて

　本書に掲載されている模試の本文の音声をご利用いただけます。音声は、音声スピードに合わせて、本文の内容を理解しながら読む速読トレーニングに使用してください。メールアドレスや表などは読み上げず、速読に必要な部分のみの音声を収録しました。音声がない部分は、一字一句読み込むのではなく、正答の根拠となる箇所だけにさっと目を通し、解答に必要な情報のみピックアップするようにしてください。

audiobook.jpとベレ出版ホームページから音声を無料でダウンロードできます。ダウンロード方法についてはベレ出版ホームページ内の『TOEIC® L&R TEST990点獲得　最強Part 7模試』のページ（https://www.beret.co.jp/books/detail/736）に解説してあります。

audiobook.jp ／ベレ出版音声DL　　共通ダウンロードコード　BFE37fuL

本書の使い方

　本書では、Part 7の4模試分を2か月間で各5回解くように設計しています。なぜ同じ問題を何度も解くのか？　それは、Part 7には同じような「型」の文書が繰り返し出題されるため、その型を体にしみこませるためには、同じ問題を繰り返し解くことが最適だと考えているからです。

　模試は実際のテストより若干難しい問題を掲載しています。特に高得点者が間違いやすい問題や、読み取りにくい文構造の文章を集めているので、繰り返し解いて難易度の高い問題にも対応できる読解力を身につけてください。

　下記に、各TESTを1回目から5回目まで繰り返し解く際の、模試の取り組み方をまとめました。

1/5回目

①別冊の「学習の進め方」に記載された制限時間を確認して問題を解く

②答えを見ずに、制限時間なしで問題をもう一度解きなおす

③答え合わせ

④語注の単語を確認。意味を何となくではなく、正確に理解しているか確認する

⑤文構造を意識しながら精読→通読

⑥音声のスピードに合わせながら、本文を読む

　音声のスピードに合わせて読んでも内容が頭に入ってくるまで続ける

⑦本文を見て、音声を聞きながら音読する（オーバーラッピング）

2/5回目

①別冊の「学習の進め方」に記載された制限時間を確認して問題を解く

②答えを見ずに、制限時間なしで問題をもう一度解きなおす

③答え合わせ（1/5回目との差を比較）

④単語を確認。意味を何となくではなく、正確に理解しているか確認する

⑤音声のスピードに合わせながら、本文を読む

　音声のスピードに合わせて読んでも、頭に入ってくるまで続ける

⑥本文を見て、音声を聞きながら音読する（オーバーラッピング）

3/5〜5/5回目以降

①別冊の「学習の進め方」に記載された制限時間を確認して問題を解く

②答え合わせ

③苦手な問題を中心に単語の再確認

④問題の内容を全部覚えてしまった人は、設問の先読みをせず本文だけを読んで、

　どこが正答の根拠になっているか把握する

990点獲得のための学習記録

本書は、2か月で4模試分のPart 7の問題を5回解くように、Day 1 〜Day60までのスケジュールを作成しています。
間違えた問題には×、勘で解いて正解してしまった問題には△を記入してください。
問題解答後に、毎回結果を記録しておきましょう。

TEST 1		1回目	2回目	3回目	4回目	5回目
	147					
	148					
	149					
	150					
	151					
	152					
	153					
	154					
	155					
	156					
	157					
	158					
	159					
	160					
	161					
	162					
	163					
	164					
	165					
	166					
	167					
	168					
	169					
	170					
	171					
	172					
	173					
	174					
	175					
	176					
	177					
	178					
	179					
	180					
	181					
	182					
	183					
	184					
	185					
	186					
	187					
	188					
	189					
	190					
	191					
	192					
	193					
	194					
	195					
	196					
	197					
	198					
	199					
	200					

TEST 2		1回目	2回目	3回目	4回目	5回目
	147					
	148					
	149					
	150					
	151					
	152					
	153					
	154					
	155					
	156					
	157					
	158					
	159					
	160					
	161					
	162					
	163					
	164					
	165					
	166					
	167					
	168					
	169					
	170					
	171					
	172					
	173					
	174					
	175					
	176					
	177					
	178					
	179					
	180					
	181					
	182					
	183					
	184					
	185					
	186					
	187					
	188					
	189					
	190					
	191					
	192					
	193					
	194					
	195					
	196					
	197					
	198					
	199					
	200					

TEST 3		1回目	2回目	3回目	4回目	5回目
	147					
	148					
	149					
	150					
	151					
	152					
	153					
	154					
	155					
	156					
	157					
	158					
	159					
	160					
	161					
	162					
	163					
	164					
	165					
	166					
	167					
	168					
	169					
	170					
	171					
	172					
	173					
	174					
	175					
	176					
	177					
	178					
	179					
	180					
	181					
	182					
	183					
	184					
	185					
	186					
	187					
	188					
	189					
	190					
	191					
	192					
	193					
	194					
	195					
	196					
	197					
	198					
	199					
	200					

TEST 4		1回目	2回目	3回目	4回目	5回目
	147					
	148					
	149					
	150					
	151					
	152					
	153					
	154					
	155					
	156					
	157					
	158					
	159					
	160					
	161					
	162					
	163					
	164					
	165					
	166					
	167					
	168					
	169					
	170					
	171					
	172					
	173					
	174					
	175					
	176					
	177					
	178					
	179					
	180					
	181					
	182					
	183					
	184					
	185					
	186					
	187					
	188					
	189					
	190					
	191					
	192					
	193					
	194					
	195					
	196					
	197					
	198					
	199					
	200					

990点獲得のための
Part 7攻略アドバイス

990点獲得のための特別な学習方法はありません。
990点獲得のためには、全力で一切妥協をせず、ストイックに勉強し続けることが必要です。
900点を突破しても、点数が上がったり下がったりを繰り返してなかなか目標とする結果が得られないことも多いと思います。
そんな時でもあきらめずに、目標達成まで努力し続けられる人が990点を獲得することができます。
ここでは皆さんに990点獲得のための5つのアドバイスをいたします。
本書はPart 7の問題を集めた模試ですが、全パートに共通するアドバイスです。

1. 多読多聴を地道に毎日続ける

　英語は、スポーツです。毎日トレーニングすれば、徐々にスキルが上がっていきますが、やらなくなってしまった途端すぐに感覚を忘れてしまいます。つまり、英語の音声を1日でも聞かなければリスニング力はすぐ落ちてしまいますし、毎日英文を読まなければ、読解力は簡単に衰えてしまいます。

　どんなに忙しい時でも、少しで良いので毎日「英語を聞く時間」、「英文を読む時間」を作ってください。毎週日曜日に2時間リスニングをするより、毎日10分リスニングをするほうが力になります！

　また、TOEIC L&R TESTより難しい長文や音声に挑戦することも有効です。本番より難しい文章と音源を毎日練習することで、本番のテストが簡単に感じられます。本書では難易度の高い文章を集めているので、何度も読み返して多読のトレーニングに使用してみてください。

2. 語彙力を上げる

　990点を目指す方の多くは、すでに高い語彙力をお持ちの方も多いでしょう。ただし、何となく意味が分かる単語をそのまま放置していないでしょうか。リスニングや長文の問題を進める時、意味を曖昧に理解している単語が登場しても前後の文脈を見れば文章の内容を理解することができると思います。その状態でも正答を導くことができる問題もありますが、990点獲得を目指すのであればすべての単語の意味を明確に理解する必要があります。

　問題を解いた後に解説を読んで満足するのではなく、復習として単語の意味を理解しているか、曖昧になっているところがないかを確認しましょう。単語の意味を意識して復習すると、単語の意味を曖昧に理解しているために落としている問題が意外と多いことに気づく方も多いと思います。

3．文法をしっかり理解する

　文法も語彙力と同様で曖昧な文法項目を徹底的につぶしてください。Part 5は、お持ちの問題集の正答の根拠がすべて説明できるように、正解した問題もしっかり復習してください。Part 7では、1文1文の構造や、文中の表現、単語の発音、正答の根拠、選択肢と本文の言い換えを確認する「精読」を行ってください。問題を解く際に、さっと読んでしまったものでも、改めて読むと文構造が難しくしっかり理解していなかった文が見つかると思います。

4．時間を常に意識して問題を解く

　TOEIC L&R TESTにおいて、タイムマネージメントはもっとも重要なスキルの1つです。普段行うトレーニングの際にも、しっかり時間を計って問題を解く癖をつけましょう。制限時間を守って各パートをトレーニングしていくことで、それぞれの問題を解くリズムが自分の中でできてくるはずです。時間の感覚を身につけることで本番でもトレーニング時と同じように問題を解くことができます。リーディングの時間配分の目安は、Part 5=1問20秒、Part 6=1問30秒、Part 7=1問1分です。

　また、時間配分が苦手な方が模試に挑戦する際は、本番と同じように日曜日の13時から模試を2時間で解いてください。人が体感する時間は日や状況によって左右されます。模試を解く際にはできるだけ本番の状況に似せたほうが良い練習になります。ですから本番通り12時半に着席し、そこから30分間はスマホを使用しないなど、空白の時間を作ってください。音量の調節、本人確認、冊子の配布などがあるこの30分の間にリラックスしつつ、13時に向けて集中力を上げていく練習をしてみてください。

5．TOEIC L&R TESTを知ること

　各パートの問題のタイプ、出題傾向を知り、作問者がどういう意図で各問題を出しているかを分析すると、各問題の正答のパターンが見えてきます。繰り返し模試や参考書を解くことで、よく一緒に使われる単語の組み合わせやストーリー展開も見えてくるので、初見の問題でもある程度展開を予想することができます。

　本書では、Part 7の問題を6タイプに分けて解説しています。各タイプの問題の解き方を意識して問題を解いてみてください。TOEIC L&R TESTの傾向が必ずわかるはずです。

Part 7 問題のタイプ分けと
それぞれの解き方

本書では、Part 7の問題を以下の6つのタイプに分けています。タイプごとに解き方が異なるので、それぞれの対策を知っていれば自信をもって解答することができます。設問を先に読んで、即座にどのタイプの問題かを判断して解答しましょう。

① 同義語問題

文中の単語・イディオムと同じ意味の単語を選ぶ問題。問題となる単語・イディオムは「多義語」であるため、文中でどのように使われているのかを見極めて意味を選ぶ必要があります。

② NOT問題

本文に当てはまらないものを、選択肢から選ぶ問題。選択肢4つのうち3つは本文の内容と等しいので、NOT問題の場合は先に選択肢をすべて読んでから本文を読むと正答を見つけやすくなります。

③ 文挿入問題

特定の文を、本文中の正しい場所に入れる問題。代名詞や挿入文の固有名詞などからヒントを得て解く問題です。この問題がある大問の場合、挿入文➡1問目の設問➡本文の順で問題を読みましょう。挿入文をどこに入れるかは、本文をすべて読み、他の設問を終えてから考えます。

④ 意図問題

チャットやテキストメッセージチェーンで必ず登場する問題。ピックアップされている英文の前後の文脈をしっかり理解し、発言者の意図を理解して答える必要があります。

⑤ 設問に着目する問題

本文と設問を読めば、選択肢を見なくても正答がわかる問題。例えば、Who most likely is Mr. Guputa? という質問に対して本文を読めばGuputaさんの職業は選択肢がなくても答えられます。この問題は正解の根拠が簡単に見つかるので、根拠を見つけたらすぐに解答しましょう。

⑥ 選択肢に着目する問題

本文と設問を読んでも正答を選ぶことができない問題。「選択肢に着目する問題」の中にも、正答の根拠の見つけ方で以下の2種類に分けることができます。
  1. purpose など目的を問う設問で、ピンポイントに正答の根拠があるか、
     本文全体を読んで目的を推測する必要がある問題。
  2. imply, suggestなどを使う設問で、本文中に根拠が明確に存在しておらず、
     ヒントの周りの文からある程度予測をして正答を導き出す問題。
2は、本文を読んだだけでは根拠がどこにあるか明確にわからないので段落を1つ読んで、選択肢を確認、根拠が見つかればそこで解答し、見つからなければ次の段落を読むという進め方をします。

TEST 1

解答&解説

Questions 147-148 refer to the following e-mail.

E-Mail Message

To: Bob McCann <bmccann@cityld.com>
From: Philippa Hardgrave <phardgrave@springfieldsoftware.com>
Subject: Delivery times
Date: June 18

Dear Mr. McCann,

I am the manager of Springfield Software in Office 16 at Holyfield Tower in Upper Stanton. I am writing with regard to the delivery of food and drinks your company prepares every day. My employees enjoy the meals you provide and it makes life very convenient for them. I am also happy to have your staff visit my employees at their desks as they tend to take shorter lunches and return to work sooner. Nevertheless, the time of your arrival is starting to become a problem. The morning hours are when we have the highest volume of work and it is important that staff focus on their tasks. Recently, lunch deliveries have been occurring as early as 10:30 A.M. and it is becoming a distraction.

I would appreciate it if you could rearrange your route so that you arrive at Springfield after 12:00 in the future.

Sincerely,

Philippa Hardgrave

問題 **147-148** は次の E メールに関するものです。

宛先：Bob McCann <bmccann@cityld.com>

送信者：Philippa Hardgrave <phardgrave@springfieldsoftware.com>

件名：配達時間

日付：6 月 18 日

McCann 様

私は Upper Stanton にある Holyfield タワー内、オフィス 16 にある Springfield ソフトウェア社のマネージャーをしております。あなたの会社が毎日作る飲食物の配達に関してメールを書いております。当社の従業員は貴社が提供する食事を楽しんでおり、それは彼らの生活をとても便利にしています。当社の従業員は短めの昼食を取り、すぐに仕事に戻る傾向があるので、私は貴社のスタッフが彼らのデスクまで来てくださっていることにも満足しております。しかしながら、あなた方の到着時間が問題になり始めています。午前中は当社の業務量が最も多い時間なので、従業員は業務に集中することが重要です。最近は、昼食の配達が午前 10 時 30 分と早くなっていて、それが集中をそぐものになってきています。

これからは経路を再調整して Springfield に 12 時以降に到着していただけると助かります。

よろしくお願いいたします。

Philippa Hardgrave

147 Who most likely is Mr. McCann?

(A) The owner of a food company

(B) A convenience store manager

(C) A research assistant

(D) A local politician

McCann さんとは誰だと考えられますか。

(A) 食品会社のオーナー

(B) コンビニの店長

(C) 研究助手

(D) 地元の政治家

正解 **A**　設問に着目する問題

I am writing with regard to the delivery of food and drinks your company prepares every day. とあり、Eメールの受信者である **McCann** さんは調理をしてそれを配達する会社の人間と分かる。　正解は (A) の食品会社のオーナーが最も適切。

☐
☐
☐

148 What is the purpose of the e-mail?

(A) To ask for improvements to a product

(B) To explain the reason for a delay

(C) To offer to help with a project

(D) To ask for later delivery

Eメールの目的は何ですか。

(A) 製品の改良を依頼すること。

(B) 遅延の理由を説明すること。

(C) プロジェクトの支援を申し出ること。

(D) より後の配達を求めること。

正解 **D**　設問に着目する問題

Eメールの目的が何かということが問われている。Eメールや、手紙などの文書の目的は、冒頭付近に書かれていることが多いが、このEメールでは、冒頭では日頃の感謝を述べ、最後に目的を述べている。ランチの配達が従業員の仕事への集中をそいでいるという状況を述べた後、I would appreciate it if you could rearrange your route so that you arrive at Springfield after 12:00 in the future. と依頼している。正解は (D)。

☐
☐
☐

☐　improvement　　　　　　　　改善、改良

語彙チェック

☐　with regard to 〜　　　　　〜に関して

☐　prepare　　　　　　　　　　（食事）を作る

☐　convenient　　　　　　　　　便利な

☐　tend to *do*　　　　　　　　　〜する傾向がある

☐　nevertheless　　　　　　　　しかしながら

☐　distraction　　　　　　　　　気を散らすもの

Questions 149-150 refer to the following text-message chain.

HARRY BUTLER (7:50 P.M.)
I'm still in New York now. My flight was canceled due to the inclement weather.

TINA KAPOOR (7:51 P.M.)
Don't you have a meeting tomorrow with Dean Pharmaceutical?

HARRY BUTLER (7:53 P.M.)
Yes, at 3 P.M. I'm trying to book the earliest flight for tomorrow, but I might not be able to make it.

TINA KAPOOR (7:55 P.M.)
It might work. There should be an early morning flight which can bring you here on time.

HARRY BUTLER (8:05 P.M.)
You're right. They got me a seat for tomorrow morning. I'll be arriving at the office around noon.

TINA KAPOOR (8:07 P.M.)
Great. You can have some time to prepare for the meeting then.

問題 **149-150** は次のテキストメッセージのやりとりに関するものです。

HARRY BUTLER　（午後 7 時 50 分）
今まだニューヨークにいるよ。僕のフライトが悪天候のためキャンセルになったんだ。

TINA KAPOOR　（午後 7 時 51 分）
Dean 製薬会社と明日、会議があるんじゃなかった？

HARRY BUTLER　（午後 7 時 53 分）
うん、午後 3 時に。明日の一番早い時間のフライトを予約しようとしているけど、もしかしたら間に合わないかもしれない。

TINA KAPOOR　（午後 7 時 55 分）
うまくいくかもしれないわよ。時間通りにこちらに着くことができる早朝のフライトがあるはずだわ。

HARRY BUTLER　（午後 8 時 05 分）
君の言うとおりだった。明日の朝の席を用意してもらった。オフィスに正午ぐらいに着ける。

TINA KAPOOR　（午後 8 時 07 分）
よかった。それなら、いくらか会議のために準備をする時間もあるわ。

149 What problem does Mr. Butler mention?

(A) Some seats were overbooked.

(B) A flight was called off.

(C) A colleague will arrive late.

(D) Some furniture has been damaged.

Butler さんは何の問題について述べていますか。

(A) 一部の席が定員以上の予約をされた。

(B) フライトがキャンセルされた。

(C) 同僚が遅れて到着する。

(D) 一部の家具が破損している。

正解 B

設問に着目する問題

7 時 50 分に Butler さんは、My flight was canceled due to the inclement weather. 「僕のフライトが悪天候のためキャンセルになったんだ」と発言している。よって (B) が正解。

☐ colleague 　　　　　　　　　同僚

150 At 7:55 P.M. why does Ms. Kapoor write, "It might work"?

(A) She believes that Mr. Butler can get a job.

(B) She likes the painting of Mr. Butler.

(C) She thinks Mr. Butler can arrive on time.

(D) She wants Mr. Butler to take over her duties.

午後 7 時 55 分に Kapoor さんはなぜ "It might work" と書いていますか。

(A) Butler さんが職を得ることができると信じているから。

(B) Butler さんの絵画が好きだから。

(C) Butler さんが時間通りに到着すると思っているから。

(D) Butler さんに彼女の職務を引き継いでほしいから。

正解 C

意図問題

Butler さんは Yes, at 3 P.M. I'm trying to book the earliest flight for tomorrow, but I might not be able to make it. と翌日の会議の時間に間に合うかどうかを心配している。それに対する応答が It might work. であるが、work は「機能する、うまくいく」という意味があるので、これは、明日のフライトでも大丈夫だということを伝えていると考えられる。続いての発言 There should be an early morning flight which can bring you here on time. も明日早朝のフライトなら時間は大丈夫だという根拠を伝えているので、正解は (C)。

☐ take over 〜 　　　　　　　〜を引き継ぐ

語彙チェック

☐ inclement weather 　　　　悪天候

☐ pharmaceutical company 　製薬会社

Questions 151-152 refer to the following notice.

Branson Soap Factory Tours

On May 19, the Goldberg Cultural Revival Society is hosting a tour of the Branson Soap Factory. The soap factory, which was once among the most famous in the country, has been vacant for more than 50 years. It is one of many local businesses that failed when the temptation of cheap imported goods attracted customers away. The Goldberg Cultural Revival Society is looking to purchase the building and restart the soap factory. The money raised from the tour will be used to fund our various cultural awareness projects and attract new members.

People or businesses interested in becoming a partner in the revived Branson Soap Company can contact our corporate operations manager at 555-8392.

問題 **151-152** は次のお知らせに関するものです。

Branson ソープ工場見学ツアー

5 月 19 日に、Goldberg 文化復興協会は Branson ソープ工場のツアーを開催します。このソープ工場は、かつては国内で最も有名な工場の 1 つでしたが、50 年以上使用されていません。安価な輸入品の誘惑に顧客が引き寄せられてしまったときに衰退した多くの地域企業の 1 つです。Goldberg 文化復興協会はこの建物を買い取ってソープ工場を再開するつもりです。ツアーで集められた資金は当協会の多様な文化理解プロジェクトへの資金提供や、新会員の勧誘に使われます。

復活後の Branson ソープ社のパートナーになることに関心がおありの方や企業は、当協会の企業運営マネージャー宛てに 555-8392 までご連絡ください。

151 What is a purpose of the event?

(A) To display the factory for investors

(B) To attract employees to a local business

(C) To raise money for an organization

(D) To teach people traditional production methods

イベントの目的は何ですか。

(A) 投資家に工場を見せること。

(B) 従業員を地域企業に引き付けること。

(C) 組織のためにお金を集めること。

(D) 人々に伝統的な生産方法を教えること。

正解 C

設問に着目する問題

文化復興協会が工場見学ツアーを行うお知らせである。The money raised from the tour will be used to fund our various cultural awareness projects「ツアーで集められた資金は当協会の多様な文化理解プロジェクトへの資金提供に使われる」とある。協会のために資金を集めることが 1 つの目的と考えられるので、(C) が正解。the Goldberg Cultural Revival Society を organization と抽象的に言い換えている。organization「組織」。

☐ display　　　　　　　　　　～を展示する、掲示する
☐ investor　　　　　　　　　　投資家

152 What is indicated about the event organizers?

(A) They are members of the Goldberg City Council.

(B) They specialize in importing goods.

(C) They will provide refreshments for participants.

(D) They are attempting to buy an abandoned factory.

イベントの主催者について何が示されていますか。

(A) 彼らは Goldberg 市議会の一員である。

(B) 彼らは品物の輸入を専門としている。

(C) 彼らは参加者に軽食を提供する。

(D) 彼らは見捨てられた工場を買おうとしている。

正解 D

選択肢に着目する問題

設問文の organizer は「主催者」という意味で、工場見学の主催者、つまり the Goldberg Cultural Revival Society を指している。be looking to do は「～することを検討している」という意味なので、The Goldberg Cultural Revival Society is looking to purchase the building and restart the soap factory. で、建物を買い取ってソープ工場を再開するつもりだと分かる。be looking to do を be attempting to do と言い換え、50 年前から使用されていない建物を an abandoned factory と表現している (D) が正解。

☐ specialize in ～　　　　　　～を専門に扱う
☐ refreshment　　　　　　　　軽食

語彙チェック
☐ vacant　　　　　　　　使用されていない
☐ temptation　　　　　　誘惑
☐ raise　　　　　　　　　（資金など）を集める
☐ awareness　　　　　　認知、認識

Questions 153-154 refer to the following advertisement.

Help Wanted

Van Hausen Repair and Maintenance specializes in providing affordable maintenance work on various equipment after the manufacturer's warranty has expired. We fix all range of items including refrigerators, air-conditioners, and office equipment. [154]We currently have an opening in our photocopier division. Experience working as a technician for one of the major manufacturers and an electrician's certificate are a must. Working hours are 9:00 A.M. to 5:00 P.M. Monday through Friday. [153]You may also be required to carry out emergency repairs on either Saturday or Sunday from time to time. In such cases, a generous overtime rate will be provided as compensation. To apply, visit our Web site at www.vanhausenrandm.com and follow the links.

問題 **153-154** は次の広告に関するものです。

従業員求む

Van Hausen 修理店はメーカーの保証期限が切れた様々な機器の手頃な価格での補修作業の提供を専門としています。冷蔵庫、エアコン、オフィス用品を含む幅広い物品を修理いたします。当店では現在コピー機部門に欠員があります。主要メーカーの 1 社で技術者として働いた経験と、電気技師免許が必須です。就業時間は月曜日から金曜日の午前 9 時から午後 5 時までです。ときどき土曜日あるいは日曜日に緊急修理を行うよう求められることもありえます。そうした場合、大幅な時間外手当が報酬として支給されます。応募するには、当社のウェブサイト www.vanhausenrandm.com にアクセスし、リンクをたどってください。

語彙チェック

☐	affordable	手頃な価格の
☐	warranty	保証
☐	opening	欠員
☐	must	必須のもの
☐	carry out 〜	〜を行う
☐	generous	豊富な、寛大な
☐	compensation	報酬

153 What is indicated about the position?

(A) Some contribution to volunteer activities is required.

(B) Extra payment is offered for weekend work.

(C) Employees must own a full set of tools.

(D) Training will be offered in the evenings.

職について何が示されていますか。

(A) ボランティア活動への貢献が求められる。

(B) 週末の業務には追加報酬が提供される。

(C) 従業員は道具一式を所持していなければならない。

(D) 研修が夕方に行われる。

正解 **B**

選択肢に着目する問題

Help Wanted「従業員求む」は求人広告で使われる定番表現。就業時間は平日の9時から5時と述べられているが、緊急修理のため土日勤務の可能性があると付け加えられている。それに関して In such cases, a generous overtime rate will be provided as compensation.「そうした場合、大幅な時間外手当が報酬として支給される」と述べられており、それを Extra payment is offered for weekend work と言い換えている (B) が正解。(A) の volunteer activities、(C) の tools、(D) の training については言及がないので、不適切。

☐ contribution　　　　　　　　貢献

---

154 What equipment will the new technician be hired to maintain?

(A) Cameras

(B) Air-conditioners

(C) Photocopiers

(D) Elevators

新しい技術者は何の機器を整備するために雇われますか。

(A) カメラ

(B) エアコン

(C) コピー機

(D) エレベーター

正解 **C**

設問に着目する問題

冒頭でこの企業の仕事内容が述べられており、その後、特に現在募集対象の分野について、We currently have an opening in our photocopier division.「当店では現在コピー機部門に欠員がある」と説明がある。したがって、正解は (C)。

Questions 155-157 refer to the following article.

DEVONSHIRE (November 21) — Toby Wood, the president of Wood Education, has announced that the Wood School of Business on Whelan Street will be moving to a larger building on Frampton Avenue. This is a result of the business being acquired by Kirkland University, which also owns the building on Frampton Avenue. Mr. Wood will continue in his position as president until he retires next month. The Wood family has run the Wood School of Business for almost 60 years and this is the first time a non-family member will take control.

In an interview, Mr. Wood stated that he believed the school was in good hands and hoped that the stronger association with the university would ensure the school's future prosperity. A letter explaining the decision and how it would affect students was sent out to all concerned last week. The move is scheduled to take place in time for the start of the new school year in February.

問題 **155-157** は次の記事に関するものです。

DEVONSHIRE（11月21日）—　Wood Education 社の社長である Toby Wood 氏は、Whelan 通りにある Wood ビジネススクールが Frampton 通りのより大きな建物に移転することを発表した。これは Frampton 大通りのその建物を所有している Kirkland 大学に事業が買収された結果である。Wood 氏は来月退職するまで社長として務め続ける。Wood 家は Wood ビジネススクールを 60 年近く経営しており、今回初めて一族以外の人間がかじ取りをすることになる。

インタビューで Wood 氏は、学校は安泰であると思うし、大学とのさらに強力な結びつきができれば学校の将来の繁栄も保証されると期待している、と述べた。その決定と、それが学生にどのような影響を及ぼすかについて説明した手紙は、先週、関係者一同に送付された。移転は 2 月の新年度の始まりに間に合うように行われる予定である。

155 Where would the article most likely appear?

(A) In an academic journal

(B) In a local newspaper

(C) In a job-offering magazine

(D) In an online catalog

この記事はどこに掲載されると考えられますか。

(A) 学術雑誌

(B) 地域新聞

(C) 求人情報誌

(D) オンラインカタログ

正解 B

設問に着目する問題

記事がどこに掲載されるものかが問われている。冒頭で Toby Wood, the president of Wood Education, has announced that the Wood School of Business on Whelan Street will be moving to a larger building on Frampton Avenue. とニュースの概要が述べられているが、移転の場所が「Whelan 通りから Frampton 大通りへ」と説明されていることから、地域住民に向けられている記事と考えられる。したがって、(B) の In a local newspaper が正解。

☐ academic　　　　　　　　　　　学問の

156 According to the article, what will likely happen in December?

(A) A school will move to a new location.

(B) A new course will be offered at a university.

(C) An executive will leave a business.

(D) An award will be given to a business owner.

記事によると、12 月におそらく何が起こりますか。

(A) 学校が新しい場所に移転する。

(B) 新しいコースが大学で提供される。

(C) 幹部が退職する。

(D) 会社の経営者が賞を授与される。

正解 C

設問に着目する問題

12 月に何が起こるかが問われている。記事内には December という語はないが、日付が 11 月 21 日とある。Mr. Wood will continue in his position as president until he retires next month. と述べられており、12 月には Mr. Wood が退職することが分かる。冒頭にあるように、Mr. Wood は the president of Wood Education なので、president を executive、retire を leave a business とそれぞれ言い換えている (C) が正解。executive「（会社などの）幹部」。

157 What is indicated about students of Wood School of Business?

(A) They have already been informed of the news.

(B) They will receive a discount on their tuition fees.

(C) They will be able to take part in university courses.

(D) They were invited to vote on the decision.

Wood ビジネススクールの学生について、何が示されていますか。

(A) 彼らはすでにそのニュースを知らされている。

(B) 彼らは授業料の割引を受ける。

(C) 彼らは大学のコースに参加することができる。

(D) 彼らはその決定について投票するよう求められた。

正解 A

選択肢に着目する問題

記事の後半に、A letter explaining the decision and how it would affect students was sent out to all concerned last week. 「その決定と、それが学生にどのような影響を及ぼすかについて説明した手紙は、先週、関係者全員に送付された」と記載がある。この all concerned は all who are concerned「関係する人全員」の who are が省略された形で、ここでは学生も当然含まれることになる。つまり、学生宛てには先週移転を知らせる手紙が送付されていることになるので、(A) が正解。

☐ tuition　　　　　　　　　　　授業料

語彙チェック

☐ in good hands　　安泰で　　　　　　☐ prosperity　　　　繁栄

☐ association　　　　結びつき　　　　　☐ all concerned　　関係者一同

☐ ensure　　　　　　〜を保証する

Questions 158-160 refer to the following notice.

The Halliburton Corporate Fitness Center Has Reopened!

Until it closed last month, many employees were taking advantage of the corporate gym. Unfortunately, the running costs had made it unfeasible for the company to continue. However, due to popular demand, the gym has reopened this week with one small change. The gym is now also available for employees of other tenants in the building. They will be charged membership fees depending on their frequency of use. The gym is still free for Halliburton staff, but this means that you will need to swipe your employee card to gain entry from now on.

To make the fitness center accessible to other users, we have had to relocate it. It can now be found in Office 3 on the building's first floor. We have arranged for Jim Cavalier, a local health expert, to visit the gym once a week to provide free consultations to users. If you would like to make an appointment, please check the schedule posted on the wall near the entrance. Users will be assisted on a first-come-first-served basis. Mr. Cavalier is the owner of Althex Fitness and Health on Rosemary Street, East Bronson. He is widely respected in sporting circles so we hope you make good use of this opportunity.

問題 **158-160** は次のお知らせに関するものです。

Halliburton 社フィットネスセンターが再開しました！

先月の閉鎖まで、多くの従業員が社用ジムを利用していました。残念ながら、運営コストのために会社はそれを継続することができなくなってしまいました。しかし、たくさんのご要望のために、1つ小さな変更を加えて今週ジムは再開しました。これから、ジムは建物の他のテナントの従業員にも利用可能になりました。彼らは利用頻度によって異なる会費を徴収されます。ジムは Halliburton 社のスタッフは変わらず無料ですが、このことにより、これからは入室するためには社員証を読み取り機に通す必要があります。

他の利用者がアクセスできるよう、フィットネスセンターを移転しなければなりませんでした。今では、フィットネスセンターは建物1階のオフィス3にあります。地元の健康専門家である Jim Cavalier さんに、週に1度ジムを訪れて利用者に無料相談の機会を提供してもらうよう手配しました。予約したい場合、玄関付近の壁に掲示したスケジュールをチェックしてください。利用者は先着順で支援を受けることになります。Cavalier さんは East Bronson の Rosemary 通りにある Althex Fitness and Health のオーナーです。彼はスポーツ界で広く尊敬を集めていますので、この機会を十分に利用していただきたいと思います。

158 What is a purpose of the notice?

(A) To promote a local business

(B) To suggest a fitness program

(C) To announce the distribution of employee cards

(D) To explain a change in policy

お知らせの目的は何ですか。

(A) 地域ビジネスを促進すること。

(B) フィットネスプログラムを提案すること。

(C) 社員証の配布について告知すること。

(D) 方針の変更を説明すること。

正解 D

設問に着目する問題

お知らせのタイトルに Fitness Center Has Reopened「フィットネスセンターが再開」とある。また the gym has reopened this week with one small change「1 つ小さな変更を加えて今週ジムは再開した」とあり、続けてその変更の内容について、他社の人も利用可能になったこと、入室の際に社員証が必要であること、場所の変更などが説明されているので、お知らせの目的は、ジムの再開と変更点の説明と分かる。(D) が正解。

☐ promote ～を促進する
☐ distribution 配布

159 What is indicated about the fitness center?

(A) It is in a new location.

(B) It was shut down due to a lack of interest.

(C) It has been designed by Jim Cavalier.

(D) It offers subsidized rates to employees.

フィットネスセンターについて何が示されていますか。

(A) 新しい場所にある。

(B) 関心が集められず閉鎖された。

(C) Jim Cavalier によって設計された。

(D) 従業員には補助金による割引料金を提供する。

正解 A

選択肢に着目する問題

To make the fitness center accessible to other users, we have had to relocate it.「他の利用者がアクセスできるよう、フィットネスセンターを移転しなければならなかった」とあるので、新しい場所に移ったと判断できるため、(A) が正解。Until it closed last month, many employees were taking advantage of the corporate gym. とあり、人気があったと判断できるため、(B) は不適切。Jim Cavalier さんが設計したという言及はないので、(C) は不適切。The gym is still free for Halliburton staff とあるので、(D) も不適切。

☐ lack 欠如
☐ subsidized 補助を受けた

160 What is true about Mr. Cavalier?

(A) He has joined the staff of Halliburton.

(B) He is a professional athlete.

(C) He is replacing another expert.

(D) He is self-employed.

Cavalier さんについて正しいものは何ですか。

(A) 彼は Halliburton 社のスタッフに加わった。

(B) 彼はプロの運動選手である。

(C) 彼は別の専門家に取って代わる。

(D) 彼は自営業者である。

正解 D

選択肢に着目する問題

Cavalier さんについては、お知らせの後半に記載がある。Mr. Cavalier is the owner of Althex Fitness and Health on Rosemary Street「Cavalier さんは Rosemary 通りにある Althex Fitness and Health のオーナーだ」と説明があり、人に雇われているのではなく自らが経営者と分かる。そのことを、self-employed と言い表している (D) が正解。self-employed「自営の、自営業の」。

【語彙チェック】
☐ unfeasible 実行不可能な
☐ swipe （カードなどを）機械に通す
☐ gain entry 入る
☐ accessible 利用可能な、到達できる
☐ make good use of ～ ～を有効に利用する

Questions 161-163 refer to the following information from a Web page.

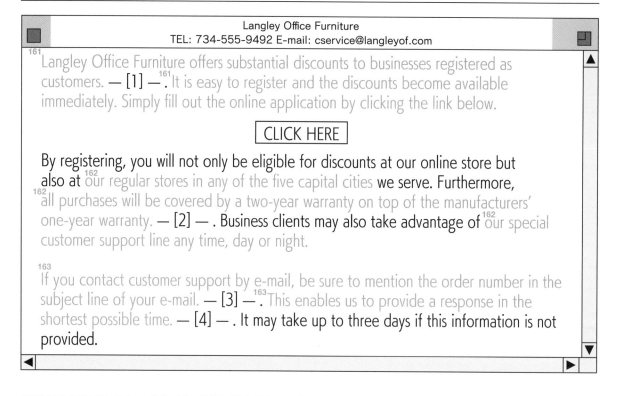

Langley Office Furniture
TEL: 734-555-9492 E-mail: cservice@langleyof.com

161 Langley Office Furniture offers substantial discounts to businesses registered as customers. — [1] —. It is easy to register and the discounts become available immediately. Simply fill out the online application by clicking the link below.

CLICK HERE

By registering, you will not only be eligible for discounts at our online store but also at our regular stores in any of the five capital cities we serve. Furthermore, all purchases will be covered by a two-year warranty on top of the manufacturers' one-year warranty. — [2] —. Business clients may also take advantage of our special customer support line any time, day or night.

If you contact customer support by e-mail, be sure to mention the order number in the subject line of your e-mail. — [3] —. This enables us to provide a response in the shortest possible time. — [4] —. It may take up to three days if this information is not provided.

問題 **161-163** は次のウェブページの情報に関するものです。

Langley オフィス家具社
電話番号:734-555-9492　E メール:cservice@langleyof.com

Langley オフィス家具社は顧客登録されている企業のお客様に大幅割引をご提供しております。登録は簡単で、すぐに割引をご利用になれます。以下のリンクをクリックしてオンライン申込用紙にご記入ください。

ここをクリック

登録すると、当社のオンラインストアだけでなく、5 つの主要都市にある当社の正規店での割引資格を得られます。さらに、すべてのご購入品には 1 年間のメーカー保証に加え、2 年間の保証をおつけします。企業のお客様は昼夜いつでも、当社の特別顧客サポート電話もご利用いただけます。

E メールで顧客サポートにご連絡いただく場合は、E メールの件名に必ず注文番号を入れてください。＊当社のシステムが確実にそれを関係するサポート職員に自動的に送られるようにします。これにより可能な限り最短でお返事することができます。この情報が提供されない場合、最大 3 日間かかる可能性があります。

161

What is the purpose of the information?

(A) To express appreciation to loyal customers

(B) To attract new customers to a business

(C) To explain the process for requesting a product return

(D) To announce a change to a product lineup

案内の目的は何ですか。

(A) 常連客に謝意を表すこと。

(B) 会社に新規顧客を引き付けること。

(C) 返品依頼の手順について説明すること。

(D) 製品ラインナップの変更を告知すること。

正解 B

設問に着目する問題

案内の目的が何かということが問われている。様々な文書の目的は、冒頭付近に書かれていることが多い。この案内でも冒頭で、Langley Office Furniture offers substantial discounts to businesses registered as customers.「Langley オフィス家具社は顧客登録されている企業のお客様に大幅割引をご提供している」と述べ、登録が簡単ですぐに割引が受けられると、企業に対し顧客登録をするよう勧誘しており、それが案内の目的であると考えられる。そのことを To attract new customers to a business と言い換えている (B) が正解。

☐ appreciation　　　　謝意
☐ loyal customer　　　常連客、得意客

162

What is NOT mentioned about Langley Office Furniture?

(A) It manufactures its own brand of furniture.

(B) It has offices in multiple cities.

(C) It offers extended warranties.

(D) It provides 24-hour customer support.

Langley オフィス家具社について述べられていないことは何ですか。

(A) それは自社ブランドの家具を製造している。

(B) それは複数の都市に営業所がある。

(C) それは延長保証を提供している。

(D) それは 24 時間の顧客サポートを提供している。

正解 A

NOT 問題

(B) は our regular stores in any of the five capital cities「5 つの主要都市にある当社の正規店」と一致する。(C) は all purchases will be covered by a two-year warranty on top of the manufacturers' one-year warranty とあり、通常の 1 年に加え 2 年の保証がつくので、一致する。(D) は our special customer support line any time, day or night「昼夜いつでも、当社の特別顧客サポート電話」と記載があるので一致する。家具の製造については言及がないので、(A) が正解。

☐ extended　　　　延長された

163

In which of the positions marked [1], [2], [3], and [4] does the following sentence best belong?

"Our system ensures that it is automatically sent to the relevant support worker."

(A) [1]　　(B) [2]　　(C) [3]　　(D) [4]

[1] , [2], [3], [4] と記載された箇所のうち、次の文が入るのに最もふさわしいのはどれですか。

「当社のシステムが確実にそれを関係するサポート職員に自動的に送られるようにします」

(A) [1]　　(B) [2]　　(C) [3]　　(D) [4]

正解 C

文挿入問題

挿入文に relevant support worker という語句があるので、サポートに言及している箇所に入ると予想できる。If you contact customer support by e-mail, be sure to mention the order number in the subject line of your e-mail. と述べられている。この文の後の [3] に挿入文を入れると、挿入文の it が E メールを指し、それが関連するサポート職員に自動的に送られるとなる。さらに、[3] の直後の This enables の This が、挿入文全体を指して、「そのことが最短での返事を可能にする」というようにつながり、文脈が通る。正解は (C)。ensure that ～「～ということを確実にする」。

語彙チェック

☐ substantial　　　　かなりの
☐ be eligible for ～　　～の資格がある

☐ furthermore　　　　さらに
☐ take advantage of ～　　～を利用する、～の特典を生かす

Questions 164-167 refer to the following e-mail.

To:	Fred Yates <fyates@veritasmotors.com>
From:	Roberta Wilson <rwilson@scarboroughbc.com>
Date:	May 6
Subject:	Scarborough Business Center
Attachment:	📎 pamphlet

Dear Mr. Yates,

Thank you for your e-mail of May 5. Attached you will find a pamphlet for our new meeting spaces at 34 Fielding Street. I understand your company is considering reserving one of our meeting rooms every Sunday for an indefinite period. This is not something we have done in the past. Nevertheless, I am very interested in discussing the possibility with you when you visit our current facility at 234 Grundy Street, Chicago, on May 9. I would be happy to pick you up from the station so please let me know your arrival time.

I have taken the liberty of reserving the room you mentioned for the next six months starting on May 14. As we have not received a formal request from you, there will be no charge if you choose not to use the room. I am open to discussing discounts and we can be flexible with some of our conditions of use in consideration of this long-term agreement. Nevertheless, I hope you will keep in mind that Scarborough Business Center is already one of the most reasonably priced providers of meeting space in Chicago.

Sincerely,

Roberta Wilson
Scarborough Business Center

問題 **164-167** は次の E メールに関するものです。

宛先：Fred Yates <fyates@veritasmotors.com>
送信者：Roberta Wilson <rwilson@scarboroughbc.com>
日付：5 月 6 日
件名：Scarborough ビジネスセンター
添付：パンフレット

Yates 様

5 月 5 日に E メールをいただきありがとうございました。わたくしどもの 34 Fielding 通りの新しい会議場のパンフレットを添付いたしましたのでご覧ください。貴社がわたくしどもの会議室を毎週日曜日、無期限に予約することをお考えであることを理解しております。これは過去に例のないことです。ですが、私は 5 月 9 日に、シカゴの Grundy 通り 234 番地にある現在の当施設をご訪問いただく際にその可能性についてお話し合いをすることにたいへん関心があります。喜んで駅にお迎えに上がりますので、到着時刻をお知らせください。

私の一存で、5 月 14 日から 6 か月間、おっしゃっていた部屋を予約しております。正式なご依頼をまだいただいていませんので、もしその部屋をお使いにならないようでしたら、代金の請求はいたしません。割引についてのお話し合いもさせていただきますし、このような長期の契約だということを考慮しますと使用条件の一部についても融通をきかせることができます。ですが、Scarborough ビジネスセンターはすでにシカゴで最も手頃な価格で会議場を提供する会社の 1 つであることを念頭に置いていただけますように。

よろしくお願いいたします。

Roberta Wilson
Scarborough ビジネスセンター

語彙チェック

☐ indefinite	限定されていない、無限の		☐ condition	条件
☐ nevertheless	しかしながら		☐ in consideration of ～	～を考慮して
☐ take the liberty of *doing*	勝手に～する		☐ reasonably priced	手頃な価格の
☐ flexible	柔軟な			

164

What is included with the e-mail?

(A) A brochure

(B) A receipt

(C) A travel itinerary

(D) A reservation confirmation

E メールに含まれているものは何ですか。

(A) パンフレット

(B) 領収書

(C) 旅行日程表

(D) 予約確認書

正解 A

設問に着目する問題

E メールの件名の下の Attachment「添付」にパンフレットとある。それを brochure と言い換えている (A) が正解。本文に Attached you will find 〜とあるが、これは Attached please find 〜と同じく、添付物がある場合の定番の表現。手紙に同封物がある場合は、Enclosed you will find 〜と表現する。brochure「パンフレット」。

165

When will Mr. Yates meet with Ms. Wilson?

(A) On May 3

(B) On May 6

(C) On May 9

(D) On May 14

Yates さんが Wilson さんに会うのはいつですか。

(A) 5 月 3 日

(B) 5 月 6 日

(C) 5 月 9 日

(D) 5 月 14 日

正解 C

設問に着目する問題

E メールの受信者である Yates さんに対し、送信者の Wilson さんは you visit our current facility at 234 Grundy Street, Chicago, on May 9 と述べている。続けて Wilson さんは I would be happy to pick you up from the station と言っているので、Wilson さん自ら Yates さんを駅まで迎えに行くことが分かる。したがって、Yates さんは 5 月 9 日に Wilson さんに会うことになるので、正解は (C)。

166

What is NOT implied about Scarborough Business Center?

(A) It offers meeting rooms for corporate clients.

(B) It is relocating soon.

(C) It is open in the evenings.

(D) It charges cancellation fees.

Scarborough ビジネスセンターについて示唆されていないことは何ですか。

(A) それは法人の依頼人に会議室を提供している。

(B) それはまもなく移転する。

(C) それは夕方に営業している。

(D) それはキャンセル料を請求する。

正解 C

NOT 問題

E メールは Scarborough ビジネスセンターから顧客に宛てられたものである。(A) は第 1 段落の I understand your company is considering reserving one of our meeting rooms から、顧客の企業が会議室を予約すると分かり、一致する。(B) は第 1 段落の our new meeting spaces at 34 Fielding Street. と our current facility at 234 Grundy Street, Chicago からビジネスセンターは現在の場所から新しい場所へ移転すると判断できる。(D) は第 2 段落の As we have not received a formal request from you, there will be no charge if you choose not to use the room. から、通常はキャンセルチャージがあると分かる。(C) の「夕方に営業している」に関しての記載はないので、(C) が正解。

167

What most likely is Ms. Wilson's job?

(A) Training officer

(B) Salesperson

(C) Analyst

(D) Event planner

Wilson さんの仕事は何だと考えられますか。

(A) 指導員

(B) 営業担当者

(C) アナリスト

(D) イベントプランナー

正解 B

設問に着目する問題

E メールの送信者である Scarborough ビジネスセンターの Wilson さんが顧客に対し、I am open to discussing discounts and we can be flexible with some of our conditions of use in consideration of this long-term agreement.「割引についてのお話し合いもさせていただきますし、このような長期の契約だということを考慮しますと使用条件の一部についても融通をきかせることができる」と割引についての話や使用条件に関する交渉が可能であることなどを提案しているので、(B) の Salesperson「営業担当者」が正解。

Day 5

Questions 168-171 refer to the following text-message chain.

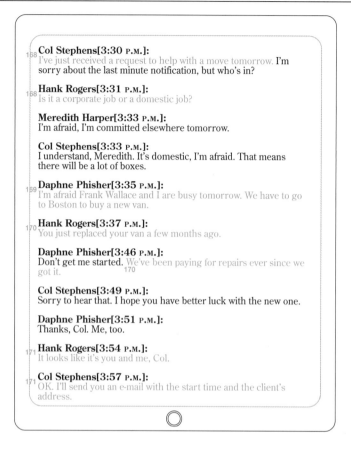

168 **Col Stephens[3:30 P.M.]:**
I've just received a request to help with a move tomorrow. I'm sorry about the last minute notification, but who's in?

168 **Hank Rogers[3:31 P.M.]:**
Is it a corporate job or a domestic job?

Meredith Harper[3:33 P.M.]:
I'm afraid, I'm committed elsewhere tomorrow.

Col Stephens[3:33 P.M.]:
I understand, Meredith. It's domestic, I'm afraid. That means there will be a lot of boxes.

169 **Daphne Phisher[3:35 P.M.]:**
I'm afraid Frank Wallace and I are busy tomorrow. We have to go to Boston to buy a new van.

170 **Hank Rogers[3:37 P.M.]:**
You just replaced your van a few months ago.

Daphne Phisher[3:46 P.M.]:
Don't get me started. We've been paying for repairs ever since we got it. 170

Col Stephens[3:49 P.M.]:
Sorry to hear that. I hope you have better luck with the new one.

Daphne Phisher[3:51 P.M.]:
Thanks, Col. Me, too.

171 **Hank Rogers[3:54 P.M.]:**
It looks like it's you and me, Col.

171 **Col Stephens[3:57 P.M.]:**
OK. I'll send you an e-mail with the start time and the client's address.

問題 **168-171** は次のテキストメッセージのやりとりに関するものです。

Col Stephens [午後 3 時 30 分]：
明日の引っ越し手伝いの要請を今受け取りました。直前のお知らせで申し訳ないけど、誰が行きますか？
Hank Rogers [午後 3 時 31 分]：
それは法人の仕事ですか、それとも個人宅の仕事ですか？
Meredith Harper [午後 3 時 33 分]：
残念ですが、明日は他の場所に行くことになっています。
Col Stephens [午後 3 時 33 分]：
分かりました、Meredith。残念ながら、個人宅です。つまり、箱がたくさんあるということです。
Daphne Phisher [午後 3 時 35 分]：
残念ながら、Frank Wallace と私は明日は忙しいです。私たちは新しいトラックを買いにボストンまで行かなければなりません。
Hank Rogers [午後 3 時 37 分]：
あなたたちは数か月前にトラックを買い替えたばかりですよね。
Daphne Phisher [午後 3 時 46 分]：
言わせないでください。買ってからずっと修理にお金を払い続けているのです。
Col Stephens [午後 3 時 49 分]：
それは残念なことですね。新しいトラックはもっといいものだといいですね。
Daphne Phisher [午後 3 時 51 分]：
ありがとう、Col。私もそう願っています。
Hank Rogers [午後 3 時 54 分]：
どうもあなたと私のようですね、Col。
Col Stephens [午後 3 時 57 分]：
分かりました。開始時間と依頼者の住所を E メールで送ります。

語彙チェック
- [ ] notification　通知
- [ ] domestic　家庭の、国内の
- [ ] commit　〜と約束する
- [ ] ever since 〜　〜以来ずっと

168 Where do the writers most likely work?

(A) At car dealerships

(B) At an airline

(C) At moving companies

(D) At a cleaning service

書き手たちはどこで働いていると考えられますか。

(A) 自動車販売店

(B) 航空会社

(C) 引っ越し業者

(D) 清掃業者

正解 C

設問に着目する問題

書き手たちがどのような業種で働いているかが問われているので、決め手となるキーワードや話の流れなどから判断する。Stephens さんが最初に I've just received a request to help with a move tomorrow. と述べている。Rogers さんがそれに対して a corporate job or a domestic job 「法人の仕事か、それとも個人宅の仕事か」と質問している。これらのことから、彼らの業務は引っ越しを請け負うことだと判断でき、(C) が正解。その後のやりとりでトラックを新しく買うということなども、正解を選ぶ決め手となっている。

169 Why is Frank Wallace going to Boston?

(A) To give a presentation

(B) Io meet with a client

(C) To visit some family members

(D) To purchase a vehicle

Frank Wallace はなぜボストンに行きますか。

(A) プレゼンテーションをするため。

(B) 顧客に会うため。

(C) 家族を訪れるため。

(D) 乗り物を購入するため。

正解 D

設問に着目する問題

Frank Wallace は、テキストメッセージの書き手ではないが、Phisher さんが I'm afraid Frank Wallace and I are busy tomorrow. We have to go to Boston to buy a new van. と書いていることから、Wallace さんと Phisher さんは一緒に新しいトラックを買うためにボストンに行くと分かるので、正解は (D)。buy を purchase、van を vehicle と言い換えている。

170 At 3:46 P.M., what does Ms. Phisher mean when she says, "Don't get me started"?

(A) She will make her own way to a work location.

(B) She has had a lot of expenses recently.

(C) She would like to take a rest.

(D) She is not interested in a new product.

午後 3 時 46 分に Phisher さんが "Don't get me started" と書く際、何を意図していますか。

(A) 彼女は自分で勤務地へ向かう。

(B) 彼女は最近出費が多かった。

(C) 彼女は休息を取りたい。

(D) 彼女は新製品に興味がない。

正解 B

意図問題

明日の引っ越しに行けない理由をシカゴにトラックを買いに行くためと説明する Phisher さんに対し、Rogers さんは「数か月前にトラックを買い替えたばかりですよね」と、なぜ買い替える必要があるのか不思議に思っている。それに対する応答が Don't get me started 「言わせないでください」である。その後、We've been paying for repairs ever since we got it. 「買ってからずっと修理にお金を払い続けている」と、前に買ったトラックは修理にお金がかかり過ぎる、つまり出費が多いと言っているので正解は (B)。

171 Who will assist Mr. Stephens tomorrow?

(A) Ms. Phisher

(B) Mr. Rogers

(C) Mr. Wallace

(D) Ms. Harper

明日、誰が Stephens さんを手伝いますか。

(A) Phisher さん

(B) Rogers さん

(C) Wallace さん

(D) Harper さん

正解 B

設問に着目する問題

Stephens さんが冒頭で明日の引っ越し業務は誰が可能なのか呼び掛けており、それぞれが明日の予定などを述べている。最終的には、Rogers さんが It looks like it's you and me, Col. と、Stephens さんに向けて書いており、それに対して Stephens さんも「分かりました。開始時間と依頼者の住所を E メールで送る」と返していることから、引っ越しは Rogers さんと Stephens さんで行うことが分かる。正解は (B)。

Questions 172-175 refer to the following article.

Hobart, September 12—Mike Sylva only intended to stay in Hobart for three months after his company transferred him there 15 years ago. Today, he is still here and he is now the owner of one of the city's most successful cafés. — [1] — . This is a far cry from what he could have imagined when he first arrived to help open a veterinary hospital for a large national chain.

— [2] — . Twenty years earlier, while he was still in veterinary school, Sylva met fellow student and musician, Il Sok Kim. His friendship with Il Sok led to his appreciation of music and eventually resulted in him learning to play the guitar and joining a band. The pair lost contact when Il Sok quit school to follow his musical ambitions.

— [3] — . The two immediately rekindled their friendship. Il Sok's laidback lifestyle appealed to Sylva, who had put his career before anything else. They started playing together again and by the time Sylva was scheduled to return to the company's head office in Sydney, they had formed a band.

Sylva elected to stay in Hobart and work at the veterinarian clinic, but he soon found that that was taking too much of his time. — [4] — . He used all of his savings to buy the café and started to run the business. He has completely revamped the menu and updated the interior. At night, he serves amazing meals with top class musical entertainment by local performers and his best friend, Il Sok. The restaurant is called Treble Clef and it is open from 7:00 A.M. to 10:00 P.M. every day except Tuesday.

問題 **172-175** は次の記事に関するものです。

Hobart、9 月 12 日―15 年前に会社の都合で Hobart に異動になったとき、Mike Sylva はそこに 3 か月間滞在するだけのつもりだった。今日、彼はいまだにここにおり、街で最も成功しているカフェの 1 つのオーナーである。これは、大規模国内チェーンの動物病院を開設する手伝いをしに初めてやってきたときに彼が想像できただろうこととは大違いである。

20 年前、彼がまだ獣医学校に在籍していたとき、Sylva は同級生でミュージシャンの Il Sok Kim と出会った。Il Sok との友情により、彼は音楽鑑賞をたしなむようになり、最終的にはギターを習得してバンドに参加するようになった。Il Sok が音楽的野心を追求するために退学したときに 2 人の連絡は途切れた。

* だから、Sylva が新設の動物病院の隣のカフェを訪れて旧友が飲み物を給仕し、客とおしゃべりしているのを見つけたとき、それは運命のように感じられた。2 人はすぐに友情を復活させた。Il Sok の気楽なライフスタイルは、キャリアを最優先してきた Sylva には魅力的だった。彼らは再び一緒に演奏をし始め、Sylva が会社のシドニー本社に戻るよう予定されていたときには、彼らはバンドを組んでいた。

Sylva は Hobart に留まって動物病院で働くことを選んだが、まもなく彼は、それでは自分の時間がとられ過ぎると分かった。彼は貯金のすべてを使ってカフェを買い取り経営を始めた。彼はメニューを完全に改良し、内装を新しくした。夜にはすばらしい食事を、地域の演奏家と彼の親友 Il Sok による最高級の音楽演奏とともに提供している。レストランの店名は Treble Clef、午前 7 時から午後 10 時まで、火曜日を除き毎日営業している。

語彙チェック

☐ intend to *do*	～するつもりである
☐ far cry from ～	～とは大違いである
☐ veterinary	獣医(の)
☐ appreciation	鑑賞すること
☐ eventually	最終的に
☐ rekindle	～に再点火する、よみがえらせる
☐ laidback	リラックスした
☐ elect to *do*	～することを選ぶ
☐ veterinarian	獣医
☐ revamp	～を改良する

172 What is the main purpose of the article?

(A) To profile a local business person

(B) To promote a new veterinary clinic

(C) To explain the benefits of living in Hobart

(D) To introduce a popular new pastime

記事の主な目的は何ですか。

(A) 地域の実業家の人物紹介をすること。

(B) 新しい動物病院の宣伝をすること。

(C) Hobart に住む利点を説明すること。

(D) 人気の新しい娯楽を紹介すること。

正解 **A**

設問に着目する問題

様々な文書の目的は、冒頭付近に書かれていることが多い。この記事の主な目的も、最初に述べられている。Mike Sylva さんについて述べられているこの記事では、彼がもともとは 3 か月の滞在のつもりで Hobart に来たが、15 年経った今も、この地でカフェのオーナーをしていると述べられている。その後も、そうなったいきさつなどが説明されている。正解は (A)。profile「〜の紹介を書く」。

173 Who is Il Sok Kim?

(A) A veterinarian

(B) A promoter

(C) A restaurant owner

(D) A musical performer

Il Sok Kim とは誰ですか。

(A) 獣医

(D) 興行者

(C) レストランのオーナー

(D) 音楽の演奏家

正解 **D**

設問に着目する問題

Il Sok さんが誰かと聞いている。このタイプの問題は彼の職業、あるいは他の登場人物との関係を問うていることが多い。ざっと選択肢を確認して問われているのがどちらかを確認してから本文を読み進めるのがポイント。第 2 段落に Il Sok quit school to follow his musical ambitions と述べられている。さらに第 4 段落で、with top class musical entertainment by local performers and his best friend, Il Sok とあることから、Il Sok さんが (D) A musical performer だと分かる。

174 Why did Mr. Sylva leave his job?

(A) It did not allow him enough freedom.

(B) It was not paid well enough.

(C) It was in a very secluded region.

(D) It did not make use of his qualifications.

Sylva さんはなぜ仕事をやめたのですか。

(A) それは彼に十分な自由を与えなかったから。

(B) それはあまり給料がよくなかったから。

(C) それは非常に人里離れた場所にあったから。

(D) それは彼の適性を生かさなかったから。

正解 **A**

設問に着目する問題

動物病院で働く Sylva さんは転勤で Sydney へ戻ることになるが、そのころには Il Sok さんとバンドを組むようになっており、彼は Hobart の動物病院で働くことを選ぶ。しかし、he soon found that that was taking too much of his time と述べられており、働きながら音楽をやるには自由な時間がないことに不便を感じていたことが分かる。それを、抽象的に It did not allow him enough freedom. と表現している (A) が正解。

175 In which of the positions marked [1], [2], [3], and [4] does the following sentence best belong?

"So, it felt like fate when Sylva visited the café next to the newly opened veterinary clinic to find his old friend serving drinks and chatting with patrons."

(A) [1]   (B) [2]   (C) [3]   (D) [4]

[1] , [2], [3], [4] と記載された箇所のうち、次の文が入るのに最もふさわしいのはどれですか。

「だから、Sylva が新設の動物病院の隣のカフェを訪れて旧友が飲み物を給仕し、客とおしゃべりしているのを見つけたとき、それは運命のように感じられた」

(A) [1]   (B) [2]   (C) [3]   (D) [4]

正解 **C**

文挿入問題

挿入文では Sylva visited the café next to the newly opened veterinary clinic to find his old friend「Sylva が新設の動物病院の隣のカフェを訪れて旧友を見つけた」とあり、「それは運命のように感じられた」と述べられている。The pair lost contact when Il Sok quit school to follow his musical ambitions. とあることから、彼らは学生時代以降は連絡を取っていないことが分かる。したがって、この文の後の空所 [3] に挿入文を入れると、長い期間を経て偶然に再会したことを挿入文中の fate「運命」が指すことになり、文脈が通る。また、[3] の後ろの The two immediately rekindled their friendship. の The two も Sylva さんと Il Sok さんを指すことになる。これらのことから、(C) が正解。fate「運命」、patron「常連客」。

Questions 176-180 refer to the following e-mail and article.

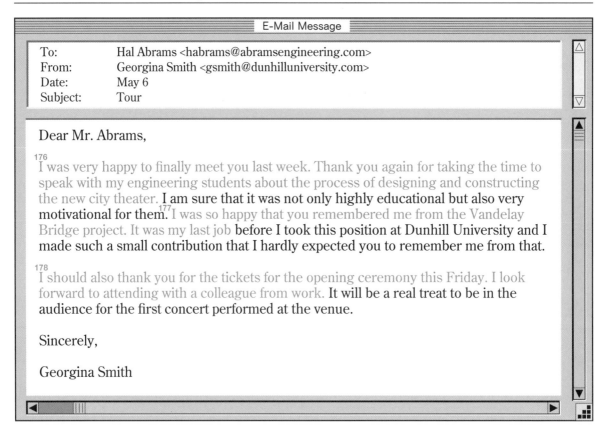

	E-Mail Message	
To:	Hal Abrams <habrams@abramsengineering.com>	
From:	Georgina Smith <gsmith@dunhilluniversity.com>	
Date:	May 6	
Subject:	Tour	

Dear Mr. Abrams,

176 I was very happy to finally meet you last week. Thank you again for taking the time to speak with my engineering students about the process of designing and constructing the new city theater. I am sure that it was not only highly educational but also very motivational for them. 177 I was so happy that you remembered me from the Vandelay Bridge project. It was my last job before I took this position at Dunhill University and I made such a small contribution that I hardly expected you to remember me from that.

178 I should also thank you for the tickets for the opening ceremony this Friday. I look forward to attending with a colleague from work. It will be a real treat to be in the audience for the first concert performed at the venue.

Sincerely,

Georgina Smith

Bronsonville Theater Opening Soon

By Greta Holmes

May 7—The new Bronsonville Theater is a marvel of engineering. 179 The amazing egg-shaped building is certainly eye-catching, but that is not all it has going for it. It promises the best acoustic features of any major indoor performance space in the world, 180 on paper at least. 178 We won't know if it measures up to expectations until it 179 opens on May 8. The chief engineer on the project, Hal Abrams, took over from Jon Gregory, who had to leave the project due to scheduling issues brought on by construction delays. 177 Abrams came directly from the famous Vandelay Bridge project he was in charge of in Amsterdam. Under his excellent leadership, the construction got back on schedule and 179 the construction company has even qualified for an early completion bonus.

問題 **176-180** は次の E メールと記事に関するものです。

宛先：Hal Abrams <habrams@abramsengineering.com>
送信者：Georgina Smith <gsmith@dunhilluniversity.com>
日付：5 月 6 日
件名：ツアー

Abrams 様

先週ようやくお会いできてとてもうれしかったです。新しい街の劇場の設計と建築の工程について私の工学科学生とお話ししてくださったことに改めてお礼を申し上げます。非常に教育上有益だっただけでなく、彼らにとっては強い動機づけとなるものだったと確信しております。Vandelay 橋のプロジェクトのことで私を覚えていてくださって、とてもうれしく思いました。それは Dunhill 大学でこの職につく前に最後にした仕事で、私はほんの少ししか貢献できなかったので、まさか私のことをそのことで覚えていてくださるとは思いませんでした。

また、今週金曜日の開場式のチケットもありがとうございます。職場の同僚と一緒に出席させていただくのを楽しみにしております。その舞台で上演される最初のコンサートの聴衆の一員となれるのは本当にすばらしいことでしょう。

敬具

Georgina Smith

Bronsonville 劇場、オープン間近

Greta Holmes

5 月 7 日—新しい Bronsonville 劇場は工学技術の驚異である。見事な卵型の建物は間違いなく人目を引き付けるものだが、それだけが強みではない。少なくとも理論上は、世界の主要な屋内公演場の中で最もすばらしい音響特性を約束している。5 月 8 日にオープンするまで、それが期待にかなうものであるかどうかは分からない。

当プロジェクトのチーフエンジニアである Hal Abrams は、工事の遅れによってもたらされたスケジュール問題のためにプロジェクトを去らねばならなかった Jon Gregory の後を継いだ。Abrams はアムステルダムで担当していた有名な Vandelay 橋のプロジェクトから直接やってきた。彼のすばらしいリーダーシップのもと、工事はスケジュールの遅れを取り戻し、建設会社は早期完成ボーナスを獲得しさえした。

176 What is the purpose of the e-mail?

(A) To express gratitude for a past event

(B) To alert employees about a policy change

(C) To request assistance with a project

(D) To remind customers to submit orders

E メールの目的は何ですか。

(A) 過去の出来事について感謝を伝えること。

(B) 方針の変更について従業員に注意を喚起すること。

(C) プロジェクトに支援を依頼すること。

(D) 顧客に注文を出すことを思い出させること。

正解 A

設問に着目する問題

E メールの目的が何かということが問われている。E メールや、手紙などの文書の目的は、冒頭付近に書かれていることが多く、この問題の正解の根拠も、冒頭近くに登場している。I was very happy to finally meet you last week. Thank you again for taking the time to speak with my engineering students about the process of designing and constructing the new city theater. とあり、E メールの受取人に対し、先週学生と話をしてくれたことに対して礼を述べているので、(A) が正解。gratitude「感謝の気持ち」。

□ alert 〜に注意喚起する、警告する
□ submit 〜を提出する

---

177 What is suggested about Ms. Smith and Mr. Abrams?

(A) They studied together at university.

(B) They will present an award at a banquet.

(C) They are employed by the same company.

(D) They both worked on a project in Amsterdam.

Smith さんと Abrams さんについて何が分かりますか。

(A) 彼らは大学で一緒に勉強していた。

(B) 彼らは祝宴で賞を授与する。

(C) 彼らは同じ会社に雇われている。

(D) 彼らは 2 人ともアムステルダムのプロジェクトで働いた。

正解 D

選択肢に着目するクロス問題

Smith さんと Abrams さんがどういう知り合いなのか、どういう関係なのかが問われている。E メールは、Smith さんから Abrams さんに宛てられたもので、Smith さんが I was so happy that you remembered me from the Vandelay Bridge project. It was my last job と述べていることから、2 人は Vandelay 橋プロジェクトの仕事に一緒に関わっていたと考えられる。また、記事の中では、Abrams came directly from the famous Vandelay Bridge project he was in charge of in Amsterdam. と書かれており、Vandelay 橋プロジェクトはアムステルダムでのプロジェクトと分かる。したがって、正解は (D)。

---

178 When most likely will Ms. Smith next visit the Bronsonville Theater?

(A) On May 6

(B) On May 7

(C) On May 8

(D) On May 9

Smith さんは次にいつ Bronsonville 劇場を訪れると考えられますか。

(A) 5 月 6 日

(B) 5 月 7 日

(C) 5 月 8 日

(D) 5 月 9 日

正解 C

クロス問題

E メールの後半で Smith さんは I should also thank you for the tickets for the opening ceremony this Friday. I look forward to attending with a colleague from work. と述べており、劇場の開場式に参加するつもりであることが分かる。記事には、オープン間近の Bronsonville 劇場に関することが述べられており、その劇場のすばらしさについて、We won't know if it measures up to expectations until it opens on May 8. と記されており、5 月 8 日が開場式と判断できるので、正解は (C)。

179 What is NOT indicated about the Bronsonville Theater?

(A) It has a very striking appearance.

(B) The city council paid for the construction.

(C) Its chief engineer changed during the project.

(D) The construction company received an additional payment.

Bronsonville 劇場について示されていないことは何ですか。

(A) それは非常に目立つ外観である。

(B) 市議会がその建築費を支払った。

(C) プロジェクトの途中でチーフエンジニアが変わった。

(D) 建設会社が追加報酬を受け取った。

正解 **B**

NOT 問題

Bronsonville 劇場については、主に記事で述べられている。(A) は The amazing egg-shaped building is certainly eye-catching「見事な卵型の建物は間違いなく人目を引き付ける」と一致する。(C) は The chief engineer on the project, Hal Abrams, took over from Jon Gregory「当プロジェクトのチーフエンジニアである Hal Abrams は、Jon Gregory の後を継いだ」と一致する。(D) は the construction company has even qualified for an early completion bonus「建設会社は早期完成ボーナスを獲得しさえした」と一致する。(B) に関しての記載はないので、(B) が正解。city council「市議会」。

☐ striking 人目を引く、目立つ
☐ appearance 外観

180 In the article, the phrase "on paper" in paragraph 1, line 7 is closest in meaning to

(A) in print

(B) as shown

(C) in theory

(D) for now

記事の第 1 段落・7 行目にある on paper に最も意味が近いのは

(A) 印刷されて

(B) 示されている通り

(C) 理論的には

(D) 今のところ

正解 **C**

同義語問題

on paper を含む文では、この劇場の音響効果が世界一を約束するものだと述べられ、最後に on paper at least「少なくとも紙の上では」が付け足されている。その後に、それは実際の 5 月 8 日のオープンまでは分からないと続いていることから、on paper は「紙の上の計算では」、つまり「理論上は」という意味であると想像できる。正解は (C)。theory「理論」。

語彙チェック

☐ engineering	工学		☐ acoustic feature	音響特性
☐ design	～を設計する		☐ measure up to ～	(期待など)にかなう
☐ construct	～を建設する		☐ expectation	期待
☐ motivational	動機づけになる		☐ issue	問題点
☐ contribution	貢献		☐ bring on ～	～を引き起こす、もたらす
☐ hardly	ほとんど～ない		☐ in charge of ～	～を担当する
☐ treat	もてなし、楽しみ		☐ qualify for ～	～の資格を得る
☐ marvel	驚異		☐ completion	完成

Questions 181-185 refer to the following letter and e-mail.

17 March

Sean Monroe
123 Halifax Road,
London,

Dear Mr. Monroe,

Thank you for agreeing to write a segment for the *London Culinary Journal*. I am sure our readers will be excited to read an article by you especially considering your recent experiences working for Camden House in Sunbury. As your article will be under 1,500 words, we will only be able to use a two-page spread. Typically, we try to fill the page with 60 percent text and 40 percent graphical content. If you have some pictures you would like us to use or have a specific request for our photographer, please let me know as soon as possible.

The title for the article is to be *Summer in Sunbury*. You can submit the completed manuscript to us using the upload link on the Web site. For security purposes, it is important that you do not send any content for publication to us by e-mail.

Depending on the relevance of the article, we may print it in one of our other publications. If for example, the recipe has historical significance, we may feature it in *Historian Monthly*. Should such a republication occur, you will receive £750 per instance on top of the previously agreed sum of £750. You will be given an opportunity to turn down such offers before publication. Please fill out the enclosed publishing contract and send it back using the self-addressed envelope. Also, I need you to e-mail me your banking particulars as soon as possible so that I can arrange the advance payment of the originally commissioned article as we agreed by the end of the month.

Sincerely,

Tina Day

Tina Day
Editor — Coot Publishing

To:	Sean Monroe <smonroe@bluejay.com>
From:	Tina Day <tday@cootpublishing.com>
Date:	27 July
Subject:	Article

Dear Mr. Monroe,

I am happy to inform you that this month, we will be providing you payment of a total of £750 for the use of *Summer in Sunbury*. Payment will be made on the 15th of next month. Due to the popularity of the article, we would like to commission you to write a new article for our October-December issue. We would like to tentatively title it *Winter in Sunbury*. However, you may suggest a different topic and title if you have something else in mind. Please let me know if you would like to renegotiate your payment. Otherwise, we will assume the same arrangements are satisfactory.

Sincerely,

Tina Day
Editor — Coot Publishing

問題 **181-185** は次の手紙と E メールに関するものです。

3 月 17 日

Sean Monroe
Halifax 通り 123 番地
ロンドン

Monroe 様

『ロンドン料理ジャーナル』への寄稿に同意してくださってありがとうございます。特にサンベリーの Camden House で勤務されていたあなたの最近のご経験を考えますと、あなたの記事を読んで読者は間違いなく興奮するでしょう。あなたの記事は 1500 語以下になりますので、2 ページ見開き分しか利用できません。通常、わたくしどもはページの 60% を文章で、40% を絵や図で埋めるようにしております。もし使ってほしい写真をお持ちであったり、当社の写真家に具体的なご依頼があったりする場合は、できるだけ早くお知らせください。

記事の題は「サンベリーの夏」になる予定です。完成原稿はウェブサイト上のアップロードリンクを使ってご提出いただけます。安全のために、出版物のいかなる内容も E メールでは送っていただかないことが重要です。

記事の関連性によっては、わたくしどもの他の出版物の 1 つに載せる可能性があります。例えば、もしそのレシピに歴史的重要性があるなら、『月刊歴史家』で特集するかもしれません。万が一そのような再掲載があった場合、前もって同意いただいた合計額の 750 ポンドに加えて 1 件当たり 750 ポンドを受け取っていただきます。出版の前に、そのような提案を断る機会があります。同封の出版契約書にご記入いただき、返信用封筒を使って送り返してください。また、合意していた通り、もともとご依頼していた記事の前金を今月中にお支払いできるよう、あなたの銀行口座情報の詳細をできるだけ早く E メールで送っていただく必要があります。

よろしくお願いいたします。

Tina Day（署名）

Tina Day
編集者―Coot 出版

宛先：Sean Monroe <smonroe@bluejay.com>
送信者：Tina Day <tday@cootpublishing.com>
日付：7 月 27 日
件名：記事

Monroe 様

今月、「サンベリーの夏」の使用のため合計 750 ポンドをお支払いすることを喜んでお知らせいたします。支払いは来月 15 日です。この記事の人気が高いことから、10 月―12 月号の新しい記事の執筆をお願いしたいと思っております。暫定的に、記事の題名は「サンベリーの冬」としたいと思っております。しかし、もし他に何かお考えでしたら、別のテーマや題名を提案いただいてもかまいません。支払いについて再交渉されたい場合、お知らせください。そうでなければ、同じ取り決めでご満足なのだと考えます。

よろしくお願いいたします。

Tina Day
編集者―Coot 出版

181 What is the purpose of the letter?

(A) To suggest a location for a meeting

(B) To confirm the details of an assignment

(C) To request attendance at a conference

(D) To announce the adoption of a new policy

手紙の目的は何ですか。

(A) 面会場所を提案すること。

(B) 仕事の詳細を確認すること。

(C) 会議の出席を依頼すること。

(D) 新しい方針の採用を告知すること。

正解 B

設問に着目する問題

手紙の目的が何かということが問われている。E メールや、手紙などの文書の目的は、冒頭付近に書かれていることが多く、この問題の正解の根拠も、冒頭近くに登場している。冒頭で記事執筆を承諾してくれた Monroe さんに謝意を示し、期待も述べている。続いて As your article will be under 1,500 words, we will only be able to use a two-page spread. と、記事の長さとページ数について触れ、その後も写真の使用などについて説明し、執筆者の意向を尋ねている。これを、confirm the details of an assignment「仕事の詳細を確認する」と抽象的に言い換えている (B) が正解。assignment「任務」。

☐ attendance　　　　　　　　　出席
☐ adoption　　　　　　　　　採用

---

182 What is indicated about Coot Publishing?

(A) It has offices in several capital cities.

(B) It provides translations of articles online.

(C) It specializes in articles about Sunbury.

(D) It publishes magazines in various genres.

Coot 出版について何が示されていますか。

(A) いくつかの主要都市に営業所を持っている。

(B) オンラインで記事の翻訳を提供している。

(C) サンベリーについての記事に特化している。

(D) 様々なジャンルの雑誌を発行している。

正解 D

選択肢に着目する問題

手紙と E メールの差出人の情報から、Coot Publishing は、Monroe さんに記事を依頼した出版社と分かる。Monroe さんには料理雑誌への寄稿を依頼しているが、we may print it in one of our other publications. If for example, the recipe has historical significance, we may feature it in *Historian Monthly*. と、歴史関連の雑誌なども手掛けていることがうかがわれる。それを magazines in various genres と表現している (D) が正解。(A) の事務所の場所、(B) の翻訳については言及がない。

---

183 What does Ms. Day ask Mr. Monroe to send by e-mail?

(A) His bank account details

(B) Information about Camden House

(C) Photographs of his work

(D) His employment history

Day さんは Monroe さんに E メールで何を送るよう求めていますか。

(A) 彼の銀行口座の詳細

(B) Camden House についての情報

(C) 彼の作品の写真

(D) 彼の雇用履歴

正解 A

設問に着目する問題

出版社の Day さんが執筆者の Monroe さんに何を E メールで送付するよう頼んでいるかが問われている。正解の根拠は手紙の最後に示されている。I need you to e-mail me your banking particulars as soon as possible「あなたの銀行口座情報の詳細をできるだけ早く E メールで送っていただく必要がある」とあるので、(A) が正解。particulars は通常複数形で「詳細」という意味になり、選択肢では details と言い換えられている。なお、(C) の写真は content for publication と考えられ、セキュリティの観点から、E メールでは送付しないようにという記述があるため、不適切。

184 What is suggested about Mr. Monroe's article?

(A) It was used in multiple publications.

(B) Its publication was delayed.

(C) It has been reviewed in a newspaper.

(D) Its length was over the agreed number of words.

Monroe さんの記事について何が分かりますか。

(A) それは複数の出版物で使用された。

(B) その出版は遅れた。

(C) それは新聞で論評された。

(D) その長さが決められた語数を超えた。

正解 **A**

選択肢に着目するクロス問題

手紙の後半で、記事の報酬に関して他の出版物に再掲載される場合は、1件につき750ポンドがさらに支払われ、『ロンドン料理ジャーナル』に寄稿した分の元の原稿料は今月（3月中）に支払われると述べられている。Eメールの冒頭を見ると、I am happy to inform you that this month, we will be providing you payment of a total of £750 for the use of *Summer in Sunbury*. Payment will be made on the 15th of next month. とあり、next month つまり8月に追加の £750 が支払われる予定だと分かる。このことから、*Summer in Sunbury* の記事が他の出版物にも使用されたと判断できる。(A) が正解。

185 According to the e-mail, why might Mr. Monroe contact Ms. Day?

(A) To thank her for paying him a commission

(B) To ask for higher compensation

(C) To introduce another writer

(D) To offer advice on a publication date

Eメールによると、Monroe さんはなぜ Day さんに連絡を取る可能性がありますか。

(A) 手数料を支払ってくれたお礼をするため。

(B) より高額な報酬を要求するため。

(C) 別の執筆者を紹介するため。

(D) 発行日についての助言をするため。

正解 **B**

設問に着目する問題

この問題の正解根拠はEメールの最後の部分にある。Eメール送信者の Day さんは、Please let me know if you would like to renegotiate your payment. 「支払いについて再交渉されたい場合、お知らせください」と述べている。記事提供者の Monroe さんにとって支払いの再交渉は、報酬の値上げを意味することになるので、(B) が正解。compensation「報酬」。

語彙チェック

☐ segment	部分、ひとコマ		☐ previously	前もって、以前に
☐ culinary	料理の		☐ turn down ～	～を却下する、辞退する
☐ spread	見開き、広がり		☐ contract	契約、契約書
☐ typically	通常は		☐ particulars	詳細、明細
☐ content	内容		☐ advance payment	前払い金
☐ specific	具体的な、特定の		☐ commission	～を依頼する
☐ manuscript	原稿		☐ issue	（刊行物などの）号
☐ relevance	関連性		☐ tentatively	暫定的に
☐ significance	重要性		☐ renegotiate	～を再交渉する
☐ feature	～を特集する		☐ assume	～と推測する、と思う
☐ republication	再発表、再出版		☐ satisfactory	満足のいく、納得の
☐ instance	事例、場合			

Questions 186-190 refer to the following receipt and e-mails.

Customer name: Robert Paulson Account number: U7384834 Date: June 7	**Galvonesta Online Shopping**

Quantity	Description	Price
1	GHT Cordless drill	$143.00
1	¹⁸⁸ GHT Stepladder (180cm)	¹⁸⁸$87.00
1	GHT Disk saw	$210.00
1	Brianbuilt Wire cutters	$54.00

	Subtotal:	$494.00
¹⁸⁷ Galvonesta Members' Discount (5%):		¹⁸⁷$24.70
	¹⁸⁶ Delivery:	¹⁸⁶$0.00
	Amount paid:	**$469.30**

¹⁹⁰You may access this receipt at any time by checking the archived orders under the account tab of Galvonesta Online Shopping. Items to be returned must be in their original packaging and they must be returned with all of their parts intact. Customer support can provide return mailing labels which enable customers to return items without paying for postage.

To:	Robert Paulson <rpaulson@firecrab.com>
From:	Marla Carter <macarter@galvonesta.com>
Date:	June 12
Subject:	Returned goods
Attachment:	📎 form

Dear Mr. Paulson,

I am sorry to learn one of the items you ordered was not entirely satisfactory. Please use the attached form to submit a return request. Once that has been received by us, ¹⁸⁸we will refund the $87 purchase price. When we receive the product back, we will investigate the problem and contact the manufacturer to ensure that it does not happen again.

In case you require a replacement, please allow me to recommend the Faraday 500. It ¹⁸⁹is a fine alternative to the GHT model and very similarly priced. You will see that it has excellent reviews and a 36-month warranty.

Sincerely,

Marla Carter

問題 **186-190** は次の領収書と 2 通の E メールに関するものです。

数量	品名	価格
	お客様氏名:Robert Paulson	**Galvonesta オンラインショッピング**
	顧客番号:U7384834	
	日付:6 月 7 日	
1	GHT コードレスドリル	143.00 ドル
1	GHT 脚立(180cm)	87.00 ドル
1	GHT 丸のこぎり	210.00 ドル
1	Brianbuilt ニッパー	54.00 ドル
	小計:	494.00 ドル
	Galvonesta 会員割引(5%):	24.70 ドル
	配送料:	0.00 ドル
	支払額:	**469.30 ドル**

この領収書は、Galvonesta オンラインショッピングのアカウントタブの下の注文記録を確認することでいつでもご覧いただけます。返品する商品はもともとの梱包に入っていて、すべての部品が無傷の状態で返品されなければなりません。顧客サポート係か、お客様か郵送料を払わずに返品できる返送用の送り状をご用意できます。

宛先:Robert Paulson <rpaulson@firecrab.com>
送信者:Marla Carter <macarter@galvonesta.com>
日付:6 月 12 日
件名:返品
添付:書式

Paulson 様

ご注文いただいた品の 1 つが全面的にご満足いただけるものではなかったということで、申し訳ございません。添付の書式を使って返品依頼をご提出ください。それをわたくしどもで受け取りましたら、87 ドルのご購入金額を返金いたします。商品を受け取りましたら、問題を調査してメーカーに問い合わせ、もうこのようなことが絶対に起こらないようにいたします。

交換品が必要な場合、Faraday 500 をお薦めいたします。GHT モデルの代替品として申し分なく、価格も同程度です。高く評価されており、36 か月の保証期間つきであることがご確認いただけると思います。

よろしくお願いいたします。

Marla Carter

To:	Marla Carter <macarter@galvonesta.com>
From:	Robert Paulson <rpaulson@firecrab.com>
Date:	June 13
Subject:	RE: Returned goods

Dear Ms. Carter,

Thank you for processing my refund so quickly. It was much faster and simpler than I had imagined. As I am purchasing these items for work, it is necessary for me to view the updated receipt. Please advise me on how to do that.

Sincerely,

Robert Paulson

宛先：Marla Carter <macarter@galvonesta.com>
送信者：Robert Paulson <rpaulson@firecrab.com>
日付：6月13日
件名：RE：返品

Carter 様

こんなに早く返金手続きをしてくださってありがとうございます。想像していたよりもずっと早く、簡単でした。これらの商品は仕事のために購入していますので、私は最新の領収書を見る必要があります。どのようにして入手したらよいか教えてください。

よろしくお願いいたします。

Robert Paulson

語彙チェック

stepladder	脚立		once	ひとたび〜すると
disk saw	丸のこぎり		ensure that 〜	〜ということを保証する
archived	保存された、記録された		replacement	代用品、交換
intact	無傷なままの		alternative	代替品
entirely	完全に、まったく		process	〜を処理する
satisfactory	満足な		view	〜を見る
submit	〜を提出する			

186

What is indicated about Galvonesta?

(A) It ships some purchases free of charge.

(B) It purchases goods from local manufacturers.

(C) It advertises its services on the radio.

(D) It only sells GHT brand products.

Galvonesta 社について何が示されていますか。

(A) それはいくつかの購入品を無料で配送している。

(B) それは地元のメーカーから商品を購入している。

(C) それはラジオで自社のサービスを宣伝している。

(D) それは GHT ブランドの製品しか販売していない。

正解 A

選択肢に着目する問題

領収書から Galvonesta はオンラインショッピングの店と判断できる。領収書の Delivery「配送料」の項目が 0 ドルとなっていることから、それを ship ～ free of charge「無料で～を配送する」と言い換えている (A) が正解。商品の仕入れ先や広告に関しては言及がないため、(B)、(C) は不適切。領収書の Description「品名」の 4 つ目に GHT 以外と思われる商品が含まれているので、(D) も不適切。ship「～を配送する」。

187

What is suggested about Mr. Paulson?

(A) He has purchased goods online before.

(B) He was introduced to Galvonesta by a colleague.

(C) He requires an express shipment.

(D) He is a registered customer of Galvonesta.

Paulson さんについて何が分かりますか。

(A) 彼は以前にもオンラインで商品を購入したことがある。

(B) 彼は同僚に Galvonesta 社に紹介された。

(C) 彼は速達での配送を必要としている。

(D) 彼は Galvonesta 社の登録顧客である。

正解 D

選択肢に着目する問題

領収書内で、Paulson さんは、Galvonesta Members' Discount (5%) として 24.70 ドルの値引きがされていることから、オンラインショップの登録顧客と判断できる。したがって (D) が正解。登録しているからといって、以前にオンラインで買い物をしているかどうかは分からないので、(A) は不適切。(B)、(C) に関しては言及がない。

188

Which item was Mr. Paulson dissatisfied with?

(A) Cordless drill

(B) Stepladder

(C) Disk saw

(D) Wire cutters

Paulson さんはどの商品について不満ですか。

(A) コードレスドリル

(B) 脚立

(C) 丸のこぎり

(D) ニッパー

正解 B

設問に着目するクロス問題

Paulson さん宛ての E メールの件名に着目すると Returned goods「返品」とあり、E メール冒頭で返品の手続きを説明している。この問題の正解の根拠は返品される商品の金額にある。we will refund the $87 purchase price とあり、87 ドルが返金されることが分かるが、領収書を見ると、87 ドルの商品は GHT Stepladder (180cm) なので、正解は (B)。

189 In the first e-mail, the word "fine" in paragraph 2, line 2 is closest in meaning to

(A) excellent

(B) delicate

(C) penalty

(D) responsible

1通目のEメールの第2段落・2行目にある "fine" に最も意味が近いのは

(A) すばらしい

(B) 繊細な

(C) 処罰

(D) 責任がある

正解 A

同義語問題

fine が含まれるEメールの前半では、一部の商品の返品の手続きについて述べられていて、後半では返品される品物の alternative「代替品」として特定の商品をショップが推薦している。ショップが顧客に勧めているので、よい代替品という意味だと考えられる。したがって、(A) の excellent が正解。

190 What will Ms. Carter most likely advise Mr. Paulson to do?

(A) Write a product review

(B) Read some operating instructions

(C) Access the Web site

(D) Attend a workshop

Carter さんは Paulson さんに何をするよう助言すると考えられますか。

(A) 製品のレビューを書く。

(B) 取扱指示書を読む。

(C) ウェブサイトにアクセスする。

(D) 講習会に参加する。

正解 C

設問に着目するクロス問題

Paulson さんからのEメールで、Paulson さんは、it is necessary for me to view the updated receipt. Please advise me on how to do that. と、最新の領収書の取得方法を尋ねている。この問題の正解の根拠は、領収書の欄外の記述にある。そこには You may access this receipt at any time by checking the archived orders under the account tab of Galvonesta Online Shopping.「この領収書は、Galvonesta オンラインショッピングのアカウントタブの下の注文記録をチェックすることでいつでもご覧いただけます」とあり、ウェブサイトで閲覧するよう助言すると思われる。正解は (C)。

☐ operating instructions　　　　　取扱指示書

Questions 191-195 refer to the following Web page and e-mails.

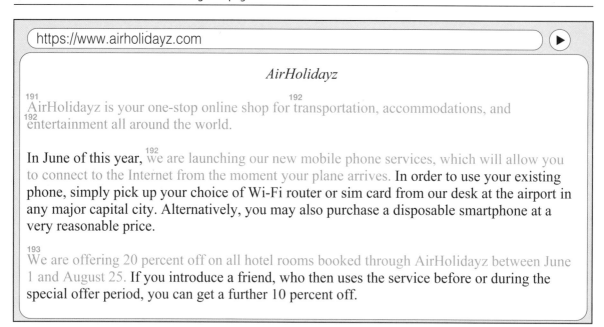

https://www.airholidayz.com ▶

AirHolidayz

[191] AirHolidayz is your one-stop online shop for [192] transportation, accommodations, and [192] entertainment all around the world.

In June of this year, [192] we are launching our new mobile phone services, which will allow you to connect to the Internet from the moment your plane arrives. In order to use your existing phone, simply pick up your choice of Wi-Fi router or sim card from our desk at the airport in any major capital city. Alternatively, you may also purchase a disposable smartphone at a very reasonable price.

[193] We are offering 20 percent off on all hotel rooms booked through AirHolidayz between June 1 and August 25. If you introduce a friend, who then uses the service before or during the special offer period, you can get a further 10 percent off.

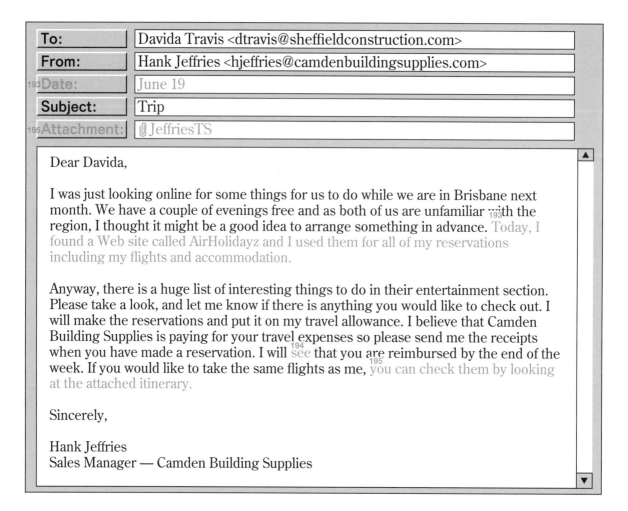

To:	Davida Travis <dtravis@sheffieldconstruction.com>
From:	Hank Jeffries <hjeffries@camdenbuildingsupplies.com>
[193] Date:	June 19
Subject:	Trip
[195] Attachment:	📎 JeffriesTS

Dear Davida,

I was just looking online for some things for us to do while we are in Brisbane next month. We have a couple of evenings free and as both of us are unfamiliar [193] with the region, I thought it might be a good idea to arrange something in advance. Today, I found a Web site called AirHolidayz and I used them for all of my reservations including my flights and accommodation.

Anyway, there is a huge list of interesting things to do in their entertainment section. Please take a look, and let me know if there is anything you would like to check out. I will make the reservations and put it on my travel allowance. I believe that Camden Building Supplies is paying for your travel expenses so please send me the receipts when you have made a reservation. I will [194] see that you are reimbursed by the end of the week. If you would like to take the same flights as me, [195] you can check them by looking at the attached itinerary.

Sincerely,

Hank Jeffries
Sales Manager — Camden Building Supplies

問題 **191-195** は次のウェブサイトと 2 通の E メールに関するものです。

https://www.airholidayz.com

AirHolidayz

AirHolidayz は世界中の交通手段、宿泊、娯楽を一括でそろえているオンラインショップです。

今年 6 月、当社は新しい携帯電話サービスを開始し、それによってお客様が飛行機ご到着直後からインターネットに接続できるようになります。現在お持ちの携帯電話を利用するためには、主要首都の空港内にある当社のデスクからお好みの Wi-Fi ルーターあるいは SIM カードを受け取るだけでかまいません。または、非常にお手頃な価格で使い捨てスマートフォンを購入することもできます。

6 月 1 日から 8 月 25 日までの間、AirHolidayz を通して予約したホテルのお部屋代を 20% 割引きいたします。ご友人を紹介いただき、その方が特別提供期間の前かその間にサービスをご利用された場合、さらに 10% 割引きさせていただきます。

宛先：Davida Travis <dtravis@sheffieldconstruction.com>
送信者：Hank Jeffries <hjeffries@camdenbuildingsupplies.com>
日付：6 月 19 日
件名：出張
添付：JeffriesTS

Davida さん

私たちが来月ブリスベンの滞在中にすることをオンラインで探していました。いくつかの日の夜に予定が空いており、私たちは 2 人ともその地域をよく知らないので、前もって何か手配しておくのがよいかもしれないと思いました。今日、AirHolidayz というウェブサイトを見つけ、私はそこを使って航空便と宿泊を含めたすべての予約をしました。

とにかく、そこの娯楽欄には面白いものの膨大なリストがあります。見てみて、チェックしたいものが何かあれば教えてください。私が予約をして出張手当につけておきます。Camden 建材社があなたの出張費を支払うでしょうから、予約をしたら私に領収書を送ってください。週の終わりまでには払い戻しを受けられるように注意しておきます。私と同じ便に乗りたい場合、添付の旅程表を見ていただければ確認できます。

よろしくお願いします。

Hank Jeffries
販売部部長— Camden 建材社

To:	Hank Jeffries <hjeffries@camdenbuildingsupplies.com>
From:	Davida Travis <dtravis@sheffieldconstruction.com>
Date:	June 19
Subject:	RE: Trip

Dear Hank,

Thank you for contacting me about the trip. It had slipped my mind. I plan to register with AirHolidayz and make all of the arrangements through them. However, I was unable to read the document you sent me. Would you mind sending it again in another format?

Sincerely,

Davida Travis
Project Manager — Sheffield Construction

宛先：Hank Jeffries <hjeffries@camdenbuildingsupplies.com>
送信者：Davida Travis <dtravis@sheffieldconstruction.com>
日付：6月19日
Subject：RE：出張

Hank さん

出張についてご連絡をありがとうございます。それについて失念しておりました。AirHolidayz 社に登録してそこを通じてすべての手配を行う予定です。しかし、送付してくださった書類を読むことができませんでした。もう一度、別の形式で送付していただけませんか。

よろしくお願いします。

Davida Travis
プロジェクト管理者—Sheffield 建設会社

191

What is indicated about AirHolidayz?

(A) It does not have any offices in other countries.

(B) It offers discount airfares.

(C) It can provide international reservations.

(D) It has merged with a telephone manufacturer.

AirHolidayz 社について何が示されていますか。

(A) 外国に事務所を持っていない。

(B) それは割引航空料金を提供している。

(C) それは国際間の予約を提供できる。

(D) 電話機メーカーと合併した。

正解 C

選択肢に着目する問題

この問題の正解の根拠は AirHolidayz 社のウェブページの冒頭にある。「世界中の交通手段、宿泊、娯楽を一括でそろえているオンラインショップ」と会社を自ら説明しているので、(C) が正解。(A) に関しては、our desk at the airport in any major capital city「主要首都の空港内にある当社のデスク」と述べられているので、他国にも事務所を構えていると判断でき、不適切。discount airfares や telephone manufacturer に関しては言及がないので、(B)、(D) は不適切。

☐ airfare 航空料金
☐ merge with ~ ～と合併する

192

What is NOT a service offered by AirHolidayz?

(A) Tickets for events

(B) Transportation arrangements

(C) Communications

(D) Travel insurance

AirHolidayz 社が提供しているサービスではないものは何ですか。

(A) イベントのチケット

(B) 交通手段の手配

(C) 通信

(D) 旅行保険

正解 D

NOT 問題

この問題の正解の根拠は AirHolidayz 社のウェブページにある。(A) は冒頭に entertainment のためのオンラインショップとあるので、一致する。(B) も同じく冒頭に transportation のためのオンラインショップとあり、一致する。(C) に関しては、6 月から we are launching our new mobile phone services, which will allow you to connect to the Internet from the moment your plane arrives. と、携帯電話のインターネット接続サービスを開始しているとあるので、一致する。正解は (D)。保険に関しては言及がない。insurance「保険」。

193

What is probably true about Mr. Jeffries?

(A) He is an employee of Sheffield Construction.

(B) He received a discount on his lodgings.

(C) He made Ms. Travis' travel arrangements for her.

(D) He has been to Brisbane in the past.

Jeffries さんについて正しいと思われることは何ですか。

(A) Sheffield 建設会社の従業員である。

(B) 宿泊料金を割引された。

(C) Travis さんの旅行の手配をした。

(D) ブリスベンに過去に行ったことがある。

正解 B

選択肢に着目するクロス問題

Jeffries さんは Camden 建材社の人間で、顧客である Sheffield 建設会社の Travis さんとブリスベンに出張に行くことが Jeffries さんの E メールから読み取れる。Today, I found a Web site called AirHolidayz and I used them for all of my reservations including my flights and accommodation. と述べており、E メールの送信日の 6 月 19 日に出張の旅行手配を AirHolidayz 社で行ったことが分かる。AirHolidayz 社のウェブページの後半を見ると、We are offering 20 percent off on all hotel rooms booked through AirHolidayz between June 1 and August 25. とあり、割引期間に予約したことになるので、(B) が正解。Travis さんが Sheffield 建設会社の従業員なので、(A) は不適切。(C) については言及なし。both of us are unfamiliar with the region とブリスベンについて述べているので、(D) は不適切。lodging「宿、宿所」。

194 In the first e-mail, the word "see" in paragraph 2, line 5 is closest in meaning to

(A) ensure

(B) view

(C) attend

(D) conclude

1 通目の E メールの第 2 段落・5 行目にある see に最も意味が近いのは

(A) 必ず〜するようにする

(B) 〜を見る

(C) 〜に出席する

(D) 〜を終える

正解 A

同義語問題

see の前後の文脈を見てみる。Jeffries さんは、Travis さんの旅費は Camden 建材社が負担するので、Travis さんの領収書は Jeffries さんに送るよう依頼し、続けて I will see that you are reimbursed by the end of the week. と、週末までには払い戻しが行われるよう注意して見ていると述べている。この see は「〜するよう注意深く見守る」を表していると考えられる。最も意味が近いのは (A)。

---

195 What does Ms. Travis ask Mr. Jeffries to send?

(A) His contact details

(B) A discount coupon

(C) A project update

(D) His schedule

Travis さんは Jeffries さんに何を送るよう求めていますか。

(A) 彼の連絡先詳細

(B) 割引クーポン

(C) プロジェクトの最新情報

(D) 彼の予定表

正解 D

設問に着目するクロス問題

Jeffries さんの E メールの最後に you can check them by looking at the attached itinerary. 「添付の旅程表を見ていただければ確認できる」と Travis さんに伝えているが、その返答である Travis さんからの E メールの最後には I was unable to read the document you sent me. Would you mind sending it again in another format? 「送付してくださった書類を読むことができませんでした。もう一度、別の形式で送付していただけませんか」と再度 itinerary の送付を頼んでいる。itinerary を schedule と言い換えている (D) が正解。

☐ update　　　　　　　　　最新情報

Questions 196-200 refer to the following advertisement, memo, and e-mail.

Choose Spark Advertising for your next promotion!

Spark Advertising is an award-winning firm with more than 40 years in the business. We handle all types of promotion and advertising from store openings to community festivals,[196] but our main area of expertise is courses for professional development.

Visit our special Web site at www.sparkadvertising.promotion.com to learn more about our offerings.[197] There, you will find a portfolio of some of our most important work, **our mission statement,**[197] a timeline showing the main events in our corporate history, and[197] a helpful list of phone numbers and extensions so that you can get in touch with the customer service agents in the department most relevant to your needs.

In order to attract new clients, this month we are offering an all-inclusive package with one month of radio and Internet advertising and all associated production and design work for just $4,000. That is a saving of over $2,500.

To: Mel Waterhouse
From: Dourine Cleminson
Subject: Campaign
Date: December 17

Dear Mel,

Just so you know, I have arranged to have Spark Advertising handle our promotional campaign this year.[198] It will cost us only $4,000,[199] which is far cheaper than what Donaldson Associates has been charging. I would like you to attend a meeting with me and one of their representatives this Friday afternoon.

I have reserved Conference Room 3 from 3:00 P.M. She is coming all the way from Salisbury to meet with us. I would like some assistance evaluating her proposal, so[199] please invite one or two of your department members who have been involved in advertising our products over the last two years.

問題 **196-200** は次の広告、メモ、E メールに関するものです。

次の販売促進に Spark 広告会社をお選びください！

Spark 広告会社は 40 年以上の営業実績を持つ、受賞歴のある会社です。店舗の開店から地域のお祭りまで、あらゆる種類の販売促進と広告宣伝を扱っておりますが、主な専門領域は専門的能力の開発です。

特設ウェブサイト、www.sparkadvertising.promotion.com を訪れて我が社の提供するサービスについてもっと知ってください。そこには、我が社の最も重要な仕事の一部の作品選集、企業理念、企業の歴史上の主要な出来事を示す年表、また、あなたのニーズに最も関係した部署の顧客サービス係に連絡を取るのに役立つ電話番号と内線リストがあります。

新規の顧客を引き付けるために、今月は、1 か月のラジオとインターネット広告、そして関連商品すべてと、デザイン業務を含む総合パッケージをたったの 4,000 ドルでご提供しています。それは 2,500 ドル以上の節約になります。

宛先：Mel Waterhouse
差出人：Dourine Cleminson
件名：キャンペーン
日付：12 月 17 日

Mel 様

念のためお伝えしますが、今年の我が社の販売促進キャンペーンは Spark 広告会社に取り扱ってもらうよう手配しました。費用は 4,000 ドルしかかからないから、Donaldson 社が請求してきている金額よりはるかに安いです。今週金曜日の午後、あなたに私と一緒に向こうの担当者の 1 人との会議に出てもらいたいと思います。

会議室 3 を午後 3 時から予約しました。彼女ははるばるソールズベリーから私たちに会いに来てくれます。彼女の提案を評価するのに助けがほしいので、あなたの部署のメンバーで過去 2 年間、我が社の商品広告に携わってきた人を 1 人か 2 人、呼んできてください。

To:	Mel Waterhouse <mwaterhouse@hasting.com>
From:	Vera Klinger <vklinger@hasting.com>
Subject:	RE: Meeting
Date:	December 18

Dear Ms. Waterhouse,

[199] Thank you for inviting me to attend the meeting with the representative from Spark Advertising. Unfortunately, I have scheduled a dentist's appointment for that time and I am not able to reschedule. However, I am very interested in attending. Is there any [200] chance that we can change the meeting time?

Sincerely,

Vera

宛先：Mel Waterhouse <mwaterhouse@hasting.com>
送信者：Vera Klinger <vklinger@hasting.com>
件名：RE：会議
日付：12月18日

Waterhouse 様

Spark 広告会社の担当者との会議に出席するよう呼んでくださりありがとうございます。残念ながら、その時間に歯医者の予約を入れてしまっていて、予定変更ができません。しかし、出席することにはとても興味があります。会議の時間を変更できる可能性はありますか。

よろしくお願いします。

Vera

語彙チェック

☐	promotion	販売促進	☐	relevant to ～	～に関連した
☐	award-winning	受賞歴のある	☐	attract	～を引き付ける
☐	handle	～を扱う	☐	all-inclusive	すべて込みの、包括的な
☐	expertise	専門知識、専門技術	☐	associated	関連した
☐	portfolio	ポートフォリオ、作品集	☐	saving	節約
☐	mission statement	企業理念	☐	representative	担当者、代表者
☐	timeline	年表	☐	all the way	はるばる
☐	extension	内線電話	☐	evaluate	～を評価する
☐	get in touch with ～	～と連絡を取る	☐	be involved in ～	～に携わる

196

According to the advertisement, what kind of promotion does Spark Advertising specialize in?

(A) Store openings

(B) Education

(C) Community events

(D) Theater

広告によると、Spark 広告会社はどのような種類の販売促進を専門にしていますか。

(A) 店舗の開店

(B) 教育

(C) 地域のイベント

(D) 劇場

正解 B

設問に着目する問題

Spark 広告社の広告の中に、We handle all types of promotion and advertising from store openings to community festivals, but our main area of expertise is courses for professional development.「店舗の開店から地域のお祭りまであらゆる種類の販売促進と広告宣伝を扱っていますが、主な専門領域は専門的能力の開発です」と記載がある。courses for professional development を education と言い換えている (B) が正解。

197

What is NOT featured on the Spark Advertising special Web site?

(A) Directions to the company's offices

(B) Samples of work from previous projects

(C) Contact details for company representatives

(D) Information about Spark Advertising's past

Spark 広告会社の特設ウェブサイトに掲載されていないことは何ですか。

(A) 会社のオフィスへの道順

(B) 以前のプロジェクトの作品例

(C) 会社の担当者の連絡先詳細

(D) Spark 広告会社の過去についての情報

正解 A

NOT 問題

正解の根拠は広告にある。portfolio が見られると述べられているので、(B) の Samples of work と一致する。(C) は a helpful list of phone numbers and extensions と一致する。(D) は a timeline showing the main events in our corporate history「企業の歴史上の主要な出来事を示す年表」と一致する。(A) の Directions に関しての記載はないので、(A) が正解。

198

What is probably true about Ms. Cleminson's organization?

(A) It has renewed its contract with Donaldson Associates.

(B) It is based in Salisbury.

(C) It has not used Spark Advertising before.

(D) It has won a business award.

Cleminson さんの組織について正しいと思われることは何ですか。

(A) それは Donaldson 社との契約を更新した。

(B) それはソールズベリーに本拠を持つ。

(C) それは以前に Spark 広告会社を利用したことがない。

(D) ビジネス賞を受賞したことがある。

正解 C

選択肢に着目する問題

Cleminson さんはメモの差出人であり、メモの冒頭で彼の会社の販促キャンペーンを Spark 広告会社が取り扱うよう手配したと述べている。続けて It will cost us only $4,000, which is far cheaper than what Donaldson Associates has been charging.「費用は 4,000 ドルしかかからないから、Donaldson 社が請求してきている金額よりはるかに安い」とあり、今までは Donaldson 社がキャンペーンを取り扱ってきていると想像できる。今回初めて Spark 広告会社と取引すると思われるので、(C) が正解。

☐ renew 〜を更新する
☐ contract 契約

199 What is implied about Ms. Klinger?

(A) She has recently transferred to Hastings College.

(B) She attended a conference in Salisbury.

(C) She is familiar with the work of Donaldson Associates.

(D) She introduced Spark Advertising to Ms. Waterhouse.

Klinger さんについて何が示唆されていますか。

(A) 彼女は最近 Hastings 大学に異動した。

(B) 彼女はソールズベリーでの会議に出席した。

(C) 彼女は Donaldson 社の仕事をよく知っている。

(D) 彼女は Spark 広告会社を Waterhouse さんに紹介した。

正解 **C**

選択肢に着目するクロス問題

Klinger さんは社内の Waterhouse さんに宛てた E メールの中で、Thanks for inviting me to attend the meeting with the representative from Spark Advertising. と述べていることから、会議への出席を依頼されていることが分かる。また、Waterhouse さんは Cleminson さんから、please invite one or two of your department members who have been involved in advertising our products over the last two years と指示されているので、Klinger さんが過去数年間の広告担当をしていたと分かる。彼らの会社は Donaldson 社を今まで使用していたことは、メモの冒頭の which is far cheaper than what Donaldson Associates has been charging 「Donaldson 社が請求してきている金額よりはるかに安い」から分かるので、Klinger さんは Donaldson 社と広告の仕事をした経験があると判断できる。正解は (C)。be familiar with 〜「〜に精通している」。

200 In the e-mail, the word "chance" in paragraph 1, line 4 is closest in meaning to

(A) risk

(B) speculation

(C) accident

(D) possibility

E メールの第 1 段落・4 行目にある chance に最も意味が近いのは

(A) 危険

(B) 思索

(C) 偶然

(D) 可能性

正解 **D**

同義語問題

chance を含むフレーズ Is there any chance 〜? は「〜の可能性はあるか」という意味で、可能性を問うときに使用する表現。会議に出席したいが歯医者の予約が変えられず出席できない、という状況で発言しており、「会議の時間を変更することができないか」と可能性を尋ねているので、この chance は「可能性」を表している。正解は (D)。

Day 11

【TEST 1　Questions 147-175】　2/5回目

Day 11は、**Day 1〜5で解いたシングルパッセージ10題**をもう一度まとめて解く日です。**別冊TEST 1の147番〜175番（別冊P3〜13）**を解きましょう。制限時間は**29分**です。解き終わったら、解説はDay 1〜5の解説ページ（本冊P14〜33）を見て確認してください。

Day 12

【TEST 1　Questions 176-200】　2/5回目

Day 12は、**Day 6〜10で解いたマルチプルパッセージ5題**をもう一度まとめて解く日です。**別冊TEST 1の176番〜200番（別冊P14〜23）**を解きましょう。制限時間は**25分**です。解き終わったら、解説はDay 6〜10の解説ページ（本冊P34〜59）を見て確認してください。

Day 13

【TEST 1　Questions 147-200】　3/5回目

Day 13は、**Day 11〜12で解いた問題**をまとめて解く日です。**別冊TEST 1の147番〜200番（別冊P3〜23）**を解きましょう。制限時間は**54分**です。解き終わったら、解説はDay 1〜10の解説ページ（本冊P14〜59）を見て確認してください。

TEST 2

解答&解説

正解一覧					
問題番号	**正解**		**問題番号**	**正解**	
147	A		176	A	
148	D		177	D	
149	B		178	B	
150	C		179	C	
151	C		180	C	
152	D		181	B	
153	B		182	D	
154	C		183	A	
155	B		184	A	
156	C		185	B	
157	C		186	A	
158	D		187	D	
159	A		188	A	
160	D		189	A	
161	A		190	D	
162	D		191	C	
163	A		192	D	
164	A		193	B	
165	C		194	A	
166	B		195	D	
167	B		196	B	
168	C		197	A	
169	D		198	C	
170	B		199	C	
171	B		200	D	
172	D				
173	C				
174	A				
175	A				

Questions 147-148 refer to the following notice.

NOTICE

**The counter area must be kept clear
for service technicians to use at any time.**

- Please do not store delivered items, personal items, or tools on the workbench.

- Due to the sensitive nature of the equipment used in this section, you must not eat or drink here at any time.

- If you need to use the area for any purpose other than the maintenance or repair of merchandise, please contact the chief of the service department, Alex Steele.

問題 **147-148** は次のお知らせに関するものです。

お知らせ

保守技術員がいつでも使用できるよう、カウンター付近にはものを置いたままにしてはいけません。

・納品物、私物、道具類などは作業台に保管しないでください。

・当部署で使用されるのは繊細な機器のため、常時ここでの飲食はしないでください。

・商品の保守や修理以外の目的でこの場所を使用する必要があるときは、サービス部部長の Alex Steele に連絡を取ってください。

147 For whom is the notice most likely intended?

(A) Employees

(B) Customers

(C) Business owners

(D) Job applicants

お知らせは誰に向けられていると考えられますか。

(A) 従業員

(B) 顧客

(C) 企業のオーナー

(D) 求職者

正解 **A**

設問に着目する問題

お知らせの内容は、「カウンター付近にものを置かない」、「私物などを作業台に保管しない」、「飲食をしない」など、あるエリアでの注意事項である。また、使用許可のための連絡先として最後に the chief of the service department, Alex Steele とあり、社名なども入っていないため、社内の従業員に宛てたものと判断できる。正解は (A)。

148 According to the notice, what activity is forbidden in the area?

(A) Use of electronic equipment

(B) Preparation for meetings

(C) Taking breaks from work

(D) Consumption of beverages

お知らせによると、その場所ではどんな活動が禁止されていますか。

(A) 電子機器の使用

(B) 会議の準備

(C) 仕事中の休憩の取得

(D) 飲み物の摂取

正解 **D**

設問に着目する問題

禁止されている活動は何かが問われているが、お知らせでは禁止事項が箇条書きで示されている。you must not eat or drink here「ここでの飲食はしないでください」とあるので、drink を consumption of beverages と言い換えている (D) が正解。consumption「摂取」は動詞 consume の名詞形。forbidden「禁じられている」、beverage「飲み物」。

語彙チェック

☐ clear	(じゃま者などの) 妨げのない
☐ service technician	保守技術員
☐ store	~を保管する
☐ workbench	作業台
☐ sensitive	繊細な、敏感な
☐ merchandise	商品

Questions 149-150 refer to the following text-message chain.

TIM CLEM (4:20 P.M.)
That delivery of food for the party you ordered still hasn't arrived. What time was it due again?

ANDREA ORTA (4:21 P.M.)
About 20 minutes ago. I'll give them a call and find out what's going on.

ANDREA ORTA (4:25 P.M.)
They said someone's on the way. We'll just have to wait. I'll gather everyone in the conference room and we can start the party. Would you mind waiting at reception?

TIM CLEM (4:27 P.M.)
I don't mind, but what for?

ANDREA ORTA (4:28 P.M.)
We have to pay the delivery driver in cash.

TIM CLEM (4:30 P.M.)
I can hear the doorbell in the conference room. I don't think there's any need to wait in reception.

ANDREA ORTA (4:31 P.M.)
OK, then. Let's get the party started. It's time.

問題 **149-150** は次のテキストメッセージのやりとりに関するものです。

TIM CLEM　（午後 4 時 20 分）
あなたが頼んでくれたパーティー用の食べ物がまだ到着していませんよ。何時の予定でしたっけ？

ANDREA ORTA　（午後 4 時 21 分）
およそ 20 分前です。電話をしてどうなっているのか聞いてみます。

ANDREA ORTA　（午後 4 時 25 分）
こちらに向かっている途中と言っていました。待つしかないですね。私が会議室に全員を集めれば、パーティーを開始できます。受付で待っていていただけませんか。

TIM CLEM　（午後 4 時 27 分）
いいけれど、何のためにですか。

ANDREA ORTA　（午後 4 時 28 分）
配達の運転手に現金で支払わなければならないんです。

TIM CLEM　（午後 4 時 30 分）
会議室でドアベルの音は聞こえますよ。受付で待つ必要はないと思います。

ANDREA ORTA　（午後 4 時 31 分）
それなら、分かりました。パーティーを始めましょう。時間です。

149 Why does Mr. Clem start the text-message chain?

(A) To announce the start of a party
(B) To inquire about a delivery time
(C) To request money to pay for some food
(D) To ask about a menu item

Clem さんはなぜテキストメッセージのやりとりを始めていますか。

(A) パーティーの開始を知らせるため。
(B) 配達時間について問い合わせるため。
(C) 食べ物の支払いのためのお金を要求するため。
(D) メニューの品目について尋ねるため。

正解 **B**

設問に着目する問題

正解の根拠は Clem さんの最初の発言にある。That delivery of food for the party you ordered still hasn't arrived. What time was it due again?「あなたが頼んでくれたパーティー用の食べ物がまだ到着していない。何時の予定でしたか」と、食べ物の到着する時間を再確認している。inquire about 〜は「〜について問い合わせる」という意味なので、(B) が正解。

☐ item　　　　　　　　　品目

---

150 At 4:30 P.M., why does Mr. Clem write, "I can hear the doorbell in the conference room"?

(A) He believes that their doorbell is in working order.
(B) He thinks that the volume is set too high.
(C) He would prefer not to wait at reception.
(D) He is letting Ms. Orta know a delivery has arrived.

午後 4 時 30 分に Clem さんはなぜ "I can hear the doorbell in the conference room" と書いていますか。

(A) ドアベルが正常に作動していると信じているから。
(B) 音量が過大に設定されていると思っているから。
(C) 受付で待ちたいと思っていないから。
(D) Orta さんに配達が到着したことを知らせているから。

正解 **C**

意図問題

Orta さんから受付で配達を待ってほしいと依頼されたことに対する Clem さんの返事が I can hear the doorbell in the conference room. である。Clem さんは続けて、I don't think there's any need to wait in reception.「受付で待つ必要はないと思う」と書いているので、彼はパーティーが始まる会議室で待ちたいと思って書いたと考えられる。(C) が正解。

☐ in working order　　　　正常に動作している

語彙チェック
☐ due　　　　　　　　　到着予定の、予定されて
☐ reception　　　　　　受付
☐ get 〜 started　　　　〜を開始する

65

Questions 151-152 refer to the following advertisement.

Expand your business
the safe way with Carter, Inc.

¹⁵¹ Carter, Inc. provides skilled, short-term employees to businesses of any size to overcome seasonal staffing shortcomings or tentatively fill positions as they expand. Register your business online and immediately get access to our easy-to-use request system. You can easily indicate the required qualifications, set the duration of the contract, and indicate working hours. In most cases, you can expect a reply within hours. ¹⁵² Carter, Inc. ensures that it has the top people for any position by providing in-house training to every candidate. We offer courses in secretarial skills, construction work, customer service and even cooking and hospitality. That is why Carter, Inc. is the place most businesses turn to for personnel when time is of the essence.

Carter, Inc.

問題 **151-152** は次の広告に関するものです。

Carter 社とともに安全にあなたのビジネスを拡大しましょう。

Carter 社は、季節的なスタッフ不足を克服したり、事業拡大にあわせて暫定的にポジションを埋めたりするために、あらゆる規模の企業に熟練した短期の従業員を提供いたします。オンラインであなたの会社を登録し、簡単に使えるリクエストシステムにすぐにアクセスしてください。必要な要件を示し、契約期間を設定し、就業時間を示すことが容易にできます。ほとんどの場合に、数時間以内にご返答いたします。Carter 社ではすべての候補者に社内トレーニングを行うことにより、どんなポジションにもトップレベルの人材を確実にご用意しています。当社は秘書スキル、建設作業、カスタマーサービス、さらには料理やおもてなしの講座を提供しています。そのようなわけで、Carter 社は、多くの企業が、時間が非常に重要なときに、人事に関して頼って来られる会社なのです。

Carter 社

151 What is being advertised?

(A) A business consultancy

(B) Employment opportunities

(C) A temporary staffing agency

(D) Communications software

何が宣伝されていますか。

(A) 事業のコンサルタント業務

(B) 雇用機会

(C) 人材派遣会社

(D) コミュニケーションソフト

正解 **C**

設問に着目する問題

Carter, Inc. という会社の広告であるが、この会社の業務が何であるかを見極めればよい。正解の根拠は冒頭にある。provides skilled, short-term employees to businesses「企業に熟練した短期の従業員を提供」、overcome seasonal staffing shortcomings「季節的なスタッフ不足を克服」、tentatively fill positions as they expand「事業拡大にあわせて暫定的にポジションを埋めたりする」などから、Carter, Inc. は人材派遣会社であると判断できる。(C) が正解。

☐ consultancy　　　　　コンサルタント業務

152 What is indicated about Carter, Inc.?

(A) It has an agreement with a local vocational college.

(B) It can provide customer assistance 24 hours a day.

(C) It allows users to search its online database.

(D) It offers employees opportunities to improve their skills.

Carter 社について何が示されていますか。

(A) 地元の専門学校と協定を結んでいる。

(B) 24 時間いつでもカスタマーサービスを行うことができる。

(C) 使用者が会社のオンラインデータベースを検索できる。

(D) 従業員にスキル向上の機会を提供している。

正解 **D**

選択肢に着目する問題

Carter, Inc. ensures that it has the top people for any position by providing in-house training to every candidate.「Carter 社ではすべての候補者に社内トレーニングを行うことにより、どんなポジションにもトップレベルの人材を確実にご用意しています」とあり、よい人材の提供をするために、社内で様々な訓練を行っていることが分かる。正解は (D)。offer opportunities「機会を提供する」、improve skills「技術を向上させる」。

☐ vocational　　　　　職業の

語彙チェック

☐ skilled	熟練した
☐ overcome	～を克服する
☐ shortcoming	不足
☐ tentatively	暫定的に
☐ required	必須の
☐ qualification	要件、能力
☐ duration	期間
☐ ensure that ～	～ということを確実にする
☐ in-house	社内の
☐ secretarial	秘書の、秘書業務に関する
☐ hospitality	おもてなし
☐ personnel	人事課
☐ of the essence	非常に重要な

Questions 153-154 refer to the following letter.

Flanders Kitchenware
Montgomery Shopping Mall
362 Holden Rd., Seattle, WA 98019
(206) 555-8394

June 1

Mr. Hans Ferdinand
63 Hannover Avenue, Apt. 7
Seattle, WA 98018

Dear Mr. Ferdinand,

Flanders Kitchenware is proud to have you among its clientele. In the past, [154] you mentioned our store on your very popular radio cooking program on Radio 4JK. While we have never paid for your endorsements, we have benefited greatly from the publicity your show brings us. In fact, since your show was syndicated, we have been welcoming more and more clientele from outside Seattle.

For the last month, the store has been closed so that some expansion and a complete renovation could be carried out. [153] I am writing to announce that the store will be reopening on June 14. We will be holding a celebration, which includes cooking demonstrations, giveaways, and special discounts for registered customers.

We would be honored if you could visit Flanders Kitchenware on that date. [154] If you would like to broadcast the show from the store, you would be welcome to make use of any or all of our amenities as well as have the complete cooperation of our six highly capable staff members.

If you are interested, you may contact me at skildare@flanderskitchenware.com.

Sincerely,

Steve Kildare

Steve Kildare
Manager

問題 **153-154** は次の手紙に関するものです。

Flanders 台所用品店
Montgomery ショッピングモール
Holden 通り 362 番地、シアトル、WA 98019
(206) 555-8394

6 月 1 日
Hans Ferdinand 様
Hannover 通り 63 番地、7 番アパート
シアトル、WA 98018
Ferdinand 様
Flanders 台所用品店はあなたにお客様になっていただけることを誇りに思います。過去に、ラジオ 4JK でのあなたの大人気ラジオ料理番組で、あなたは私たちの店について言及してくださいました。私たちはあなたのご推薦に対して何もお支払いしたことはありませんが、あなたの番組によってもたらされた知名度により私たちは非常に利益を得ました。実際、あなたの番組が複数ネットで放送されて以来、シアトル外からますます多くのお客様をお迎えしております。
ここ 1 か月、店の拡張と全面改装のため、閉店しておりました。当店は 6 月 14 日に再開いたしますことをお知らせしようと思い、手紙を書いています。私たちは祝賀会を開き、料理の実演、景品配布、登録顧客向け特別割引をいたします。
当日、あなたに Flanders 台所用品店にいらしていただけますと光栄です。もし当店から番組を放送なさりたい場合、私たちの設備のどれでも、あるいはすべてをご自由に利用していただいてかまいませんし、当店の極めて有能な 6 人のスタッフも全面的に協力させていただきます。
ご興味がありましたら、skildare@flanderskitchenware.com までご連絡ください。
よろしくお願いします。
Steve Kildare（署名）
Steve Kildare
支配人

153 What is a purpose of the letter?

(A) To confirm a broadcast schedule

(B) To announce a special event

(C) To explain membership rules

(D) To offer payment for advertising

手紙の目的は何ですか。

(A) 放送予定を確認すること。

(B) 特別イベントを告知すること。

(C) 会員規則の説明をすること。

(D) 宣伝の報酬を提供すること。

正解 B

設問に着目する問題

手紙の目的が何かが問われている。この問題では、I am writing to ～「～するために書いている」という表現に注目できれば、正解の根拠が見つかる。I am writing to announce that the store will be reopening on June 14. We will be holding a celebration, which includes cooking demonstrations, giveaways, and special discounts for registered customers. とあり、6月14日に新装開店し、様々な祝賀イベントが顧客のために開かれることが述べられている。(B) が正解。

154 Who most likely is Mr. Ferdinand?

(A) The manager of a store

(B) An engineer of a radio station

(C) A local celebrity

(D) The owner of a construction company

Ferdinand さんとはおそらく誰ですか。

(A) 店の支配人

(B) ラジオ局の技師

(C) 地元の有名人

(D) 建設会社のオーナー

正解 C

設問に着目する問題

手紙の受取人である Ferdinand さんについて、you mentioned our store on your very popular radio cooking program on Radio 4JK「ラジオ 4JK でのあなたの大人気ラジオ料理番組で、あなたは私たちの店について言及してくれた」とある。また、来たるべき祝賀イベントにおいても、If you would like to broadcast the show from the store「もし当店から番組を放送なさりたい場合」とあることから、Ferdinand さんはラジオ番組の出演者であると判断できる。それを celebrity と言い換えている (C) が正解。celebrity「有名人」。

語彙チェック

be proud to *do*	～することを誇りに思う
clientele	顧客
endorsement	(公共媒体での商品の) 推薦
benefit	利益を得る
publicity	知れ渡ること、評判
syndicated	同時配給されている
expansion	拡張
carry out ～	～を行う
giveaway	景品、無料サンプル
be honored	光栄に思う
amenity	設備
capable	有能な

Questions 155-157 refer to the following schedule.

Raymond City
12th Annual Rhythm and Blues Festival
Sunday, September 21

10:00 A.M.– 12:00 NOON.	**Blues concert with performances by the Glendale High School Band as well as a number of excellent local amateur performers.** Tickets are free, but it is necessary to register in advance on the Web site. Gather in the Greenwood Park Center Auditorium.
11:00 A.M.– 12:00 NOON.	**A guitar lesson with Val Borland.** All are welcome! Just bring a guitar to the main tent at the entrance of Greenwood Park.
11:45 A.M.– 1:00 P.M.	Enjoy lunch served from stalls operated by local restaurants. The stalls will be located on the pathway along the Raymond River. Delicious food at competitive prices.
12:00 NOON.– 2:00 P.M.	An open-air concert **by The Blues Cats.** This wonderful band will take a break from their national tour to lend their support to the Raymond City Rhythm and Blues Festival.
2:00 P.M.– 3:30 P.M.	**Battle of the Bands.** 20 acts from in and around Raymond City will vie for the top prize and a possible recording contract with TVW Record Company. Sign up on the day. Registration forms are available from the main tent at the venue.

All events will be held at Greenwood Park on Orlando Street.
For more information, visit the festival Web site at www.raymondcrabfest.com.

問題 **155-157** は次の予定表に関するものです。

Raymond 市
第 12 回　年に一度のリズムアンドブルースフェスティバル
9 月 21 日（日曜日）

午前 10 時―正午	**Glendale 高校スクールバンドと多くの地元の優秀なアマチュア演奏家の演奏によるブルースコンサート**。入場無料ですが、事前にウェブサイトでの登録が必要です。Greenwood 公園の中央講堂に集まってください。
午前 11 時―正午	**Val Borland さんによるギターレッスン**。どなたも歓迎です！Greenwood 公園入口のメインテントにギターを持参してください。
午前 11 時 45 分―午後 1 時	地元の飲食店が出店する屋台で出される昼食をお楽しみください。屋台は Raymond 川沿いの小道に並びます。低価格のおいしいお食事です。
正午―午後 2 時	**The Blues Cats による野外コンサート**。このすばらしいバンドは国内ツアーを休んで Raymond 市のリズムアンドブルースフェスティバルに力を貸してくれます。
午後 2 時―午後 3 時 30 分	**バンド 対抗戦**。Raymond 市内外からの 20 組が 一等賞と TVW レコード会社とのレコーディング契約の可能性をかけて競い合います。当日に登録してください。登録用紙は会場のメインテントで入手可能です。

すべてのイベントは Orlando 通りの Greenwood 公園で開催されます。

さらに詳しい情報は、フェスティバルのウェブサイト www.ramondcrabfest.com にアクセスしてください。

155 According to the schedule, what will be sold at the festival?

(A) Concert tickets

(B) Meals

(C) Guitar lessons

(D) Albums

予定表によると、フェスティバルで何が販売されますか。

(A) コンサートのチケット

(B) 食事

(C) ギターレッスン

(D) アルバム

正解 **B**

設問に着目する問題

予定表の午前 11 時 45 分から午後 1 時までの欄に、Enjoy lunch served from stalls operated by local restaurants.「地元の飲食店が出店する屋台で出される昼食をお楽しみください」や、Delicious food at competitive prices.「低価格のおいしいお食事です」とある。lunch を meals と言い換えている (B) が正解。

☐
☐
☐

156 When will the outdoor event start?

(A) At 10:00 A.M.

(B) At 11:00 A.M.

(C) At 12:00 NOON.

(D) At 2:00 P.M.

屋外イベントが始まるのはいつですか。

(A) 午前 10 時

(B) 午前 11 時

(C) 正午

(D) 午後 2 時

正解 **C**

設問に着目する問題

午前中の 2 つのイベントは、それぞれ Greenwood Park Center Auditorium と main tent at the entrance of Greenwood Park とあり、講堂とテントで行われる。正午から午後 2 時に、An open-air concert「野外コンサート」が行われるので、(C) が正解。

☐
☐
☐

157 Where can people obtain a registration form for the competition?

(A) At the outdoor stage

(B) From the Web site

(C) At the park entrance

(D) On the river path

コンテストの登録用紙はどこで入手できますか。

(A) 野外ステージ

(B) ウェブサイト

(C) 公園の入口

(D) 川沿いの道

正解 **C**

設問に着目するクロス問題

予定表の中の 4 つの音楽イベントの中で、20 acts from in and around Raymond City will vie for the top prize「Raymond 市内外からの 20 組が一等賞をかけて競い合う」とあるので、competition「コンテスト」があるのは Battle of the Bands.「バンド対抗戦」と判断できる。Registration forms are available from the main tent at the venue. とあり、登録用紙は会場のメインテントで入手できる。そこで、午前 11 時からのギターレッスンの詳細を見ると、the main tent at the entrance of Greenwood Park とあるので、メインテントは Greenwood 公園入り口にあると分かる。正解は (C)。

☐
☐
☐

☐　path　　　　　　　　　　小道

語彙チェック

☐ in advance	事前に	☐ competitive	(価格などが) 競争力の高い
☐ auditorium	講堂	☐ open-air	野外の
☐ stall	屋台、売店	☐ act	芸人、出し物
☐ pathway	小道、歩道	☐ vie for ～	～を求めて競う

Questions 158-160 refer to the following e-mail.

From:	Gregory Holland <gholland@hammondfloorings.com>
To:	Norma Rose <nrose@londonhomerenovations.com.uk>
Subject:	Tiles
Date:	March 7

Dear Norma,

We were ready to send the floor tile samples you need for your promotional event on March 19 today, but unfortunately, the airports around New York have been forced to close due to the snow. We don't have word on when they will reopen. I have had to make other arrangements.

I have been in touch with another of our customers in the United Kingdom and have explained the situation to them. They are NHL Building Supplies in Glasgow, Scotland. The contact person there is Hamish McDougal and he has agreed to send the products you require by express delivery.

The cost of the items and the delivery charges will be paid for by Hammond Floorings in the United States. If there are any problems with the shipment, please contact Mr. McDougal directly. His e-mail address is hmacdougal@nhlbuildingsupplies.com.

Sincerely,

Gregory Holland
Manager — Hammond Floorings

問題 **158-160** は次の E メールに関するものです。

送信者：Gregory Holland <gholland@hammondfloorings.com>
宛先：Norma Rose <nrose@londonhomerenovations.com.uk>
件名：タイル
日付：3 月 7 日

Norma 様

3 月 19 日の貴社の販売促進イベントで必要な床タイルのサンプルを本日送る準備ができていたのですが、不運にもニューヨーク周辺の空港が降雪のために閉鎖されています。いつ再開するかについては何とも言えない状況です。他の手配をする必要がありました。

英国の別の顧客と連絡を取り、状況を説明したところです。彼らはスコットランドのグラスゴーにある NHL 建材社という会社です。あちらの担当者は Hamish McDougal で、あなたの必要な製品を速達で送ってくれることに同意してくれました。

品物の代金と配送料はアメリカの Hammond Floorings 社が支払います。荷物に関して何か問題があれば、直接 McDougal さんに連絡をしてください。彼の E メールアドレスは、hmacdougal@nhlbuildingsupplies.com です。

よろしくお願いいたします。

Gregory Holland
部長 — Hammond Floorings 社

語彙チェック

☐ promotional	販売促進の
☐ be forced to *do*	～するのを余儀なくされる
☐ due to ～	～のために
☐ be in touch with ～	～と連絡を取る
☐ contact person	連絡窓口係、担当者
☐ shipment	積み荷、発送

158 What is the purpose of the e-mail?

(A) To apologize for a shipping error

(B) To offer an alternative product

(C) To request an update on an order

(D) To explain a change in plans

E メールの目的は何ですか。

(A) 発送ミスを謝罪すること。

(B) 代替製品を提供すること。

(C) 注文の更新を依頼すること。

(D) 予定の変更を説明すること。

正解 D

設問に着目する問題

Hammond Floorings 社が床タイルのサンプルを英国の Rose さん宛てに送ろうとしたが、ニューヨークの空港が閉鎖され、送れなくなったという問題が述べられている。そのため I have had to make other arrangements. と、他の手配をし、スコットランドの会社が he has agreed to send the products you require by express delivery と、希望の商品を送付することになったといういきさつが述べられている。これらのことを、まとめて change in plans と表現している (D) が正解。発送ミスもないし、代替製品でもないので、(A) と (B) は不適切。

☐ alternative　　　　　　　　　代替品

---

159 What has Mr. McDougal agreed to do?

(A) Invoice Mr. Holland's company

(B) Represent Hammond Floorings in the United Kingdom

(C) Attend a product demonstration in London

(D) Publish product details on his company's Web site

McDougal さんは何をすることに同意していますか。

(A) Holland さんの会社に請求書を送る。

(B) 英国の Hammond Floorings 社を代表する。

(C) ロンドンでの製品のデモンストレーションに参加する。

(D) 彼の会社のウェブサイトで製品の詳細を公開する。

正解 A

設問に着目する問題

McDougal さんとは Hammond Floorings 社がタイルの供給を代わりに依頼したスコットランドにある NHL 建材社の担当者である。NHL 建材社から Rose さんにサンプルタイルが送付されることに関して、The cost of the items and the delivery charges will be paid for by Hammond Floorings in the United States. とあり、料金は Hammond Flooring 社が負担することになるので、McDougal さんは請求書を Holland さんの Hammond Floorings 社に送付すると判断できる。正解は (A)。Invoice は名詞で「送り状、請求書」、動詞では「〜に送り状を送る、請求する」という意味。

☐ represent　　　　　　　　　〜を代表する
☐ publish　　　　　　　　　　〜を公開する

---

160 What does Mr. Holland instruct Ms. Rose to do?

(A) Order through NHL Building Supplies in the future

(B) Send a refund request to Hammond Floorings

(C) Return any damaged products to the manufacturer

(D) Contact Mr. McDougal with any delivery issues

Holland さんは Rose さんに何をするよう指示していますか。

(A) 今後は NHL 建材社を通して注文をする。

(B) Hammond Floorings 社に返金依頼を送付する。

(C) 破損している製品をメーカーに返却する。

(D) 配送品の問題については McDougal さんに連絡をする。

正解 D

設問に着目する問題

この問題の正解の根拠は E メールの最後にある。E メールの書き手である Holland さんは、Rose さんに対して、If there are any problems with the shipment, please contact Mr. McDougal directly. 「荷物に関して何か問題があれば、直接 McDougal さんに連絡をしてください」とあるので、(D) が正解。any problems with the shipment が any delivery issues と言い換えられている。issue「問題点」。

Questions 161-163 refer to the following article.

Woodhill (January 16)—The Richmond Art Gallery has reopened in a new location. It is now on the corner of Walton and Norbert Streets in the building which once housed the Camden Theater. — [1] — . For more than 100 years, the Richmond Art Gallery has housed artwork from the best of our local artists as well as the great European masters.

On February 17 the gallery will host a series of paintings by Henrietta Chang. The most famous of these is her depiction of the popular city mayor, Paula Shore. — [2] — . Ms. Shore worked to diversify the city's economy so that it relied not just on manufacturing but also on culture and tourism. This shift has measurably improved the lives of our citizens. — [3] — .

The paintings on show include works spanning Ms. Chang's whole career — a period of some 60 years. Admission to the main gallery is free. However, tickets to see Ms. Chang's works cost $10. They can be purchased online at www.richmondag.com or at the ticket booth on the first floor. — [4] — . The gallery's opening hours are from 9:30 A.M. to 6:00 P.M. Monday to Friday and from 10:00 A.M. to 7:00 P.M. on Saturday and Sunday.

問題 **161-163** は次の記事に関するものです。

Woodhill（1 月 16 日）—Richmond アートギャラリーは新しい場所で再オープンした。現在は、Walton 通りと Norbert 通りの角にある、かつては Camden 劇場があった建物内にある。この、かなり広く華やかな建物は、ギャラリーに真にふさわしい壮大さを醸し出している。Richmond アートギャラリーは 100 年以上にわたり、ヨーロッパの偉大な巨匠たちに加え、優れた地元の芸術家らの作品を収蔵している。

アートギャラリーは 2 月 17 日に Henrietta Chang の一連の絵画を展示する。これらの中で最も有名なのは人気の市長である Paula Shore の肖像だ。Shore さんは、市が製造業だけでなく、文化や観光業にも依存できるようにと、市の経済を多様化するために働いた。この転換は市民生活を目に見えるほどに向上させた。

展示中の絵画には、Chang さんの全経歴約 60 年にわたる作品が含まれている。メインギャラリーへの入場は無料だ。しかしながら、Chang さんの作品を鑑賞するためのチケットは 10 ドルとなっている。それらは www.richmondag.com にてオンラインで、または 1 階のチケット売り場で購入できる。開館時間は月曜日から金曜日までが午前 9 時 30 分から午後 6 時、土曜日と日曜日が午前 10 時から午後 7 時までである。

語彙チェック

☐	house	～を収蔵する、～に家を提供する
☐	artwork	芸術作品
☐	master	巨匠、熟練工
☐	depiction	描写
☐	diversify	～を多様化する
☐	rely on ～	～に依存する
☐	measurably	目に見えるほど明らかに
☐	spanning	～にわたる

161 What is announced in the article?

(A) The commencement of a new exhibition

(B) Plans to relocate an art gallery

(C) The closure of a popular theater

(D) The retirement of a politician

記事の中では何が発表されていますか。

(A) 新しい展示の開始

(B) アートギャラリーの移転計画

(C) 人気の劇場の閉鎖

(D) 政治家の引退

正解 **A**

選択肢に着目する問題

On February 17 the gallery will host a series of paintings by Henrietta Chang. 「アートギャラリーは 2 月 17 日に Henrietta Chang の一連の絵画を展示する」とあり、特別展示が始まることが発表されている。(A) が正解。commencement は「開始」という意味。冒頭でアートギャラリーが移転後再オープンしたことが述べられているが、(B) の移転計画は、これからのことを指すので不適切。また、移転先がかつての劇場だったことも述べられているが、劇場の閉鎖に関しての言及はなく、(C) も不適切。

☐ relocate 〜を移転する
☐ closure 閉鎖

162 Who is Paula Shore?

(A) A model for a character in a novel

(B) An actress in a theatrical company

(C) A popular local artist

(D) The subject of a portrait

Paula Shore とは誰ですか。

(A) 小説内のキャラクターのモデル

(B) 劇団の女優

(C) 地元の人気アーティスト

(D) 肖像画の人物

正解 **D**

設問に着目する問題

The most famous of these is her depiction of the popular city mayor, Paula Shore. 「これらの中で最も有名なのは人気の市長である Paula Shore の肖像だ」とある。同格のコンマの前に「市長」とあり、政治家と分かるが選択肢にはない。depiction は「描写」という意味。depiction of Paula Shore で「Paula Shore の肖像画」となるので、(D) が正解。subject は「画題、題材」という意味がある。

☐ theatrical company 劇団

163 In which of the positions marked [1], [2], [3], and [4] does the following sentence best belong?

"These much larger and ornate premises lend the gallery the air of grandness it truly deserves."

(A) [1]

(B) [2]

(C) [3]

(D) [4]

[1], [2], [3], [4] と記載された箇所のうち、次の文が入るのに最もふさわしいのはどれですか。

「この、かなり広く華やかな建物は、ギャラリーに真にふさわしい壮大さを醸し出している」

(A) [1]

(B) [2]

(C) [3]

(D) [4]

正解 **A**

文挿入問題

挿入文の These much larger and ornate premises「この、かなり広く華やかな建物」が、建造物を指していることを念頭に置いて挿入箇所を検討する。挿入文を [1] に入れると、These premises は、前の文の the Camden Theater が入っていた建物、屋敷全体を示すことになり、文意が通る。したがって、正解は (A)。動詞 deserve は「〜を受けるに足る、〜にふさわしい」。ornate「華やかな」、premises「建物」、deserve「〜の価値がある、〜を受けるに足る」。

Questions 164-167 refer to the following information.

Clarkson Associates is a partnership between highly regarded business professionals each with a record of success as employees in the private sector and as advisors to a diverse range of businesses.[164] We offer tailored advice from our most suited partners to our highly valued clients. At our initial consultation, we review your company's business plan and financial statements in detail to assess our ability to bring about a positive change in your organization. Based on that assessment, we assign a specialist with the experience and expertise you need moving forward.

[165] In a recent article in *Business Brain* magazine, Clarkson Associates was acknowledged as the most sought after and demonstrably successful business consultancy in Australia.[166] The article assessed our performance guiding fledgling businesses, our knowledge of recruitment strategies, and our familiarity with the rules of trade with Australia's largest trading partners.

[167] Between March 23 and April 14, Clarkson Associates will be interviewing prospective clients. If you are interested in speaking with our team and discovering whether or not you are a match for our services, please contact our new client hotline at 02-555-3432. During the process, you will need to send representatives to our main office in central Melbourne. Please be advised that in some cases, it is necessary for prospective clients to come in for follow-up meetings on short notice.

CLARKSON ASSOCIATES

問題 **164-167** は次の案内に関するものです。

Clarkson Associates は高評価を受けているビジネスのプロ人材によるパートナーシップで、一人一人が民間企業での従業員として、また様々なビジネスへのアドバイザーとしての成功の実績を持っています。極めて大切な顧客に対し、最適なパートナーから顧客に合わせてあつらえたアドバイスを提供いたします。貴社の組織に対しよい変化をもたらせるよう当事務所の能力を見極めるために、最初のご相談のときに、貴社の経営計画と財務諸表を詳細に検討させていただきます。その評価に基づき、貴社が前進するために必要な経験と専門知識を持ったスペシャリストを割り当てます。

Business Brain 誌の最近の記事で、Clarkson Associates はオーストラリアで、最も求められ、ビジネスコンサルティング業務において確実に成功をおさめていると認められました。記事では、創業まもない企業への当事務所の指導実績、採用戦略の知識、そしてオーストラリアの最大貿易相手国との貿易ルールの熟知が評価されました。

3 月 23 日から 4 月 14 日の間に、Clarkson Associates は将来のお客様と面談を行います。もし、貴社が我がチームと話し、当事務所のサービスが貴社に合うかどうかを判断してみたいと興味をお持ちならば、当事務所の新規顧客ホットライン 02-555-3432 までご連絡ください。その過程では、貴社を代表する方がメルボルン中心部の当事務所までお越しいただくことが必要となります。場合によっては、見込み客の方にフォローアップ会議に急な呼び出しでお越しいただくことが必要になる場合があります。

CLARKSON ASSOCIATES

語彙チェック

regard	〜を評価する		assessment	評価
a diverse range of 〜	様々な〜		expertise	専門知識
tailored	あつらえた、オーダーメードの		acknowledged	広く認められた
valued	貴重な		sought after	引っ張りだこの
initial	最初の		demonstrably	確実に
financial statement	財務諸表		prospective	見込みのある、将来の
assess	〜を評価する		match	適合する人
bring about 〜	〜をもたらす		on short notice	急な依頼で

164 What is a purpose of the information?

(A) To describe a company's customer service principles

(B) To encourage people to apply for jobs at Clarkson Associates

(C) To explain regulations that apply to private businesses in Australia

(D) To report on the financial forecast for a business sector

案内の目的は何ですか。

(A) 会社の顧客サービスの原則について説明すること。

(B) Clarkson Associates の職に応募するよう人々を促すこと。

(C) オーストラリアでの民間事業に適用される規則について説明すること。

(D) ある業種の財政予測について報告すること。

正解 **A**

設問に着目する問題

冒頭で会社の説明をした後、We offer tailored advice from our most suited partners「最適なパートナーから顧客に合わせてあつらえたアドバイスを提供する」と、会社のサービスの特徴を述べている。続けて、経営計画や財務諸表の詳細な検討をベースに作業を進めていくことを説明している。会社が個別仕立てのアドバイスというサービスを原則としていることを示しているので、(A) が正解。principle「原則」。

165 What is true about Clarkson Associates?

(A) It has offices in several countries.

(B) It was founded by a property developer.

(C) It was mentioned in a magazine article.

(D) It is looking to hire more staff members.

Clarkson Associates について正しいことは何ですか。

(A) それはいくつかの国にオフィスを持っている。

(B) それは不動産開発業者によって設立された。

(C) それは雑誌の記事で言及された。

(D) それはより多くのスタッフを雇うつもりである。

正解 **C**

選択肢に着目する問題

In a recent article in *Business Brain* magazine, Clarkson Associates was acknowledged as ～「Business Brain 誌の最近の記事で、Clarkson Associates は～と認められた」とあり、ビジネス誌に掲載されたことが分かるので、(C) が正解。

166 What is NOT a service offered by Clarkson Associates?

(A) Advice for new businesses

(B) Introductions to financial lenders

(C) Assistance in finding suitable employees

(D) Provision of information about international business

Clarkson 事務所が提供していないサービスは何ですか。

(A) 新事業への助言

(B) 金融業者への紹介

(C) 適切な従業員を見つける援助

(D) 国際事業に関する情報提供

正解 **B**

NOT 問題

Clarkson Associates が提供するサービスについては、ビジネス誌に掲載された内容に詳細が示されている。(A) は our performance guiding fledgling businesses とあるので一致する。fledgling は「未熟の、駆け出しの」という意味。(C) は our knowledge of recruitment strategies とあるので一致する。(D) は our familiarity with the rules of trade with Australia's largest trading partners とあり、貿易、つまり国際事業を熟知していると分かり、一致する。(B) の金融業者への紹介に関しては言及がないので、正解は (B)。

167 What is mentioned about prospective clients?

(A) They can receive an initial consultation for free.

(B) They should call Clarkson Associates about interviews.

(C) They can attend the Clarkson Associates office of their choice.

(D) They should analyze their financial statements.

見込み客について何が述べられていますか。

(A) 彼らは初回相談を無料で受けられる。

(B) 彼らは面談について Clarkson Associates に電話するべきである。

(C) 彼らは自分たちで選んだ Clarkson Associates のオフィスに通うことができる。

(D) 彼ら財務諸表を分析するべきである。

正解 **B**

選択肢に着目する問題

設問文の prospective clients「見込み客」については、案内の後半で言及されている。Clarkson Associates 社が 3 月 23 日から 4 月 14 日の間に見込み客の面談を行うと述べられている。続いて、If you are interested in speaking with our team and discovering whether or not you are a match for our services, please contact our new client hotline at 02-555-3432. とあり、面談を希望する見込み客はホットラインに電話をするように指示されている。したがって、正解は (B)。

Day 18

Questions 168-171 refer to the following online chat discussion.

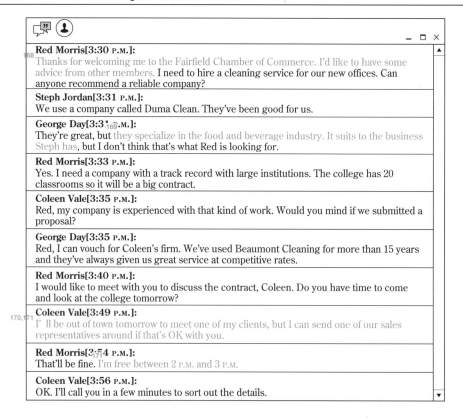

Red Morris[3:30 P.M.]:
168 Thanks for welcoming me to the Fairfield Chamber of Commerce. I'd like to have some advice from other members. I need to hire a cleaning service for our new offices. Can anyone recommend a reliable company?

Steph Jordan[3:31 P.M.]:
We use a company called Duma Clean. They've been good for us.

George Day[3:31 169 P.M.]:
They're great, but they specialize in the food and beverage industry. It suits to the business Steph has, but I don't think that's what Red is looking for.

Red Morris[3:33 P.M.]:
Yes. I need a company with a track record with large institutions. The college has 20 classrooms so it will be a big contract.

Coleen Vale[3:35 P.M.]:
Red, my company is experienced with that kind of work. Would you mind if we submitted a proposal?

George Day[3:35 P.M.]:
Red, I can vouch for Coleen's firm. We've used Beaumont Cleaning for more than 15 years and they've always given us great service at competitive rates.

Red Morris[3:40 P.M.]:
I would like to meet with you to discuss the contract, Coleen. Do you have time to come and look at the college tomorrow?

Coleen Vale[3:49 P.M.]:
170,171 I'll be out of town tomorrow to meet one of my clients, but I can send one of our sales representatives around if that's OK with you.

Red Morris[3:54 P.M.]:
171 That'll be fine. I'm free between 2 P.M. and 3 P.M.

Coleen Vale[3:56 P.M.]:
OK. I'll call you in a few minutes to sort out the details.

問題 **168-171** は次のオンラインチャットでの話し合いに関するものです。

Red Morris [午後 3 時 30 分]:
Fairfield 商工会議所に迎えていただきありがとうございます。他の会員の方々からアドバイスをいただきたいと思います。当社の新しい事務所用に清掃会社を雇う必要があります。どなたか信頼できる会社をお薦めいただけますか？

Steph Jordan [午後 3 時 31 分]:
我が社は Duma 清掃会社を利用しています。私たちにはよくしてくれていますよ。

George Day [午後 3 時 31 分]:
そこはとてもよいですが、飲食業界が専門です。Steph さんが所有している会社には合いますが、Red さんがお探しのものではないと思います。

Red Morris [午後 3 時 33 分]:
はい。大きな施設での実績がある会社を必要としています。大学には 20 教室ありますので、大きな契約になります。

Coleen Vale [午後 3 時 35 分]:
Red さん、我が社はそのような仕事の経験が豊富です。我が社が提案書を提出してもかまいませんか？

George Day [午後 3 時 35 分]:
Red さん、Coleen さんの会社は私が保証しますよ。我が社は 15 年以上 Beaumont 清掃会社を利用していますが、彼らはいつも低料金ですばらしいサービスを私たちに提供してくれています。

Red Morris [午後 3 時 40 分]:
契約の話し合いをするためにお会いしたいです、Coleen さん。明日、うちの大学を見に来る時間はありますか？

Coleen Vale [午後 3 時 49 分]:
明日は顧客の 1 人と会うために町を出ていますが、もしよろしければ営業担当者の 1 人をお送りできます。

Red Morris [午後 3 時 54 分]:
それで大丈夫です。私は午後 2 時から午後 3 時まで空いています。

Coleen Vale [午後 3 時 56 分]:
分かりました。詳細を整理するために数分後にお電話いたします。

語彙チェック

□ specialize in ～	～を専門とする	□ vouch for ～	～を保証する
□ track record	過去の実績	□ competitive rate	競争力のある、優れた価格
□ institution	施設	□ sort out ～	～を整理する

168

Who are the writers?

(A) Employees of a laundry service

(B) Real estate agents

(C) Members of a business association

(D) College students

書き手たちは誰ですか。

(A) クリーニング会社の従業員

(B) 不動産業者

(C) ビジネス協会の会員

(D) 大学生

正解 C

設問に着目する問題

この問題の正解の根拠は冒頭にある。オンラインチャットを開始した Morris さんが、チャットのメンバーたちに対し、Thanks for welcoming me to the Fairfield Chamber of Commerce. I'd like to have some advice from other members. と書いている。したがって、チャットの書き手たちは、商工会議所の会員であると判断できる。それを business association の会員と言い表している (C) が正解。association「協会」。

laundry　　　　　　洗濯物、洗濯屋
real estate　　　　不動産

169

What kind of business does Ms. Jordan most likely work for?

(A) A dry cleaning service

(B) A financial institution

(C) An online store

(D) A restaurant

Jordan さんはどのような会社で働いていると考えられますか。

(A) ドライクリーニング会社

(B) 金融機関

(C) オンラインストア

(D) レストラン

正解 D

設問に着目する問題

Morris さんの発言から、彼は清掃業者を探していてお薦めの業者を教えてほしいと会員たちにお願いしていることが分かる。Jordan さんが Duma Clean という業者の名を挙げるが、それに対して Day さんは they specialize in the food and beverage industry. It suits to the business Steph has「そこは飲食業界が専門です。Steph さんが所有している会社には合う」と述べているので、Steph つまり Jordan さんがやっている事業は飲食業界と推測できる。したがって、正解は (D)。

170

What will Ms. Vale most likely do tomorrow?

(A) She will meet with Mr. Morris.

(B) She will attend a meeting.

(C) She will interview a job applicant.

(D) She will recommend a course to some employees.

明日、Vale さんは何をすると考えられますか。

(A) 彼女は Morris さんと会う。

(B) 彼女は会議に出席する。

(C) 彼女は就職希望者に面会する。

(D) 彼女は一部の従業員に教育課程を薦める。

正解 B

設問に着目する問題

Vale さんの会社である Beaumont 清掃会社に興味を持った Morris さんは、さっそく清掃業務の契約について話し合うため、Vale さんに大学に来るよう求めるが、それに対し Vale さんは、I'll be out of town tomorrow to meet one of my clients と応答している。Vale さんは明日顧客と会議があると考えられるので、正解は (B)。

171

At 3:54 P.M., what does Mr. Morris mean when he writes, "That'll be fine"?

(A) He can welcome Ms. Vale in the afternoon.

(B) He is happy to meet Ms. Vale's colleague.

(C) He finds Ms. Vale's rates acceptable.

(D) He expects the weather to clear up.

午後 3 時 54 分に Morris さんが "That'll be fine" と書く際、何を意図していますか。

(A) 彼は午後 Vale さんを迎えることができる。

(B) 彼は Vale さんの同僚に会うことに満足している。

(C) 彼は Vale さんの価格が受け入れられると分かっている。

(D) 彼は天気が晴れると予想している。

正解 B

意図問題

Morris さんのこの発言は、直前の Vale さんの I'll be out of town tomorrow to meet one of my clients, but I can send one of our sales representatives around if that's OK with you. を受けている。Vale さんは都合がつかず、さしつかえなければ代わりの者を大学に行かせるという提案である。また、Morris さんは発言の直後に、I'm free between 2 P.M. and, 3 P.M.「午後 2 時から 3 時まで空いている」と自分の都合を伝えている。Morris さんはこの発言によって、彼女の会社の営業担当者と会うことを了承していることを伝えていると判断できるので、(B) が正解。

Questions 172-175 refer to the following article.

Nasser Aims for Mutually Assured Prosperity by Brandon Harps

Cambridge (19 November) — The Cambridge-based online bookstore Nasser was recently the subject of a documentary film which explored the company's unusual internal structure and policies with regard to profit sharing.

At the time of the company's foundation, the president instituted an unusual rule which stated that no employee may earn more than five times the wage of the lowest paid full-time employee in the business. This rule ensures that upper management may only enjoy the fruits of the company's success if they share the rewards with those lower down the chain.

— [1] — . Publishers wishing to sell books through the online service pay a commission of only five percent to the company, which is the lowest sales commission charged by any online bookstore in the country. — [2] — . Nasser is able to do this because of the incredible efficiency it is able to achieve in its warehouses and the entire supply chain. This is something only possible where every employee benefits directly from the company's profitability.

The film, directed by Claude Rossi, was shown on Channel 7 last Friday, 12 November and since then, Nasser's sales have increased by some 12 percent. It seems that the community wants to reward the company for its progressive attitude toward profit. — [3] — .

The company does not have sales or offer discounts. — [4] — . However, it does allow publishers to distribute free online content to generate interest in their products. This usually takes the form of downloadable eBooks or audio versions of underperforming titles. It appears this is one of the reasons for the business' incredible success and it is something that competitors are starting to imitate.

問題 **172-175** は次の記事に関するものです。

Nasser、相互保証の繁栄を目指す
Brandon Harps

ケンブリッジ（11 月 19 日）— ケンブリッジに本拠を置くオンライン書店 Nasser は、最近、当社の珍しい内部構造と利益分配に関する方針を探る記録映画の題材となった。

会社の創立当時に社長が、どの従業員も社内で最も賃金の低いフルタイムの従業員の 5 倍以上の賃金を得てはならないとする変わった規則を制定した。この規則により、上級管理職は下級労働者と報酬を分け合う限りにおいて会社の成功の成果を享受できるようになっている。

* この理想は従業員だけでなく供給業者にも適用される。当社オンラインサービスを通じて本を販売したい出版社が同社に支払うのはたった 5% の委託手数料であり、国内オンライン書店が請求する販売委託手数料としては最低価格である。Nasser にこれが可能なのは、同社が倉庫と供給網全体において達成できている驚くべき効率性のおかげである。これは、全従業員が社の収益性から直接利益を得ている場合にのみ可能なことである。

Claude Rossi が監督を務めるこの映画は、先週金曜日の 11 月 12 日に 7 チャンネルで放映され、それ以来、Nasser の売り上げは約 12% 伸びた。地域社会は、利益に対する進歩的な姿勢に対して、当社に報酬を与えたいと考えているようである。

当社はセールも割引もしない。しかし、出版社が自社の商品に関心を持ってもらうために無料のオンラインコンテンツを配布することは許可している。これは通常、ダウンロード可能な電子書籍や、売れ行きのよくない本のオーディオ版という形態をとる。これは当社が驚くべき成功をおさめた理由の 1 つのようであり、競合会社がまねし始めていることである。

語彙チェック

☐ aim for 〜	〜を目指す		☐ ensure that	〜ということを保証する
☐ mutually	相互に		☐ incredible	驚くべき、信じ難い
☐ assured	保証された		☐ supply chain	サプライ・チェーン、供給網
☐ prosperity	繁栄		☐ profitability	収益性
☐ subject	題材		☐ progressive	進歩的な
☐ structure	構造		☐ distribute	〜を配布する
☐ with regard to 〜	〜に関する		☐ generate	〜を生む、生み出す
☐ profit sharing	利益分配		☐ underperforming	成績の劣る、売れ行きのよくない
☐ foundation	設立、創立		☐ imitate	〜をまねる
☐ institute	〜を制定する			

172 What is the article mainly about?

(A) The dangers associated with running an online business

(B) Strategies employed by a publisher to train employees

(C) The career of a successful documentary filmmaker

(D) A company president's goal of distributing wealth fairly

主に何についての記事ですか。

(A) オンラインビジネス経営に関する危険

(B) 従業員を訓練するために出版社が実行している戦略

(C) 成功した記録映画製作者の経歴

(D) 富を公平に分配するという会社社長の目標

正解 **D** 設問に着目する問題

記事は、あるオンライン書店の利益分配に関するユニークな社内構造と方針が映画の題材になったということを述べている。そのユニークな規則というものについて、the president instituted an unusual rule which stated that no employee may earn more than five times the wage of the lowest paid full-time employee in the business と述べられており、創業者が社内の給料の差を一定以上にしないと定めたとある。そのことを、distribute wealth fairly「富を公平に分配する」と言い表している (D) が正解。wealth「富」、fairly「公平に」。

173 What is indicated about Nasser?

(A) It is the country's longest-running online bookstore.

(B) It prefers to hire graduates straight out of university.

(C) It strives to reduce wastefulness in its processes.

(D) It commissioned Claude Rossi to make its documentary.

Nasser について何が示されていますか。

(A) それは国内で最も長期間経営しているオンライン書店である。

(B) それは大学新卒者を雇うのを好む。

(C) それは作業工程において無駄を減らそうと努力している。

(D) それは Claude Rossi さんに記録映画を作ってもらうよう依頼した。

正解 **C** 選択肢に着目する問題

Nasser is able to do this because of the incredible efficiency it is able to achieve in its warehouses and the entire supply chain. とあり、Nasser が、供給業者の委託手数料を業界最低にできる原因として倉庫やサプライチェーンにおける incredible efficiency「驚くべき効率性」を挙げている。efficiency を to reduce wastefulness「無駄を減らす」と言い換えている (C) が正解。strive「努力する」、wastefulness「無駄」。

☐ commission　　　　　　　　～に依頼する

174 According to the article, why did Nasser experience an increase in sales?

(A) It enjoyed some positive publicity.

(B) It launched a new service.

(C) It received an award from the government.

(D) It ran a seasonal sale.

記事によると、Nasser はなぜ売り上げが伸びましたか。

(A) それは肯定的な評判を得たから。

(B) それは新しいサービスを開始したから。

(C) それは政府から賞を授与されたから。

(D) それは季節のセールを行ったから。

正解 **A** 設問に着目する問題

Rossi さんによる映画がテレビで放映されてから、Nasser の売り上げが伸びたと述べられている。続いて It seems that the community wants to reward the company for its progressive attitude toward profit.「地域社会は、利益に対する進歩的な姿勢に対して、その会社に報酬を与えたいと考えているようだ」とあり、特異な企業の方針が購買者の共感を呼び、購買者が会社を応援したくなったのだろうと想像できる。positive publicity は「肯定的な評判」という意味なので、(A) が正解。

175 In which of the positions marked [1], [2], [3], and [4] does the following sentence best belong?

"This ideal is not only applied to employees but also suppliers."

(A) [1]　　(B) [2]　　(C) [3]　　(D) [4]

[1] , [2], [3], [4] と記載された箇所のうち、次の文が入るのに最もふさわしいのはどれですか。

「この理想は従業員だけでなく供給業者にも適用される」

(A) [1]　　(B) [2]　　(C) [3]　　(D) [4]

正解 **A** 文挿入問題

挿入文中の This ideal とは、Nasser の創業者が設定した、給料の格差を一定以下に限定するという会社の規則と推測できる。挿入文を [1] に入れると、その規則の従業員への適用が述べられている [1] 以前の内容を受け、次に供給業者に対する適用について述べる前置きとなる。また [1] 以降でも、本の供給者である出版社の販売委託手数料を低くおさえていることを述べており、スムーズに文意が流れることが確認できる。正解は (A)。

Questions 176-180 refer to the following letter and monthly statement.

NetNex Internet Service
373 Bruce Street, Boise ID 83702

Ms. Trisha Colbert
165 Rio Bravo Drive, Apt. 201
West Boise, ID 83642
Account Number: 8423-4390-43

October 26

Dear Ms. Colbert:

You are currently signed up for our NetNex Lite plan, which is the cheapest plan we offer.[177] It allows you to use up to one gigabyte of data each month at the very low monthly rate of $10. Data used in excess of that amount will be charged at a rate of 10 cents per megabyte.[177] NetNex Internet Service is obliged to contact you by e-mail if your usage exceeds the amount included in your monthly plan. On October 20, your usage came to a total of 1.2 gigabytes.

Since that date, you have used almost 500 megabytes of data. That comes to a total of $50 to date.[179] If you were to upgrade to the NetNex Basic plan,[176] you could use three gigabytes of data for just $20 per month. I strongly[178] recommend this plan if you expect to continue using a larger amount of data. We would be willing to retroactively implement this new plan so[178] that your fee for this month would be reduced from a total of $65 to just $20. You can do this by logging onto the Web site and filling in a plan upgrade form.

Rhod Davies

Rhod Davies
Customer Service Manager

NetNex Internet Service Ms. Trisha Colbert 165 Rio Bravo Drive, Apt. 201 West Boise, ID 83642	Monthly Statement November Account Number: 8423-4390-43 [179]Service Plan: NetNex Basic plan
Service for the period: November 1 through November 30	Total Charges: [179] $32.50
This amount will be deducted from your bank account automatically on December 10. [180]If you see any discrepancies in this bill and your actual usage, please contact the customer service division at 986-555-2343 by December 31.	

NetNex インターネットサービス
Bruce 通り 373 番地、Boise　ID 83702

Trisha Colbert 様
Rio Bravo 通り 165 番地、201 番アパート
West Boise、ID 83642
アカウント番号：8423-4390-43

10 月 26 日

Colbert 様

あなたは現在、当社の最安値プランである NetNex Lite プランにご登録されています。このプランでは、月額 10 ドルという非常に低い料金で毎月 1 ギガバイトまでデータを使用することができます。その量以上のデータ使用については 1 メガバイト当たり 10 セントの料金が請求されます。あなたの使用量が月間プランに付いている量を超えた場合、NetNex インターネットサービスは E メールであなたに連絡する義務があります。10 月 20 日、あなたの使用量は合計 1.2 ギガバイトに達しました。

その日以来、あなたは 500 メガバイト近いデータを使用しました。現在までのところ、これは合計 50 ドルに達することになります。NetNex ベーシックプランにアップグレードすれば、月額たったの 20 ドルで 3 ギガバイトのデータを使用できます。より多いデータ量を使用し続けることをお望みでしたら、このプランを強くお薦めいたします。今月のあなたの料金を合計 65 ドルからたったの 20 ドルに減額できるように、この新プランをさかのぼって適用させていただくことができます。ウェブサイトにログインしてプランアップグレードの書式にご記入いただくことで、このことが可能です。

Rhod Davies（署名）
Rhod Davies
顧客サービス部部長

NetNex インターネットサービス	月次明細書
Trisha Colbert 様	11 月
Rio Bravo 通り 165 番地、201 番アパート	アカウント番号：8423-4390-43
West Boise、ID 83642	サービスプラン：NetNex ベーシックプラン
サービスの期間： 11 月 1 日から 11 月 30 日まで	総額： 32.50 ドル
上記の金額が 12 月 10 日にあなたの銀行口座より自動引き落としされます。この請求書とあなたの実際のご使用量の間に何らかの食い違いがある場合、12 月 31 日までに、顧客サービス部 986-555-2343 までご連絡ください。	

176

Why was the letter sent to Ms. Colbert?

(A) To advise that she switch to another plan

(B) To inform her about an upcoming sale

(C) To announce a change to the service agreement

(D) To request that she update her bank account information

手紙はなぜ Colbert さんに送られましたか。

(A) 彼女に別のプランに切り替えるよう助言するため。

(B) 今度のセールについて彼女に知らせるため。

(C) サービス規約の変更について告知するため。

(D) 彼女の銀行口座情報を更新するよう依頼するため。

正解 **A**

設問に着目する問題

手紙の送られた理由が何かということが問われている。この問題の正解根拠は手紙の後半部分にある。Colbert さんのインターネットサービスの使用状況と料金について知らせる内容であるが、I strongly recommend this plan if you expect to continue using a larger amount of data.「より多いデータ量を使用し続けることをお望みでしたら、このプランを強くお薦めいたします」とあり、料金をより安くするための助言がされている。正解は (A)。

177

What is implied about NetNex Internet Services?

(A) It recently changed its name.

(B) It offers special rates to customers who switch from another provider.

(C) It has multiple offices in the Boise area.

(D) It recently sent Ms. Colbert an e-mail.

NetNex インターネットサービスについて何が示唆されていますか。

(A) それは最近社名を変えた。

(B) それは別のプロバイダーから切り替えた顧客に特別料金を提供している。

(C) それは Boise の地域に複数の事務所がある。

(D) それは最近 Colbert さんに E メールを送った。

正解 **D**

選択肢に着目する問題

NetNex Internet Service is obliged to contact you by e-mail if your usage exceeds the amount included in your monthly plan.「あなたの使用量が月間プランに付いている量を超えた場合、NetNex インターネットサービスは E メールであなたに連絡する義務がある」とある。Colbert さんのプランでは、It allows you to use up to one gigabyte of data each month at the very low monthly rate of $10. という条件なので、1 ギガバイトを超えると、E メールで通知がくると考えられる。続いて On October 20, your usage came to a total of 1.2 gigabytes. と 1 ギガを超えたとあるので、(D) が正解。

178

What should Ms. Colbert do if she wishes to accept Mr. Davies' offer?

(A) Call the customer service section

(B) Complete an online application

(C) Reply to an e-mail from NetNex Internet Service

(D) Agree to pay a processing fee

Davies さんの申し出を受け入れたいと思ったら、Colbert さんは何をすべきですか。

(A) 顧客サービス部に電話をかける。

(B) オンライン申込用紙に記入する。

(C) NetNex インターネットサービスからの E メールに返信する。

(D) 手数料を支払うことに同意する。

正解 **B**

設問に着目する問題

手紙の差出人である Davies さんは、プランの変更を提案し、また We would be willing to retroactively implement this new plan so that your fee for this month would be reduced とあるように、別のプランに変更をすれば、今月分にさかのぼって、料金が引き下げられる、と申し出ている。続けて、You can do this by logging onto the Web site and filling in a plan upgrade form.「ウェブサイトにログインしてプランアップグレードの書式にご記入いただくことで、このことが可能だ」と述べているので、(B) が正解。complete「〜を仕上げる、にすべて記入する」。

☐ processing fee　　　　　　手数料

TEST 1

179 What does the monthly statement imply about Ms. Colbert?

(A) She has not paid her previous month's charges.

(B) She rejected Mr. Davies' offer.

(C) She has used more than three gigabytes of data.

(D) She has changed her home address.

Colbert さんについて月次明細書は何を示唆していますか。

(A) 彼女は前月の料金を支払っていない。

(B) 彼女は Davies さんの申し出を断った。

(C) 彼女は 3 ギガバイト以上のデータを使用した。

(D) 彼女は住所を変更した。

正解 C

選択肢に着目するクロス問題

手紙の冒頭から、Colbert さんは 10 月には NetNex Lite プランを契約していたことが分かる。月次明細書では、アカウント番号の下に NetNex Basic plan とあるので、Davies さんの申し出を受け入れて月 20 ドルで 3 ギガバイトまで使用できるプランに変更したと考えられる。また、合計請求額は 32.50 ドルなので、20 ドルの 3 ギガバイトを超えて使用したと想像できる。したがって、(C) が正解。

180 According to the monthly statement, why might Ms. Colbert call the customer service division?

(A) To revert to her original plan

(B) To request weekly billing

(C) To discuss an error in her bill

(D) To cancel her Internet service

月次明細書によると、Colbert さんはなぜ顧客サービス部に電話をする可能性がありますか。

(A) 彼女の元のプランに戻すため。

(B) 週ごとの請求書作成を依頼するため。

(C) 彼女の請求書の間違いについて話し合うため。

(D) 彼女のインターネットサービスを中止するため。

正解 C

設問に着目する問題

この問題の正解根拠は月次明細書の最後にある。Colbert さん宛ての明細書の最後に、If you see any discrepancies in this bill and your actual usage, please contact the customer service division at 986-555-2343 by December 31.「この請求書とあなたの実際のご使用量の間に何らかの食い違いがある場合、12 月 31 日までに、顧客サービス部 986-555-2343 までご連絡ください」とある。discrepancies in this bill and your actual usage を error in her bill と言い換えている (C) が正解。

| revert | 戻る |
| billing | 請求書の作成、請求書の発送 |

語彙チェック

in excess of ～	～より多く、を超過して	retroactively	さかのぼって
be obliged to *do*	～する義務がある	implement	～を実行する
be to *do*	～する予定である	discrepancy	不一致、食い違い

85

Questions 181-185 refer to the following Web page and e-mail.

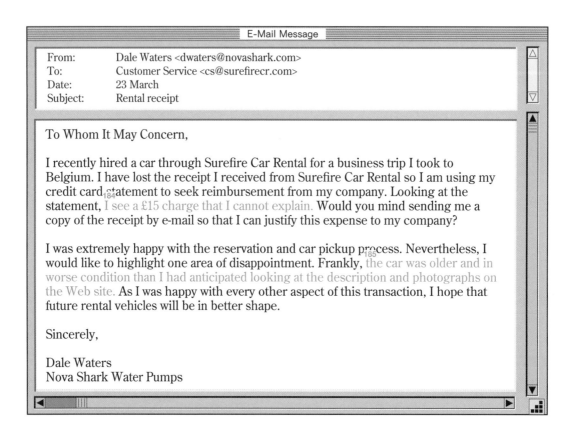

Surefire レンタカー

よくある質問	予約	ご利用方法	ホーム

料金割引はありますか？

ご出張の方には 10% の割引をご提供しています。

出張と認められるためには、お勤めの会社名で予約する必要があります。会社は事前に Surefire レンタカーの顧客として登録しなければなりません。

空港から車を利用することはできますか？

Surefire レンタカーは空港自体には営業所がありません。しかし、当社の営業所まで無料のシャトルバスをご提供しており、すべての営業所が空港から 5 分以内の場所にあります。手荷物を受け取り次第顧客サービスの番号までお電話くださり、到着ターミナルの正面からの送迎をご依頼ください。

レンタル料金には何が含まれていますか？

表示しているレンタル料金は車そのもののみの料金です。ご返却の際に燃料を補充していただかなければなりません。そうしなかった場合、燃料補充の最低料金の 50 ポンドをお支払いいただくことになります。カーナビやチャイルドシートをご希望でしたら、ご予約の際にお申し込みください。追加料金はそれぞれ 15 ポンド、20 ポンドです。この料金は期間の長さに関わらず、貸出期間全体に適用されます。

送信者：Dale Waters <dwaters@novashark.com>
宛先：Customer Service <cs@surefirecr.com>
日付：3 月 23 日
件名：レンタル領収書

関係者各位

私は最近、ベルギーへの出張旅行のために Surefire レンタカーを通じて車を借りました。Surefire レンタカーからもらった領収書を紛失してしまいましたので、会社から払い戻しを受けるためにクレジットカードの請求書を使うつもりです。請求書を見たところ、説明のできない 15 ポンドの請求があります。この出費を会社に証明できるように、E メールで領収書の写しを送っていただけますでしょうか。

予約と車の受け取りについてはたいへん満足しました。それでも、一点、残念だったことを強調しておきたいと思います。率直に言って、車は私がウェブサイトで説明や写真を見て予想していたよりも古くて状態が悪かったです。今回の取引の他のすべての面で満足したので、将来借りる車はもっとよい状態であることを願います。

よろしくお願いします。

Dale Waters
Nova Shark ウォーターポンプ社

181 According to the Web page, who is eligible for a discount?

(A) People who are registered customers of Surefire Car Rental

(B) People whose reservations are made under company name

(C) People who have used Surefire Car Rental in the past

(D) People whose rental period is longer than 10 days

ウェブページによると、割引を得られるのは誰ですか。

(A) Surefire レンタカーの登録顧客である人

(B) 会社名で予約した人

(C) 過去に Surefire レンタカーを利用したことがある人

(D) レンタル期間が 10 日以上の人

正解 B

設問に着目する問題

ウェブページでは FAQ のページが開かれている。最初の質問で割引価格について記されている。出張者に 10 パーセントの割引がされるとあるが、そのためには、it is necessary to make the booking under your company's name「お勤めの会社名で予約する必要がある」とある。正解は (B)。book と reserve の言い換えは定番。eligible for ～「～に対して資格がある」。

182 When should people arrange transportation from the airport?

(A) When they make a reservation

(B) When they learn their arrival time

(C) When their plane arrives

(D) When they have retrieved their luggage

いつ空港からの移動手段を手配すべきですか。

(A) 予約するとき。

(B) 到着時刻が分かったとき。

(C) 飛行機が到着したとき。

(D) 手荷物を回収したとき。

正解 D

設問に着目する問題

ウェブページに車両のピックアップ方法が述べられているが、空港にはレンタカー会社の事務所がないため、無料のシャトルバスを手配するよう指示されている。Simply call our customer service line as soon as you have your luggage「手荷物を受け取り次第顧客サービスの番号までお電話ください」とあり、自分の手荷物を受け取ることを retrieve という動詞で表現している (D) が正解。retrieve「～を取り戻す」。

183 What is implied about Surefire Car Rental?

(A) Its cars are supposed to be returned with a full tank of fuel.

(B) Its cars come with free extras.

(C) It offers a wide variety of makes and models.

(D) It provides 24-hour customer support.

Surefire レンタカーについて何が示唆されていますか。

(A) その車は燃料が満杯の状態で返却されることになっている。

(B) その車には無料の追加装備が付いている。

(C) それは幅広い種類のメーカーや型式のものを提供している。

(D) それは 24 時間顧客サポートを提供している。

正解 A

選択肢に着目する問題

ウェブページのレンタル料金には何が含まれているかという項目のところに、燃料に関しての記述がある。You must refill the car with fuel when you return it.「ご返却の際に燃料を補充していただかなければならない」と説明されており、使用した分の燃料を補充し、満タンで返却すべきであることが分かる。正解は (A)。

184 What is most likely true about Mr. Waters?

(A) He requested a navigation system with his rental.

(B) He failed to refill the car with fuel before returning it.

(C) He traveled to Belgium for personal reasons.

(D) He has rented from Surefire Car Rental before.

Waters さんについて何が正しいと考えられますか。

(A) 彼はレンタルの際にカーナビを申し込んだ。

(B) 彼は返却の前に燃料を補充し損ねた。

(C) 彼は個人的な理由でベルギーへ旅行した。

(D) 彼は以前に Surefire レンタカーからレンタルしたことがある。

正解 A

選択肢に着目するクロス問題

Waters さんは E メールで I see a £15 charge that I cannot explain と書いており、15 ポンド分の請求の明細が分からないようだ。そこで、レンタカー会社のウェブページを見ると、2 つのオプションについての記述がある。If you would like to use navigation systems or child seats, …There is an additional charge of £15 and £20 respectively. 「カーナビやチャイルドシートをご希望でしたら、…追加料金はそれぞれ 15 ポンド、20 ポンドです」とあるので、15 ポンドのカーナビを申し込んだと判断できる。正解は (A)。

185 What does Mr. Waters mention about the car he rented?

(A) It was returned to a rental agency in Belgium.

(B) It did not live up to his expectations.

(C) It had excellent fuel economy.

(D) It was more expensive than his travel budget allowed for.

Waters さんは彼が借りた車について何を述べていますか。

(A) それはベルギーのレンタル業者に返却された。

(B) それは彼の期待に沿わなかった。

(C) それは燃費がたいへんよかった。

(D) それは彼の旅行予算が許容していたよりも高価だった。

正解 B

選択肢に着目する問題

Waters さんがレンタルした車についての感想は E メールの後半に述べられている。the car was older and in worse condition than I had anticipated looking at the description and photographs on the Web site 「車は私がウェブサイトで説明や写真を見て予想していたよりも古くて状態が悪かった」とある。これを、live up to ~ 「(期待などに)に沿う、かなう」という動詞句を使って表現している (B) が正解。

☐ fuel economy　　　　　　　　　燃費

Questions 186-190 refer to the following notice, letter, and e-mail.

Join the Gladwell Humane Society

By becoming a member of the Gladwell Humane Society, you can help support a large number of worthwhile local causes both financially and through activities run by the society. As a member of the society, you can take advantage of many benefits provided by like-minded local businesses and even the local government. These benefits include discounts on goods and services and free tickets to many events. Of course, these benefits are only available to current members and it is necessary to devote a certain number of hours each month to maintain your membership.

Membership Levels:

Gold — For members who contribute over 12 hours of service a week. Benefits include all silver level benefits as well as a State Museum and Art Gallery membership, 10 percent off on all purchases at participating stores, including Greenmart and South Hampton Shopping Center.

Silver — For members who contribute over six hours of service a week. Benefits include all bronze level benefits as well as free use of public swimming pools and gyms. Five percent off on all purchases at participating stores, including Greenmart and South Hampton Shopping Center.

Bronze — For members who contribute over three hours of service a week. Benefits include free registration in the Annual Gladwell Fun Run and a three percent discount on council taxes.

Standard — For members who contribute to at least one event a year. You will receive a monthly newsletter which provides information about upcoming volunteer opportunities and social events.

To learn more about the club, please contact the president, Red Pearlman, at rpearlman@gladwellhumanesociety.org.

GHS The Gladwell Humane Society

Ms. Henrietta Wright
783 Hillview Terrace
Bradman, WA
98004

July 7

Dear Ms. Wright,

Please find enclosed your new membership card. I hope you will take full advantage of all the benefits it offers. You certainly deserve them. I have gotten the Art Gallery membership using mine and it has given me many hours of pleasure. I hope that you will do the same. I would be very happy if you would join me in attending an exhibition of Mr. Greg Holland's work there on July 30. I have made an arrangement with the museum curator for a private tour before the exhibition officially opens.

I have enclosed the monthly newsletter with this letter. You will notice that our next meeting is scheduled for July 27. I would like you to give a five- to ten-minute inspirational talk to the other members.

Sincerely,

Red Pearlman

Red Pearlman

問題 **186-190** は次のお知らせ、手紙、E メールに関するものです。

Gladwell 動物愛護協会にご参加ください

Gladwell 動物愛護協会の会員になることで、あなたは経済的にも、協会によって運営されている活動を通しても、多くの価値ある地域運動を支える手助けができます。協会の会員として、あなたは同じ目的を持つ地元の企業や地方自治体さえもが提供している多くの特典を利用することができます。これらの特典には、商品やサービスの割引や、多くのイベントの無料チケットが含まれます。もちろん、これらの特典は現会員のみが利用でき、会員資格を維持するには毎月一定の時間数をささげる必要があります。

会員レベル:

ゴールド — 週に 12 時間以上奉仕する会員。特典はすべてのシルバーレベルの特典に加えて州立美術館とアートギャラリーの会員資格を含む。Greenmart とサウス・ハンプトンショッピングセンターを含む加盟店でのすべての買い物が 10% 割引。

シルバー — 週に 6 時間以上奉仕する会員。特典はすべてのブロンズレベルの特典に加えて公共のプールとジムの無料使用権を含む。Greenmart とサウス・ハンプトンショッピングセンターを含む加盟店でのすべての買い物が 5% 割引。

ブロンズ — 週に 3 時間以上奉仕する会員。特典は毎年開催の Gladwell アマチュアマラソンへの無料登録と、市民税の 3% 割引を含む。

スタンダード — 少なくとも年に 1 度イベントで奉仕する会員。今後のボランティアの機会や社交イベントについての情報を提供するニュースレターを毎月受け取る。

クラブについてもっと知るためには、会長の Red Pearlman に、rpearlman@gladwellhumanesociety.org までご連絡ください。

GHS Gladwell 動物愛護協会

Henrietta Wright 様
Hillview Terrace 783 番地
Bradman、WA
98004

7 月 7 日

Wright 様

あなたの新しい会員カードを同封いたしました。そちらが提供するすべての特典をご利用いただければと思います。それらは確かにあなたにふさわしいものです。私は自分の会員資格を使ってアートギャラリーの会員になり、何時間も楽しいときを過ごさせてもらってきました。あなたも同じようになさることを願います。7 月 30 日にそこで開催される Greg Holland さんの作品展覧会に私と一緒に参加してくださるのでしたらたいへんうれしく思います。展覧会が公式に始まる前に、個人ツアーをしてもらえるよう美術館学芸員と打ち合わせをしてあります。

この手紙と一緒に月刊のニュースレターを同封いたしました。私たちの次の会合は 7 月 27 日であるとお気づきになるでしょう。あなたには他のメンバーに向けて、5 分から 10 分間、心を揺さぶるようなお話をしていただきたいと思っています。

よろしくお願いします。

Red Pearlman（署名）

Red Pearlman

To:	Red Pearlman <rpearlman@gladwellhumanesociety.org>
From:	Henrietta Wright <hwright@gladwellhumanesociety.org>
Date:	July 9
Subject:	Thank you

Dear Mr. Pearlman,

Thank you so much for your letter of July 7. I get great joy from my work with the Gladwell Humane Society.[189] Now that my working life is over, I hope to dedicate even more time to our local community. I am grateful to you and the Gladwell Humane Society for helping me do that.

Unfortunately, I[190] am unable to attend the next scheduled meeting of GHS as I will be away visiting family. However,[190] I would be honored to accompany you to the Art Gallery to see Mr. Holland's exhibition. Please let me know what time and where you would like to meet.

Regards,

Henrietta Wright

宛先：Red Pearlman <rpearlman@gladwellhumanesociety.org>
送信者：Henrietta Wright <hwright@gladwellhumanesociety.org>
日付：7 月 9 日
件名：ありがとうございます

Pearlman 様

7 月 7 日のお手紙ありがとうございます。Gladwell 動物愛護協会での仕事からたいへん大きな喜びを得ております。今や私の仕事人生も終わりましたので、地域社会のためにより多くの時間をささげていきたいと願っています。私がそうするのを助けてくださって、あなたと Gladwell 動物愛護協会に感謝しています。

残念ながら、家族を訪問するため不在にするため、次回予定されている GHS の会合には参加できません。ですが、Holland 氏の展覧会を見にあなたと一緒に美術館に行かせていただくのは光栄に思います。。何時にどこで待ち合わせをするかお知らせください。

よろしくお願いします。

Henrietta Wright

語彙チェック				
☐	humane	人道的な	☐ council tax	地方税
☐	worthwhile	価値ある	☐ deserve	～を受けるに値する
☐	cause	運動、主張	☐ curator	学芸員、館長
☐	take advantage of ～	～を利用する	☐ inspirational	感動を与えるような
☐	like-minded	同じ考えを持った	☐ dedicate	～をささげる
☐	devote	～を充てる、ささげる	☐ grateful	感謝している
☐	contribute	～を提供する、貢献する	☐ be honored to *do*	～することを光栄に思う

What is suggested about the Gladwell Humane Society?

(A) It offers entitlements to members according to their service time.

(B) It has received an achievement award from the city council.

(C) It is run by a privately-owned financial institution.

(D) It was founded by a popular politician.

Gladwell 動物愛護協会について何が分かりますか。

(A) それは奉仕した時間に応じてメンバーに特典を与える。

(B) それは市議会から特別功労賞を授与されたことがある。

(C) それは民間所有の金融機関によって運営されている。

(D) それは人気のある政治家によって設立された。

正解 A

選択肢に着目する問題

Gladwell 動物愛護協会については、お知らせの内容で述べられている。お知らせでは、協会のメンバーになるよう勧誘している。さらに it is necessary to devote a certain number of hours each month to maintain your membership「会員資格を維持するには毎月一定の時間数をささげる必要がある」とあり、続けて会員のレベルに応じてその条件と特典が述べられている。正解は (A)。

What is NOT a benefit of membership in the Gladwell Humane Society?

(A) Entry to government-run fitness centers

(B) Discounts from local retail stores

(C) A reduction of local government taxes

(D) One free ticket to movie theaters a month

Gladwell 動物愛護協会の会員特典ではないものは何ですか。

(A) 自治体が運営するフィットネスセンターへの入会

(B) 地元の小売店の割引

(C) 地方自治体の税金の割引

(D) 月あたり 1 枚の無料映画観賞チケット

正解 D

NOT 問題

協会の会員特典は、お知らせの「会員レベル」のところに述べられている。(A) はシルバー会員の free use of public swimming pools and gyms と一致する。public が government-run と言い換えられている。(B) は Five percent off on all purchases at participating stores, including Greenmart and South Hampton Shopping Center. と一致する。(C) はブロンズ会員の a three percent discount on council taxes「市民税の 3% 割引」と一致する。映画鑑賞チケットに関しては言及がないので、(D) が正解。

☐ government-run　　　　　　　　　政府経営の、国営の

What level of membership has Ms. Wright most likely received?

(A) Gold

(B) Silver

(C) Bronze

(D) Standard

Wright さんはどのレベルの会員資格を授与されていると考えられますか。

(A) ゴールド

(B) シルバー

(C) ブロンズ

(D) スタンダード

正解 A

設問に着目するクロス問題

Pearlman さんから Wright さん宛ての手紙に、I have gotten an Art Gallery membership using mine and it has given me many hours of pleasure. I hope that you will do the same.「私は自分の会員資格を使ってアートギャラリーの会員になり、何時間も楽しいときを過ごさせてもらってきた。あなたも同じようになさることを願う」とあるので、Wright さんもアートギャラリーの会員になる資格を持つと判断できる。お知らせを見ると、ゴールド会員のところに、Benefits include all silver level benefits as well as a State Museum and Art Gallery membership. とあるので、(A) が正解。

189 What is suggested about Ms. Wright?

(A) She has retired from her job.

(B) She is a founding member of GHS.

(C) She will hire an inspirational speaker.

(D) She has introduced other people to GHS.

Wright さんについて何が分かりますか。

(A) 彼女は仕事を定年退職した。

(B) 彼女は GHS の創立メンバーである。

(C) 彼女は感動的なスピーチができる人を雇う。

(D) 彼女は GHS に他の人々を紹介した。

正解 **A**

選択肢に着目する問題

正解の根拠は、彼女が Pearlman さんに送った E メールの中にある。Now that my working life is over「今や私の仕事人生も終わりましたので」と彼女が書いていることから、定年退職したと想像できる。She has retired from her job. と表現している (A) が正解。なお、Now that ～は「今や～なので」という意味で、接続詞としての役割を果たす。

190 When will Ms. Wright and Mr. Pearlman most likely meet next?

(A) On July 7

(B) On July 9

(C) On July 27

(D) On July 30

Wright さんと Pearlman さんは次にいつ会うと考えられますか。

(A) 7 月 7 日

(B) 7 月 9 日

(C) 7 月 27 日

(D) 7 月 30 日

正解 **D**

設問に着目するクロス問題

Wright さん宛ての手紙で Pearlman さんは Holland さんの展覧会について、I would be very happy if you would join me in attending an exhibition of Mr. Greg Holland's work there on July 30. と Wright さんが同行することを誘っている。また、次の会合が 7 月 27 日だと述べている。Wright さんは Pearlman さん宛ての E メールの最後で、次の会合には出席できないと述べてから、I would be honored to accompany you to the Art Gallery to see Mr. Holland's exhibition. と返事をしている。これらのことから、2 人は 7 月 30 日の展覧会で会うと判断できる。正解は (D)。

Questions 191-195 refer to the following Web page, e-mail, and ticket.

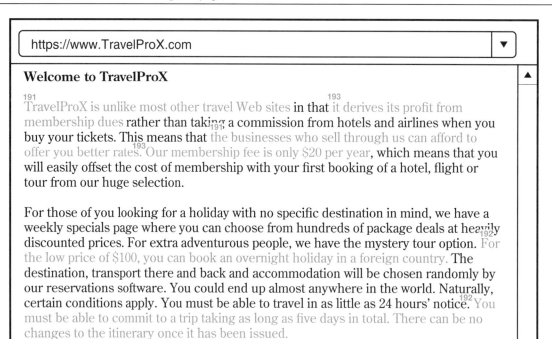

Welcome to TravelProX

TravelProX is unlike most other travel Web sites in that it derives its profit from membership dues rather than taking a commission from hotels and airlines when you buy your tickets. This means that the businesses who sell through us can afford to offer you better rates. Our membership fee is only $20 per year, which means that you will easily offset the cost of membership with your first booking of a hotel, flight or tour from our huge selection.

For those of you looking for a holiday with no specific destination in mind, we have a weekly specials page where you can choose from hundreds of package deals at heavily discounted prices. For extra adventurous people, we have the mystery tour option. For the low price of $100, you can book an overnight holiday in a foreign country. The destination, transport there and back and accommodation will be chosen randomly by our reservations software. You could end up almost anywhere in the world. Naturally, certain conditions apply. You must be able to travel in as little as 24 hours' notice. You must be able to commit to a trip taking as long as five days in total. There can be no changes to the itinerary once it has been issued.

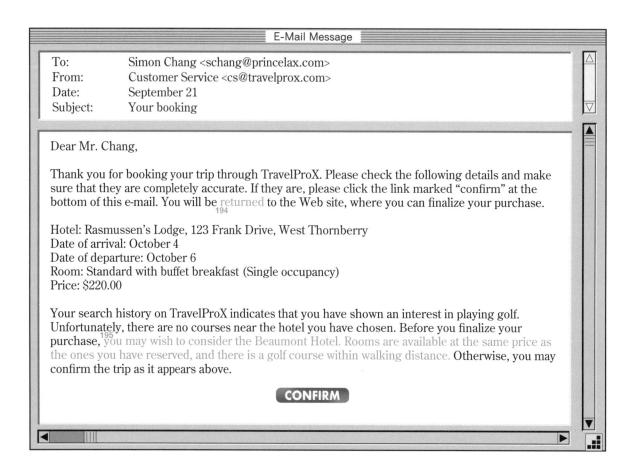

E-Mail Message

To: Simon Chang <schang@princelax.com>
From: Customer Service <cs@travelprox.com>
Date: September 21
Subject: Your booking

Dear Mr. Chang,

Thank you for booking your trip through TravelProX. Please check the following details and make sure that they are completely accurate. If they are, please click the link marked "confirm" at the bottom of this e-mail. You will be returned to the Web site, where you can finalize your purchase.

Hotel: Rasmussen's Lodge, 123 Frank Drive, West Thornberry
Date of arrival: October 4
Date of departure: October 6
Room: Standard with buffet breakfast (Single occupancy)
Price: $220.00

Your search history on TravelProX indicates that you have shown an interest in playing golf. Unfortunately, there are no courses near the hotel you have chosen. Before you finalize your purchase, you may wish to consider the Beaumont Hotel. Rooms are available at the same price as the ones you have reserved, and there is a golf course within walking distance. Otherwise, you may confirm the trip as it appears above.

CONFIRM

問題 **191-195** は次のウェブページ、E メール、チケットに関するものです。

https://www.TravelProX.com

TravelProX へようこそ

TravelProX はお客様がチケットを買った際にホテルや航空会社から手数料をもらうのではなく、会費から収益を上げているという点で、他のほとんどの旅行ウェブサイトとは違います。これはつまり、当社を通じて販売している企業はお客様によりよい料金を提供することができるということです。当社の年会費はたったの 20 ドルですので、当社の豊富な品揃えのホテル、航空便、ツアーの最初のご予約で簡単に会費の元が取れることになります。

特に決まった行き先が念頭にないまま休暇先を探していらっしゃる方のために、大幅値下げをした何百ものパッケージ旅行から選ぶことができる週ごとの特別ページをご用意しております。特に冒険がお好きな方のためには、ミステリーツアーのオプションもご用意しております。100 ドルという低料金で、外国での 1 泊旅行をご予約いただけます。行き先、行き帰りの交通手段、宿泊は当社の予約ソフトウェアによって無作為に選ばれます。世界のほとんどどこにでも行くことになる可能性があります。当然ながら、一定の条件が適用されます。お知らせがあってからたった 24 時間で旅行に出発できなければなりません。合計 5 日間にもわたる旅行に専念できなければなりません。一度出された旅程表は変更不可能です。

宛先：Simon Chang <schang@princelax.com>

送信者：Customer Service <cs@travelprox.com>

日付：9 月 21 日

件名：ご予約

Chang 様

TravelProX での旅行のご予約ありがとうございます。以下の詳細を確認いただき、完全に正しいことをお確かめください。これで正しければ、この E メールの一番下にある「確認」とマークされたリンクをクリックしてください。ウェブサイトに戻されますので、そこでご購入内容を最終確定することができます。

ホテル：Rasmussen's Lodge、Frank 通り 123 番地、West Thornberry

到着日：10 月 4 日

出発日：10 月 6 日

部屋：ビュッフェ形式の朝食つきスタンダード（1 人部屋）

価格：220.00 ドル

TravelProX でのお客様の検索履歴は、お客様がゴルフに興味をお持ちであることを示しています。残念ながら、お客様がお選びになったホテルの近辺にはゴルフコースはございません。ご購入内容を最終確定する前に、Beaumont ホテルを検討なさってはいかがでしょうか。ご予約のお部屋と同じ価格でお部屋が利用可能であり、徒歩圏内にゴルフコースがございます。そうなさらない場合、上記の通りで旅行を確定していただいてかまいません。

| 確認 |

Please print out this voucher and show it to the hotel staff at check-in.

Reservation Number: MU7482383
Reservation Type: Accommodation only
Guest Name: Simon Chang
[195]**Hotel:** Beaumont Hotel
Check-in: Friday, October 4
Check out: Sunday, October 6
Room Type: Standard
Breakfast: Included (Buffet in Stylez Restaurant on the first floor.)

このクーポン券を印刷して、チェックインの際にホテルのスタッフにご提示ください。

予約番号：MU7482383
予約タイプ：宿泊のみ
お客様氏名：Simon Chang
ホテル：Beaumont ホテル
チェックイン：10 月 4 日（金）
チェックアウト：10 月 6 日（日）
お部屋タイプ：スタンダード
朝食：含まれる（1 階の Stylez レストランでのビュッフェ）

191 What is the purpose of the Web page?

(A) To explain ways that people can make money from home

(B) To suggest positions for job seekers to apply for

(C) To describe the benefits of an online service

(D) To recommend a specific travel destination

ウェブページの目的は何ですか。

(A) 在宅でお金を稼げる方法について説明すること。

(B) 就職希望者が応募すべき職を提案すること。

(C) オンラインサービスの利点を説明すること。

(D) 特定の旅行先を薦めること。

正解 C

設問に着目する問題

文書の目的が問われている。様々な文書の目的は、冒頭付近に書かれていることが多く、この問題の正解の根拠も、ウェブページの冒頭にある。まず TravelProX is unlike most other travel Web sites「TravelProX は他のほとんどの旅行ウェブサイトとは違う」と述べられ、続いて、どのような違いがあり、どのように顧客にとって得なのかが、the businesses who sell through us can afford to offer you better rates「当社を通じて販売している企業はお客様によりよい料金を提供することができる」と説明されている。(C) が正解。

☐ job seeker　　　　　　　就職希望者

---

192 What is NOT a condition of the mystery tour?

(A) There is a fixed price.

(B) Only international destinations are available.

(C) The return date is not negotiable.

(D) All travel must be taken alone.

ミステリーツアーの条件ではないものは何ですか。

(A) 価格が決まっている。

(B) 国外の目的地のみが利用可能である。

(C) 帰ってくる日については交渉できない。

(D) すべての旅行は一人旅でなければならない。

正解 D

NOT 問題

ミステリーツアーに関してはウェブページの後半に言及がある。(A) は For the low price of $100, と一致する。(B) は you can book an overnight holiday in a foreign country と一致する。(C) は You must be able to commit to a trip taking as long as five days in total. There can be no changes to the itinerary once it has been issued.「合計 5 日間にもわたる旅行に専念できなければなりません。一度出された旅程表は変更不可能」を not negotiable を使って表現しているので、一致する。旅行人数についての条件には言及がないので、正解は (D)。

---

193 What is indicated about Mr. Chang?

(A) He reserved his transportation with TravelProX.

(B) He took out a membership in TravelProX.

(C) He has advertised his business with TravelProX.

(D) He was previously employed at TravelProX.

Chang さんについて何が示されていますか。

(A) 彼は TravelProX で交通手段を予約した。

(B) 彼は TravelProX の会員になった。

(C) 彼は TravelProX との事業を宣伝した。

(D) 彼は以前 TravelProX で雇われていた。

正解 B

選択肢に着目するクロス問題

E メールやチケットから Chang さんは TravelProX を介して旅行の予約をしたことが分かる。ウェブページを見てみると、it derives its profit from membership dues「それは会費から収益を上げている」や、Our membership fee is only $20 per year「当社の年会費はたったの 20 ドルだ」とあり、TravelProX で旅行の予約をするためには、まず会員になり、会費を支払う必要があると判断できるので、正解は (B)。take out a membership は「会員になる」という意味。

194 In the e-mail, the word "returned" in paragraph 1, line 3 is closest in meaning to

(A) sent back

(B) responded

(C) replaced

(D) looked over

E メールの第 1 段落・3 行目にある returned に最も意味が近いのは

(A) 送り返される

(B) 応答される

(C) 取って代わられる

(D) 目を通される

正解 **A**

同義語問題

旅行会社から Chang さんに送られた E メールは、Chang さんに旅行予約の内容の確認を求めている。詳細が正しければ、メール内の「確認」をクリックするよう述べられており、そうすることで、ウェブサイトに戻されて購入内容を最終確定することができるとある。つまり、be returned は、クリックするとメールからウェブサイトに「送られる」という意味を表している。正解は (A)。

195 What is most likely true about Mr. Chang's trip?

(A) He took advantage of the mystery tour option.

(B) He will travel with some family members.

(C) He will receive a reimbursement from his company.

(D) He intends to play golf during his stay.

Chang さんの旅行について正しいと考えられることは何ですか。

(A) 彼はミステリーツアーのオプションを利用した。

(B) 彼は何人かの家族と一緒に旅行する。

(C) 彼は会社から払い戻しを受ける。

(D) 彼は滞在中にゴルフをするつもりである。

正解 **D**

選択肢に着目するクロス問題

E メールでは、Chang さんの宿泊は Rasmussen's Lodge となっている。Chang さんがゴルフに興味があることを TravelProX は検索履歴から知っていて、you may wish to consider the Beaumont Hotel. Rooms are available at the same price as the ones you have reserved, and there is a golf course within walking distance と、Beaumont ホテルは同価格でしかもゴルフをすることもできると提案している。そしてチケットでは、宿泊が Beaumont ホテルとなっており、Chang さんがゴルフをするために変更したと想像できる。正解は (D)。intend to *do*「〜するつもりだ」

☐ reimbursement　　　　　　　払い戻し

Questions 196-200 refer to the following e-mails and advertisement.

To:	Claire Thompson <cthompson@thompsonco.com>
From:	Blair Goldman <bgoldman@thompsonco.com>
Date:	November 6
Subject:	Stirling Advertising Agency

Dear Ms. Thompson,

196 You asked me to send a review of the performance of Stirling Advertising Agency. **My personal opinion is that** 197 they are simply repeating different variations of the same kind of advertising they did for us in the first year. **The success we experienced then was because of the originality and the high quality of the advertisements.** 197 It seems that the new advertisements are 198 less and less successful **because the company has already used up all of its best ideas.** Stirling Advertising has been requesting a bigger budget each year and despite this, sales of our confectionaries are more and more discouraging. **The returns on our investment in advertising have been decreasing.** 200 It is a big problem as we only produce confectionary **and we've given the whole contract to one agency. In short, I believe it is time for us to replace Stirling Advertising Agency or at least offer part of the contract to another company.**

Sincerely,

Blair Goldman
Chief of Sales — Thompson Co.

To:	Blair Goldman <bgoldman@thompsonco.com>
From:	Claire Thompson <cthompson@thompsonco.com>
Date:	November 6
Subject:	RE: Stirling Advertising Agency

Thank you for your insightful review of Stirling Advertising's performance. 198 It cannot be denied that sales have declined since we started using Stirling. **However, I am not sure that this is a failing on Stirling Advertising's part. I think** 200 we should discuss the matter with our own product development department **and get their opinions. I will put Stirling Advertising Agency on notice that their performance is** under review and pressure them to produce a more successful campaign this year. 199

Claire Thompson
President — Thompson Co.

宛先：Claire Thompson <cthompson@thompsonco.com>
送信者：Blair Goldman <bgoldman@thompsonco.com>
日付：11 月 6 日
件名：Stirling 広告代理店

Thompson 様

Stirling 広告代理店の実績についての評価を送ってほしいとのご依頼でした。私の個人的な意見としては、彼らは最初の年に当社用に作成した広告と同じ種類のものの様々な変種を繰り返しているだけです。当時当社が経験した成功はその広告の独創性と高い品質のおかげでした。新しい広告は、会社が最良のアイデアをすべて使い切ってしまったため、だんだん成果が出なくなってきているようです。Stirling 広告代理店は毎年、前年より大きな予算を要求してきていますが、これにもかかわらず、当社の菓子の売り上げはだんだん思わしくないものになっています。広告への投資に対する見返りは減ってきています。当社は菓子類しか製造しておらず、契約全体を 1 社と結んでいるため、これは大きな問題です。つまり、当社はもう Stirling 広告代理店の代わりを見つけるか、少なくとも契約の一部を別の会社に提案するかすべきときだと思います。

よろしくお願いします。

Blair Goldman
販売部部長—Thompson 社

宛先：Blair Goldman <bgoldman@thompsonco.com>
送信者：Claire Thompson <cthompson@thompsonco.com>
日付：11 月 6 日
件名：RE：Stirling 広告代理店

Stirling 広告代理店の業績に対する洞察に満ちた評価をありがとうございます。Stirling を利用し始めて以来売り上げが落ちてきたことは否定できません。しかし、これが Stirling 広告代理店側の落ち度であるかどうか私には分かりません。この問題について当社の製品開発部と話し合って彼らの意見を聞くべきだと思います。私は Stirling 広告代理店に彼らの業績が検討されていることを通知し、今年はもっと成功するキャンペーンを制作するようプレッシャーをかけます。

Claire Thompson
社長 — Thompson 社

Pineapple Water
A treat to beat the summer heat!

This new sports beverage comes from Thompson Co. and has all the essential salts and minerals you need to stay active through the summer.
Don't let the heat slow you down.
Stay fit, stay active, stay hydrated!

パイナップルウォーター
夏の暑さに勝つ絶品！

この新しいスポーツドリンクは Thompson 社製で、夏を元気に過ごすために必要な塩分とミネラルが全部入っています。
暑さでへばらないで。
健康に、元気に過ごし、こまめに水分補給しましょう！

語彙チェック

☐	despite	～にもかかわらず	☐	failing	不手際、欠点
☐	confectionary	菓子	☐	put someone on notice	（人）に通告する
☐	discouraging	がっかりさせるような、思わしくない	☐	treat	ごちそう、特別な楽しみ
☐	contract	契約	☐	beverage	飲料
☐	replace	～の代わりを見つける	☐	essential	必要不可欠な
☐	insightful	洞察力のある	☐	fit	健康な、元気な
☐	deny	～を否定する	☐	hydrated	水分補給された
☐	decline	下がる、落ちる			

According to the first e-mail, what did Ms. Thompson request Mr. Goldman to do?

(A) Provide some updated sales statistics

(B) Do an evaluation of a service

(C) Announce a company's decision

(D) Offer assistance with a project

1つ目のEメールによると、Thompson さんは Goldman さんに何をするよう求めましたか。

(A) 最新の売り上げ統計を提出する。

(B) サービスの評価をする。

(C) 会社の決定を告知する。

(D) プロジェクトの援助を申し出る。

正解 B

設問に着目する問題

Thompson さんに宛てられた1つ目のEメールの冒頭で Goldman さんは You asked me to send a review of the performance of Stirling Advertising Agency.「あなたは Stirling 広告代理店の実績についての評価を送ってほしいとのご依頼でした」とある。つまり、Thompson さんが広告会社の評価を事前に Goldman さんに依頼していたことが分かる。a review of the performance of Stirling Advertising Agency を an evaluation of a service と言い換えている (B) が正解。evaluation「評価」。

☐ statistics　　　　　　　　統計資料

What is stated about Stirling Advertising Agency?

(A) It has been employed by Ms. Thompson's company for several years.

(B) It has had its budget reduced since last year.

(C) It has gradually been having greater and greater success.

(D) It has contracts with several other companies.

Stirling 広告代理店について述べられていることは何ですか。

(A) それは Thompson さんの会社に何年間か雇用されている。

(B) それは昨年以来予算が削られている。

(C) それはだんだん大きな成功を収めてきている。

(D) それは他の何社かと契約を結んでいる。

正解 A

選択肢に着目する問題

広告代理店の評価を求められた Goldman さんは1つ目のメールの中で、広告代理店について述べている。they are simply repeating different variations of the same kind of advertising they did for us in the first year.「彼らは最初の年に当社用に作成した広告と同じ種類のものの様々な変種を繰り返している」や It seems that the new advertisements are less and less successful「新しい広告は、だんだん成果が出なくなってきている」などと、過去1回ではなく、数年間にわたり、Thompson 社の広告に携わっていることが分かる。正解は (A)。

What do Mr. Goldman and Ms. Thompson agree about?

(A) Stirling Advertising Agency's responsibility for sales

(B) A prediction for the company's future profits

(C) The company's current sales performance

(D) The marketing strategy for a product

Goldman さんと Thompson さんは何について意見が一致していますか。

(A) Stirling 広告代理店の売り上げに関する責任

(B) 会社の将来の収益に関する予測

(C) 会社の現在の販売業績

(D) 製品のマーケティング戦略

正解 C

設問に着目するクロス問題

Goldman さんはEメールの中で、Stirling Advertising has been requesting a bigger budget each year and despite this, sales of our confectionaries are more and more discouraging. と、Stirling 広告代理店の予算要求が増えているのに、菓子の売り上げが下がっていると述べ、Thompson さんもEメールの中で、It cannot be denied that sales have declined since we started using Stirling. と、売り上げが落ちていることを述べている。したがって、両者とも、会社の菓子の売り上げが落ちていることを指摘しているので、(C) が正解。

☐ prediction　　　　　　　予測

199 In the second e-mail, the word "under" in paragraph 1, line 5 is closest in meaning to

(A) covered by

(B) secondary to

(C) subject to

(D) available for

2 通目の E メールの第 1 段落・5 行目にある under に最も意味が近いのは

(A) 〜に補償されて

(B) 〜に次いで

(C) 〜の影響下に

(D) 〜に利用可能で

正解 **C**

同義語問題

under を含む文では、社長である Thompson さんが、広告代理店に対し彼らの業績を検討中であると伝えると述べ、そうすることでもっとよい広告を制作するようプレッシャーを与えると続けている。したがって、under は「〜の最中にある、の支配下にある」という意味であると想像できる。この under に最も近いのは「〜の影響下に」という意味の subject to。正解は (C)。

200 What is most likely true about Thompson Co.?

(A) It is no longer using Stirling Advertising Agency.

(B) It has stopped producing some of its products.

(C) It has reduced its product development department.

(D) It is experimenting with a new product type.

Thompson 社について正しいと考えられることは何ですか。

(A) それはもう Stirling 広告代理店を利用していない。

(B) それは製品の一部を生産するのをやめた。

(C) それは製品開発部を縮小した。

(D) それは新しい種類の製品を試している。

正解 **D**

選択肢に着目するクロス問題

菓子の売り上げが落ちていることに関して、Goldman さんは、It is a big problem as we only produce confectionary と、菓子のみ製造していることも問題点として挙げている。社長の Thompson さんも、広告だけでなく、we should discuss the matter with our own product development department と、製品開発も考えていく必要があると述べている。そして新しい広告を見ると、This new sports beverage comes from Thompson Co. とあり、菓子でないスポーツ飲料製品が開発販売されたことが分かる。(D) が正解。experiment with 〜「〜を試してみる」。

Day 24

【TEST 2 Questions 147-175】　2/5回目

Day 24は、**Day 14〜18で解いたシングルパッセージ10題**をもう一度まとめて解く日です。**別冊TEST 2の147番〜175番（別冊P27〜37）**を解きましょう。制限時間は**29分**です。解き終わったら、解説はDay 14〜18の解説ページ（本冊P62〜81）を見て確認してください。

Day 25

【TEST 2 Questions 176-200】　2/5回目

Day 25は、**Day 19〜23で解いたマルチプルパッセージ5題**をもう一度まとめて解く日です。**別冊TEST 2の176番〜200番（別冊P38〜47）**を解きましょう。制限時間は**25分**です。解き終わったら、解説はDay 19〜23の解説ページ（本冊P82〜107）を見て確認してください。

Day 26

【TEST 2 Questions 147-200】　3/5回目

Day 26は、**Day 24〜25で解いた問題**をまとめて解く日です。**別冊TEST 2の147番〜200番（別冊P27〜47）**を解きましょう。制限時間は**54分**です。解き終わったら、解説はDay 14〜23の解説ページ（本冊P62〜107）を見て確認してください。

TEST 3

解答&解説

Questions 147-148 refer to the following advertisement.

Wesson A to B

Our highly-trained employees will ensure that your prized possessions make it to their destination in one piece. [147] Whether you are relocating your apartment down the street or a fully furnished house across the country, Wesson A to B is the clever choice.

We offer:

Free same-day price estimates

[148] 24-hour service

[147] Furniture assembly and disassembly at both ends

Comprehensive insurance for your belongings

Call a customer service representative at 555-4782 to make an appointment.
Payment can be made by credit card or bank transfer.
www.wessonatob.com

問題 **147-148** は次の広告に関するものです。

Wesson A to B

我が社の高度に訓練された従業員はあなたの大切な所有物を無事に目的地までお届けすることを保証します。アパートのお部屋を通り沿いに引っ越すにしろ、家具付き一軒家を国を横断して引っ越すにしろ、Wesson A to B 社は賢い選択です。

ご提供するもの：

無料の即日価格見積もり
24 時間サービス
出発時および到着時の家具の組み立てと解体
所有物の総合保険

顧客サービス担当者に 555-4782 まで電話でご予約ください。
クレジットカードか銀行振込でお支払いいただけます。
www.wessonatob.com

147

What is being advertised?

(A) A moving company

(B) A travel agency

(C) A shuttle bus service

(D) A local competition

何が広告されていますか。

(A) 引っ越し会社

(B) 旅行会社

(C) シャトルバスサービス

(D) 地元のコンペ

正解 A

設問に着目する問題

Whether you are relocating your apartment down the street or a fully furnished house across the country, Wesson A to B is the clever choice. 「アパートのお部屋を通り沿いに引っ越すにしろ、家具付き一軒家を国内を横断して引っ越すにしろ、Wesson A to B 社は賢い選択だ」とある。また、提供するサービスの内容である、家具の組み立てや解体などからも引っ越し会社の広告と分かる。正解は (A)。

148

What is indicated about the company?

(A) It is looking to update its equipment.

(B) It has recently expanded.

(C) It has been nominated for an award.

(D) It can provide its service in the evenings.

会社について何が示されていますか。

(A) それは設備を最新式のものにするつもりである。

(B) それは最近拡大した。

(C) それは賞に推薦されたことがある。

(D) それは夕方にサービスを提供することができる。

正解 D

選択肢に着目する問題

提供するサービスが箇条書きにされているが、24-hour service「24時間サービス」とあり、夜間の作業も可能であることが分かる。正解は (D)。

| ☐ | be looking to *do* | ～する予定だ、するつもりだ |
| ☐ | expand | 拡大する |

語彙チェック

☐	ensure that ～	～ということを確実にする
☐	prized	貴重な
☐	possession	所有物、財産
☐	furnished	家具付きの
☐	assembly	組み立て
☐	comprehensive	総合的な、包括的な
☐	belongings	所有物、持ち物

Questions 149-150 refer to the following text-message chain.

> **BRENDA CARTER 3:51 P.M.**
> Vladimir, are you busy this evening?

> **VLADIMIR DRAGO 3:53 P.M.**
> I don't have any jobs, but I was looking forward to going home.

> **BRENDA CARTER 3:53 P.M.**
> I have a delivery job for you. It's a big one at short notice so we can offer you higher rates than usual.

> **VLADIMIR DRAGO 3:54 P.M.**
> What's the job?

> **BRENDA CARTER 3:59 P.M.**
> We need you to deliver some building materials to an address on Tambourine Mountain by 8:00 P.M.

> **VLADIMIR DRAGO 4:02 P.M.**
> Can I take them home with me and deliver them first thing in the morning?

> **BRENDA CARTER 4:03 P.M.**
> We can't have that, I'm afraid. Our insurance doesn't allow that kind of thing.

> **VLADIMIR DRAGO 4:20 P.M.**
> I'll be there at 5:00 P.M. It'll take me a while to get back to the shipping center at this time of day.

問題 **149-150** は次のテキストメッセージのやりとりに関するものです。

BRENDA CARTER　　午後 3 時 51 分
Vladimir、今日の夕方は忙しいかしら？
VLADIMIR DRAGO　　午後 3 時 53 分
仕事はありませんが、家に帰るのを楽しみにしていました。
BRENDA CARTER　　午後 3 時 53 分
あなたに配達の仕事があるの。急な大仕事だから、いつもより高い料金を提案できるわ。
VLADIMIR DRAGO　　午後 3 時 54 分
何の仕事ですか？
BRENDA CARTER　　午後 3 時 59 分
午後 8 時までに、Tambourine Mountain のある住所まで建築資材を配達してもらう必要があるの。
VLADIMIR DRAGO　　午後 4 時 2 分
家に持ち帰って朝一番に配達することはできますか？
BRENDA CARTER　　午後 4 時 3 分
残念だけど、それはできないの。うちの保険はそうしたことを許可していないわ。
VLADIMIR DRAGO　　午後 4 時 20 分
午後 5 時にそこへ行きます。この時間だと運送センターに戻るのにしばらくかかるでしょう。

149 What is the purpose of the text-message chain?

(A) To request a refund

(B) To arrange a delivery

(C) To explain a new policy

(D) To offer some advice

テキストメッセージのやりとりの目的は何ですか。

(A) 返金を依頼すること。

(B) 配達の手配をすること。

(C) 新しい方針を説明すること。

(D) 助言をすること。

正解
B

設問に着目する問題

Brenda から、急な配送業務ができないか打診された Vladimir は、報酬を高めに受け取れることもあり、I'll be there at 5:00 P.M. と言って、最終的にその業務を引き受けている。Brenda は配送会社で Vladimir の上司と推測でき、急な配送業務を手配するために、このやりとりを開始したと考えられる。したがって、正解は (B)。

150 At 4:03 P.M., what does Brenda mean when she writes, "We can't have that"?

(A) Some equipment is no longer in production.

(B) A reservation has already been accepted.

(C) They do not have permission for an action.

(D) A device has been reserved by another group.

午後 4 時 3 分に Brenda が "We can't have that" と書く際、何を意図していますか。

(A) 一部の設備はもう生産されていない。

(B) 予約はすでに受け付けられた。

(C) 彼らはある行動の許可をもらっていない。

(D) ある装置が別のグループに予約されてしまった。

正解
C

意図問題

I was looking forward to going home と書いている Vladimir は、今晩は早く帰宅したかったと分かる。夕方に急な仕事を頼まれて、Can I take them home with me and deliver them first thing in the morning? と、明日の朝一番で配達可能か Brenda に尋ねた際の彼女の応答が We can't have that である。Brenda は続けて Our insurance doesn't allow that kind of thing.「うちの保険はそうしたことを許可していない」と書いていることから、彼女は Vladimir が朝配送をすることは許可されていないということを伝えるために書いたと考えられる。正解は (C)。permission「許可」。

☐ in production　　　　　生産されている
☐ device　　　　　　　　装置

語彙チェック
☐ building material　　　建築資材
☐ while　　　　　　　　少しの時間

Questions 151-152 refer to the following letter.

Harmony Textiles
563 Dawson Creek Road,
Stanford, QLD 4563

June 19

Dear Ms. Kline,

¹⁵¹Thank you for contacting me about launching your new enterprise in China. While I am deeply honored that Mr. Holmes recommended me, I regret that I may not be the best person for the job. ¹⁵²I have never worked in the textile business before and have no contacts in the industry.

I have an acquaintance by the name of Roger Lim, who is much more suited to the role. Please contact him at rlim@limconsultancy.com.

I am sorry that I am unable to assist you with this project and hope that you will contact me again if something more suited to my skillset comes along.

Sincerely,

Trevor Wang

Trevor Wang

問題 **151-152** は次の手紙に関するものです。

Harmony 織物社
Dawson Creek 通り 563 番地
Stanford, QLD 4563

6 月 19 日

Kline 様

中国での貴社の新事業開始についてご連絡をいただきありがとうございます。Holmes さんにご推薦いただいたということで非常に光栄ではありますが、残念ながら、私はその仕事に最もふさわしい人物ではないかもしれません。私は繊維業では働いた経験がなく、業界との接点もありません。

Roger Lim という名の知り合いがおりまして、彼の方がその役割により適しています。rlim@limconsultancy.com まで、彼と連絡を取ってください。

このプロジェクトに関してお手伝いできず残念ですが、もし私のスキルにより適したことが出てきましたら、またご連絡いただければと思います。

よろしくお願いします。

Trevor Wang （署名）

Trevor Wang

151 What is implied about Ms. Kline?

(A) She is currently living in China.

(B) She is employed by Mr. Holmes.

(C) She plans to open a new business.

(D) She is looking to hire a secretary.

Kline さんについて何が示唆されていますか。

(A) 彼女は現在中国に住んでいる。

(B) 彼女は Holmes さんに雇われている。

(C) 彼女は新事業を起こすつもりである。

(D) 彼女は秘書を雇うつもりである。

正解 **C**

選択肢に着目する問題

Kline さんに宛てられた手紙の冒頭にこの問題の正解の根拠がある。Thank you for contacting me about launching your new enterprise in China.「中国での貴社の新事業開始についてご連絡をいただきありがとう」とあり、Kline さんは新事業を始めるにあたって、Wang さんに連絡をしたと判断できる。正解は launch your new enterprise を open a new business と言い換えている (C)。

---

152 Why is Mr. Wang unable to assist Ms. Kline?

(A) He has too much on his schedule.

(B) He has committed to help a competitor.

(C) He does not take international contracts.

(D) He lacks appropriate experience.

Wang さんはなぜ Kline さんを手伝うことができないのですか。

(A) 彼は予定が詰まり過ぎているから。

(B) 彼は競合他社を手伝うと約束しているから。

(C) 彼は国際契約を結ばないから。

(D) 彼は適切な経験がないから。

正解 **D**

設問に着目する問題

事業の支援をお願いされた Wang さんが、それを辞退している。自分が最適な人物ではないと述べた後、I have never worked in the textile business before and have no contacts in the industry.「私は繊維業では働いた経験がなく、業界との接点もない」と繊維業界での経験がないことを理由として挙げている。そのことを He lacks appropriate experience. と表現している (D) が正解。lack「〜を欠く」。

☐ commit to *do* 　　　　　〜すると約束する
☐ competitor 　　　　　　競合他社

語彙チェック

☐ textile 　　　　　　　　織物（の）
☐ launch 　　　　　　　　〜を開始する
☐ enterprise 　　　　　　事業、企業
☐ be honored that 〜 　　〜ということを光栄に思う
☐ acquaintance 　　　　　知り合い
☐ skillset 　　　　　　　（仕事に必要な）知識や技能
☐ come along 　　　　　　やってくる、現れる

Questions 153-154 refer to the following postcard.

Snaptech

Dear Valued Customer:

Snaptech prides itself on its excellent product quality and customer service, so it pains us to admit that a product recall is necessary for one of our recently released products. Purchasers of the U766X mini projector are being asked to return their devices to have the battery replaced. The turnaround should take no more than two weeks. We understand that two weeks is too long to be without this important device for some people. By way of compensation, we are offering a price reduction of 20 percent on your next purchase of a Snaptech device. Simply show this postcard to the clerk when you make your purchase. Please keep in mind that this discount is only available from official retailers of Snaptech products.

Sincerely,

Dale Shepheard
CEO — Snaptech

問題 **153-154** は次のはがきに関するものです。

Snaptech

大切なお客様へ:

Snaptech 社は非常に優れた品質と顧客サービスを誇っておりますので、最近発売した商品の 1 つに関して商品回収が必要であると認めるのは心苦しいことです。U766X 小型プロジェクターを購入されたお客様に、電池交換のために装置を返品していただきますようお願い申し上げます。2 週間以内にお返しできるはずです。このような重要な装置なしでの 2 週間というのは一部の方々にとっては長過ぎるということは承知しております。埋め合わせに、Snaptech 製品の次回購入時に 20% の価格割引をご提供いたします。ご購入の際、店員にこのはがきを提示していただくだけで結構です。この割引は Snaptech 製品の正規販売店のみでご利用いただけますのでご注意ください。

よろしくお願いいたします。

Dale Snepheard
Snaptech 社　最高経営責任者

153 What are customers asked to do?

(A) Download a users' manual

(B) Return a product

(C) Send in a warranty form

(D) Register as customers

顧客は何をするよう求められていますか。

(A) 取扱説明書をダウンロードする。

(B) 製品を返品する。

(C) 保証書式を送付する。

(D) 顧客として登録する。

正解 B

設問に着目する問題

このはがきは Snaptech 社の最高経営責任者から、Valued Customer「大切なお客様」に宛てられたもので、Purchasers of the U766X mini projector are being asked to return their devices to have the battery replaced. とあり、電池交換の必要があるため、小型プロジェクターの購入者は製品を返品するよう求められていることが分かる。その前に a product recall is necessary という表現も出てきていることから、(B) が正解となる。

☐ send in ～ 　　　　　　　　　～を送付する、提出する

154 What compensation is offered?

(A) A full refund of the purchase price

(B) A product upgrade

(C) A discount on a future purchase

(D) A written apology

どのような埋め合わせが提案されていますか。

(A) 購入金額の全額返金

(B) 製品のアップグレード

(C) 将来の購入の割引

(D) 書面での謝罪

正解 C

設問に着目する問題

リコールの compensation「埋め合わせ」については、By way of compensation, we are offering a price reduction of 20 percent on your next purchase of a Snaptech device.「埋め合わせに、Snaptech 製品の次回購入時に 20 パーセントの価格割引をご提供いたします」とあり、同社製品の next purchase「次回の購入」には割引が提供されるので、(C) が正解。

語彙チェック

☐ valued	大切な
☐ pride oneself on ～	～を自慢する、誇りに思う
☐ pain	～に苦痛を与える
☐ admit	～を認める
☐ turnaround	(作業)時間、ターンアラウンド
☐ by way of compensation	埋め合わせとして
☐ retailer	小売業者、販売店

Day 29

Questions 155-157 refer to the following advertisement.

Would you like to improve your confidence in the kitchen?

If so, ¹⁵⁵ you need to attend a session with a qualified chef.

¹⁵⁶ **Saul White,** a highly respected chef who has worked in five-star hotels around the world, is giving an introductory cooking class at the Vandelay Convention Center.

¹⁵⁶ Chef White's appearance fees and the rent on the hall have been covered by the Regent Cooking School so anyone is welcome to attend for free. We simply ask that you register in advance as seats are limited. To register you must contact the Regent Cooking School enrollments office directly. ¹⁵⁷ You can do so by calling 555-7432, sending an e-mail to enrollments@regentcs.com, or by sending a text message with your name to 030-555-5150.

An Afternoon with Chef Saul White
Brought to you by
Regent Cooking School

問題 **155-157** は次の広告に関するものです。

台所での自信を高めたいですか？
それなら、有能な料理人との講習会に出席する必要があります。

世界中の 5 つ星ホテルに勤めてきた非常に尊敬を集めている料理人である **Saul White** さんが、Vandelay 会議センターで料理入門教室を開講します。

White シェフの出演料とホールの部屋代は Regent 料理学校が負担していますので、どなたでも無料でご参加いただけます。席数は限られておりますので、あらかじめご登録をお願いいたします。ご登録の際は Regent 料理学校の入学課に直接ご連絡ください。連絡は 555-7432 までお電話いただくか、enrollments@regentcs.com まで E メールをいただくか、または 030-555-5150 までお名前を入れてテキストメッセージを送信してください。

Saul White シェフとの午後
Regent 料理学校が提供いたします

155

What is being advertised?

(A) A documentary

(B) A seminar

(C) An online service

(D) A recipe book

何が広告されていますか。

(A) 記録映画

(B) セミナー

(C) オンラインサービス

(D) 料理本

正解 B

設問に着目する問題

冒頭で、台所での自信を高めるために、you need to attend a session with a qualified chef とあり、有能な料理人とのセッション、つまり料理セミナーの宣伝だと推測できる。その後も、シェフである White さんの経歴や、セミナーへの費用、登録の仕方などが述べられていることから、(B) が正解。

156

What is indicated about Saul White?

(A) He will be paid for his appearance.

(B) He has appeared at Vandelay Convention Center before.

(C) He is a full-time employee of Regent Cooking School.

(D) He has recently published a book.

Saul White さんについて何が示されていますか。

(A) 彼は出演料を支払われる。

(B) 彼は以前 Vandelay 会議センターに現れたことがある。

(C) 彼は Regent 料理学校の常勤職員である。

(D) 彼は最近本を出版した。

正解 A

選択肢に着目する問題

Saul White, a highly respected chef 〜 is giving an introductory cooking class とあり、シェフである White さんが料理クラスを行うことが分かる。また、Chef White's appearance fees and the rent on the hall have been covered by the Regent Cooking School とあるので、appearance fees「出演料」が、Regent 料理学校から White さんに支払われると判断できる。正解は (A)。以前同じ会議センターに登場したかどうかについては言及がないので、(B) は不適切。

157

What registration method is NOT mentioned?

(A) Sending a text-message

(B) Calling a cooking school

(C) Writing an e-mail

(D) Sending a fax

どの登録方法が述べられていませんか。

(A) テキストメッセージの送信

(B) 料理学校への電話

(C) E メールを書くこと

(D) ファックスの送信

正解 D

NOT 問題

広告の終盤で、講習会に登録するために料理学校に連絡するよう求められている。You can do so by に続き、連絡方法がいくつか述べられている。(A) は by sending a text message with your name to 030-555-5150 と述べられている。(B) は by calling 555-7432 と述べられている。(C) は sending an e-mail to enrollments@regentcs.com と述べられている。ファックスについては言及がないので、(D) が正解。

語彙チェック

☐	qualified	能力のある、資格を有した
☐	introductory	入門の、初歩の
☐	appearance fee	出演料
☐	in advance	事前に
☐	enrollment	入学、入会

Questions 158-160 refer to the following letter.

Holyfield Museum of Modern Art
56 Harborview Road, Sydney, NSW 2003, Australia

Ms. Yoko White
45 Giordano Court
Sydney, NSW 2012

May 2

Dear Ms. White,

As a member of the Holyfield Museum of Modern Art Society (HMMAS),[158] you will be eager to know the status of our plans to add an additional wing to the museum. I am happy to inform you that the work is complete and that we will be opening our first exhibition in the space on Friday, July 17. The exhibition is called *Art in Nature* and it features photographs of plants and animals taken with a special zoom lens.[159] The exhibition features works by Neil Davis, Bob Chang, Helen Unaday, as well as three other photographers.

[159] As a platinum member, you are entitled to attend a special pre-opening event on the evening of Thursday, July 16. I strongly encourage you to attend as the preview audience who will not be restricted from approaching the artworks, and none of them will be shielded by the glass barriers we put up for the public exhibition. Furthermore,[160] the museum's head guide will be taking visitors around each of the works explaining them and their place within the context of the exhibition. This will be led by Ms. Dotty Smith, who has been with the museum for more than 20 years.

Tickets for the general public to see *Art in Nature* will be available online or from the museum box office.[159] The exhibition will be on display for only two weeks so please be sure not to miss this brief opportunity to see some very exciting artworks.

Sincerely,

Rose McTavish

Rose McTavish
Museum Curator

問題 **158-160** は次の手紙に関するものです。

Holyfield 現代美術館
Harborview 通り 56 番地、シドニー、NSW 2003、オーストラリア

Yoko White 様
Giordano Court 45 番地
シドニー、NSW 2012

5 月 2 日

White 様

Holyfield 現代美術館(HMMAS)の会員として、美術館に追加の棟を建設する計画の状況についてお知りになりたいことと存じます。建設作業は完了し、7 月 17 日の金曜日にその場所での最初の展覧会を開催することを喜んでお知らせいたします。展覧会は Art in Nature と題され、特殊なズームレンズで撮影された動植物の写真を特集します。展覧会は Neil Davis、Bob Chang、Helen Unaday とその他 3 人の写真家の作品を特集します。

プラチナメンバーとして、あなたは 7 月 16 日、木曜日夕方の特別プレオープンイベントに出席する資格をお持ちです。お客様には限りなく美術作品に近づくことができる、内覧会の観客としてのご出席を強くお勧めしておりまして、すべての作品は一般公開時にはおつけしているガラスの保護バリアで覆われていない状態になります。さらに、当館のガイド長がご来場者様をお連れして各作品をまわり、作品と展示の文脈におけるその位置づけをご説明いたします。当館に 20 年以上勤務している Dotty Smith さんがガイドを務めます。

Art in Nature 展の一般チケットはオンラインあるいは当館のチケット売り場で入手可能です。展覧会は 2 週間だけの開催ですので、非常に刺激的な芸術作品を見ることのできるこの短い機会をお見逃しなく。

よろしくお願いいたします。

Rose McTavish(署名)

Rose McTavish
美術館館長

158 Why was the letter written?

(A) To request payment of membership dues

(B) To announce the release of a new product

(C) To thank a visitor for writing a review

(D) To provide a situation update

手紙はなぜ書かれましたか。

(A) 会費の支払いを依頼するため。

(B) 新製品の発売を発表するため。

(C) 訪問者に批評を書いてくれたお礼をするため。

(D) 最新の状況を知らせるため。

正解 **D**

設問に着目する問題

E メールや手紙などの文書の目的は、冒頭付近に書かれていることが多く、この問題の正解の根拠も冒頭近くに登場している。you will be eager to know the status of our plans to add an additional wing to the museum. I am happy to inform you that the work is complete「美術館に追加の棟を建設する計画の状況についてお知りになりたいことと存じます。建設作業は完了したことを喜んでお知らせいたします」とあり、メンバーである White さんに、工事が完了したことを伝えている。provide a situation update と表現している (D) が正解。

membership due	会費

159 What is NOT mentioned about *Art in Nature*?

(A) It will be touring several countries.

(B) A preview will be shown to certain people.

(C) It is a collaborative exhibition.

(D) The artworks will be shown temporarily.

Art in Nature 展について述べられていないことは何ですか。

(A) それはいくつかの国をまわる。

(B) 内覧会がある特定の人々に見せられる。

(C) それは協同の展覧会である。

(D) 芸術作品は一時的に展示される。

正解 **A**

NOT 問題

美術館の増設工事が完了したことが述べられた後、そこで行われる Art in Nature 展について説明されている。(B) は、As a platinum member, you are entitled to attend a special pre-opening event と一致する。pre-opening event を preview と言い換えている。(C) は The exhibition features works by Neil Davis, Bob Chang, Helen Unaday, as well as three other photographers. と一致する。(D) は The exhibition will be on display for only two weeks と一致する。(A) に関しては言及がないので、正解は (A)。tour「～を巡回する」。

certain	特定の
collaborative	協同の
temporarily	一時的に

160 Who is Dotty Smith?

(A) A television personality

(B) A member of HMMAS

(C) A nature photographer

(D) A tour guide

Dotty Smith とは誰ですか。

(A) テレビタレント

(B) HMMAS の会員

(C) 自然写真家

(D) ツアーガイド

正解 **D**

設問に着目する問題

プラチナメンバーはプレオープンイベントに出席できると説明があり、それについて、the museum's head guide will be taking visitors around each of the works explaining them and their place within the context of the exhibition「当館のガイド長がご来場者様をお連れして各作品をまわり、作品と展示の文脈におけるその位置づけをご説明する」とある。続けて、This will be led by Ms. Dotty Smith とあるので、それを担当するガイド長というのが Dotty Smith さんであると分かる。正解は (D)。

語彙チェック

be eager to *do*	しきりに～したがる		shield	～を保護する
status	状況		context	文脈
feature	～を特集する		general public	一般の人
be entitled to *do*	～する資格がある		curator	館長、学芸員
restrict *A* from *doing*	A が～するのを制限する			

Questions 161-163 refer to the following notice.

Important Notice

Every day, certain [161] rides at the park are closed for maintenance. [161] You will be pleased to learn that today, all of our most popular rides are available for you to enjoy. — [1] — . [161,162] These include the Whizzer, Gold Rush Roller Coaster, and The Mighty Drop. — [2] — . However, [162] Wild Water and Radical Race will be shut while workers conduct an inspection and mechanical upkeep. Work on the latter will not be finished early enough for visitors to ride it before closing time. We regret any inconvenience this causes.

[163] You can get information about which rides are scheduled for maintenance by looking at the Web site at www.lunaland.com. — [3] — . Visitors who have purchased their one-day tickets online may ask for a refund before entering the park if the ride they intended to enjoy is unavailable. Naturally, this does not apply to season or lifetime pass holders. — [4] — .

Management

問題 **161-163** は次のお知らせに関するものです。

重要なお知らせ

毎日、園内の特定の乗り物が補修管理のために休業しています。今日は、最も人気のある乗り物のすべてがお楽しみいただけますので喜んでいただけると思います。これらは Whizzer、Gold Rush Roller Coaster、The Mighty Drop を含みます。しかし、Wild Water と Radical Race は作業員が検査と機械の保全を行っている間は運休いたします。後者に関する作業は閉園時間前にお乗りいただけるほど早くは終わらないでしょう。これによりご不便をおかけして申し訳ありません。

どの乗り物が補修管理予定なのかの情報は、ウェブサイト www.lunaland.com を見ていただくことで入手できます。＊ですから、家を出る前にあなたのお気に入りのアトラクションの状態を確認することをお勧めします。お楽しみになる予定だった乗り物がご利用いただけない場合、オンラインで1日券を購入したお客様は、入園前に返金を要求することができます。当然ながら、これはシーズンパスや生涯パスをお持ちの方には適用されません。

管理部

161

For whom is the notice most likely intended?

(A) Amusement park guests

(B) Maintenance workers

(C) Bus drivers

(D) Ticket sellers

お知らせは誰に向けられていると考えられますか。

(A) 遊園地の客

(B) 補修管理作業員

(C) バスの運転手

(D) チケット販売員

正解 A

設問に着目する問題

rides at the park「園内の乗り物」や、Gold Rush Roller Coaster, and The Mighty Drop などから、遊園地に関してのお知らせと判断できる。You will be pleased to learn that today, all of our most popular rides are available for you to enjoy.「今日は、最も人気のある乗り物のすべてがお楽しみいただけますので喜んでいただけると思います」とあり、来園者に向けたお知らせと分かる。(A) が正解。

162

According to the notice, what attraction is NOT available today?

(A) The Whizzer

(B) Gold Rush Roller Coaster

(C) Wild Water

(D) Radical Race

お知らせによると、今日はどのアトラクションが利用できませんか。

(A) The Whizzer

(B) Gold Rush Roller Coaster

(C) Wild Water

(D) Radical Race

正解 D

設問に着目する問題

今日は人気のアトラクションは利用でき、それらは These include the Whizzer, Gold Rush Roller Coaster, and The Mighty Drop. とあるので、(A)、(B) は利用できる。However と続けて Wild Water and Radical Race は検査、保全中は運休するとある。さらに、Work on the latter will not be finished early enough for visitors to ride it before closing time.「後者に関する作業は閉園時間前にお乗りいただけるほど早くは終わらない」と付け加えられており、前者の Wild Water は作業が終われば運転されると判断できるので、(D) が正解。

163

In which of the positions marked [1], [2], [3], and [4] does the following sentence best belong?

"Therefore we encourage you to check the status of your favorite attractions before leaving home."

(A) [1]

(B) [2]

(C) [3]

(D) [4]

[1] , [2], [3], [4] と記載された箇所のうち、次の文が入るのに最もふさわしいのはどれですか。

「ですから、家を出る前にあなたのお気に入りのアトラクションの状態を確認することをお勧めします」

(A) [1]

(B) [2]

(C) [3]

(D) [4]

正解 C

文挿入問題

挿入文の文頭の Therefore は「それ故に、その結果として」と前後の論理関係を説明する副詞。よって、空所の前の文の内容が挿入文の理由、原因となる。挿入文を [3] に入れると、前文の You can get information about which rides are scheduled for maintenance by looking at the Web site「どの乗り物が補修管理予定なのかの情報は、ウェブサイトを見ていただくことで入手できる」が、挿入文の we encourage you to check the status of your favorite attractions before leaving home「家を出る前にあなたのお気に入りのアトラクションの状態を確認することをお勧めする」の理由となる。(C) が正解。

語彙チェック

☐ conduct	～を行う	☐ the latter	(2 つのうち) 後者
☐ inspection	検査	☐ apply to ～	～に適用する
☐ upkeep	維持、保全		

Questions 164-167 refer to the following article.

Papua New Guinea Awards Young Entrepreneur at Gala Event

The Port Moresby Chamber of Commerce last night [164] awarded a young entrepreneur from Porebada for his contribution to the local community and our local economy. [165,167] Reece Carmody's company, Luscious Balms has been making skin cream from several plant species native to the area. After a series of fortunate incidents, the creams caught the attention of several international news and current affairs programs, which ran positive stories making Luscious Balms a highly sought-after brand. The production requirements have forced Carmody to expand his operations three times in the last two years and [164] employ more than 200 additional staff. He is now the region's largest employer and that is what earned him the Businessperson-of-the-Year award this year.

[165] The company now has factories in Port Moresby and Hula as well as [166] the most recently opened plant in Kokoda. It was there that the awards ceremony was held as a joint celebration of the plant's opening and Mr. Carmody's achievements for the community. During his acceptance speech, [167] Mr. Carmody talked about his plans for the future, expressing his belief that the company needed to expand into other product lines.

While he would not go into detail, he did mention that he was negotiating the purchase of an abandoned food processing plant in central Port Moresby. He said that he believed that people around the world would soon be enjoying delicacies from the forests of Papua New Guinea.

問題 **164-167** は次の記事に関するものです。

パプアニューギニアが若い起業家を祝賀行事で表彰

Port Moresby 商工会議所は昨夜、Porebada 出身の若き起業家を地域社会と地元経済への貢献のため表彰した。Reece Carmody の会社、Luscious Balms は地域固有のいくつかの植物種由来の皮膚用クリームを生産している。一連の幸運な出来事の後、そのクリームはいくつかの国際ニュースや時事問題番組の注目を集め、肯定的に報じられたため、Luscious Balms は引っ張りだこのブランドになった。生産要求に応えるため、Carmody は事業を過去 2 年間で 3 倍に拡大し、追加で 200 人以上のスタッフを雇わなければならなかった。今や彼は地域最大の雇用主であり、そのため今年の年間実業家賞を獲得した。

会社は現在 Port Moresby と Hula に工場を持っており、最近では Kokoda にも工場を開設した。工場の開設と Carmody 氏の地域社会への業績を合わせて祝うものとして、授賞式が行われたのはその場所である。受賞スピーチでは、Carmody 氏は将来的な計画について話し、会社は他の商品ラインに拡大していく必要があるとの信念を表明した。

詳細は語らなかったものの、彼は Port Moresby の中心地にある打ち捨てられた食品加工工場の購入を交渉中であると述べた。まもなく世界中の人々がパプアニューギニアの森の珍味を楽しむようになると信じていると彼は言った。

語彙チェック		
☐	gala	祝祭
☐	contribution	貢献
☐	species	(生物分類の)種
☐	native to ～	～原産の
☐	incident	出来事
☐	sought-after	引っ張りだこの
☐	earn A B	A に B をもたらす
☐	product line	商品ライン
☐	abandoned	放棄された、廃墟となった
☐	processing plant	加工工場
☐	delicacy	珍味

164 Why was Reece Carmody given an award?

(A) He has provided many jobs in Papua New Guinea.

(B) He donated money to support the local community.

(C) He encouraged businesses to join the chamber of commerce.

(D) He won a design competition.

Reece Carmody さんはなぜ賞を受賞しましたか。

(A) 彼はパプアニューギニアで多くの仕事を提供したから。

(B) 彼は地域社会を支えるためにお金を寄付したから。

(C) 彼は商工会議所に加わるよう企業に勧めたから。

(D) 彼はデザインコンペで優勝したから。

正解 A

設問に着目する問題

冒頭で Carmody さんの受賞の理由として for his contribution to the local community and our local economy「地域社会と地元経済への貢献のため」と述べられている。さらに、その具体的な内容として、employ more than 200 additional staff「追加で 200 人以上のスタッフを雇用」とある。また、He is now the region's largest employer and that is what earned him the Businessperson-of-the-Year award this year. と、地域で最大の雇用主になったことが、年間実業家賞を彼にもたらしたとあるので、(A) が正解。

165 Who is Reece Carmody?

(A) An importer of products from Papua New Guinea

(B) The owner of a manufacturing plant

(C) The chairperson of the chamber of commerce

(D) An expert in farming processes

Reece Carmody とは誰ですか。

(A) パプアニューギニアからの製品輸入業者

(B) 製造工場のオーナー

(C) 商工会議所の議長

(D) 農作業の専門家

正解 B

設問に着目する問題

表彰された若い起業家 Reece Carmody についての記事である。Reece Carmody's company, Luscious Balms has been making skin cream とあり、彼の会社は皮膚用クリームを製造していることが分かる。The company now has factories in Port Moresby and Hula からも、彼の会社は工場を持っていると判断できるので、(B) が正解。

166 Where was the award presented?

(A) In Port Moresby

(B) In Porebada

(C) In Kokoda

(D) In Hula

賞はどこで授与されましたか。

(A) Port Moresby

(B) Porebada

(C) Kokoda

(D) Hula

正解 C

設問に着目する問題

It was there that the awards ceremony was held as a joint celebration of the plant's opening and Mr. Carmody's achievements for the community.「工場の開設と Carmody 氏の地域社会への業績を合わせて祝うものとして、授賞式が行われたのはその場所である」とある。there はその前文の the most recently opened plant in Kokoda を指しているので、Kokoda にある工場と分かる。正解は (C)。

167 What is indicated about Luscious Balms?

(A) It will change ownership soon.

(B) It will diversify its product range.

(C) It has received government support.

(D) It is opening its own retail stores.

Luscious Balms について何が示されていますか。

(A) それは所有者をまもなく変える。

(B) それは製品範囲を多様化する。

(C) それは政府の支援を受けてきた。

(D) それは独自の小売店を開店する。

正解 B

選択肢に着目する問題

Reece Carmody's company, Luscious Balms とあるので、Luscious Balms は Carmody さんの会社の名前であると分かる。Carmody さんは授賞式でのスピーチで talked about his plans for the future, expressing his belief that the company needed to expand into other product lines と、会社の将来について、他の商品ラインに進出することを述べている。そのことを、diversify「～を多様化する」という動詞を使って言い表している (B) が正解。

Questions 168-171 refer to the following online chat discussion.

Colin Sorenson [3:30 P.M.]:
It's getting close to summer and a lot of people are going to start placing orders soon. Perhaps we should offer a discount to people who order early.

Harry Rollins [3:31 P.M.]:
I agree. That way we can space out the work over the busy season a bit better.

Lisa Wang [3:31 P.M.]:
Perhaps we should put an advertisement in this month's issue of House and Garden. A lot of new home builders read that magazine and they'll be thinking of swimming with their families over summer.

Colin Sorenson [3:33 P.M.]:
Sounds good, Lisa. Can you call them and find out about the cost of placing a full-page advertisement?

Lisa Wang [3:35 P.M.]:
Sure thing.

Donna Petrov [3:38 P.M.]:
Instead of offering a discount, how about offering free upgrades? A deluxe filter or an automated cleaning system might appeal to busy people who don't have time for cleaning.

Harry Rollins [3:42 P.M.]:
That's an idea! Otherwise, we could offer a free set of a parasol and two chairs to set by the water.

Colin Sorenson[3:45 P.M.]:
These are all good ideas. Let's get together on Tuesday morning to discuss it before we make any decisions.

Donna Petrov [3:46 P.M.]:
I know Harry and Lisa are free. I've got to visit a client in Melville. How's Wednesday?

Colin Sorenson [3:49 P.M.]:
I'm sure that'll be fine. They'll be around until Thursday.

問題 **168-171** は次のオンラインチャットでの話し合いに関するものです。

Colin Sorenson [午後 3 時 30 分]
夏が近づいてきて、もうすぐ多くの人々が発注を出し始めるでしょう。もしかしたら、早期に発注した人に割引を提供すべきかもしれないですね。
Harry Rollins [午後 3 時 31 分]
賛成です。そうすれば、もう少しうまく繁忙期の仕事を一定の期間を置いて行うことができるでしょう。
Lisa Wang [午後 3 時 31 分]
もしかしたら、House and Garden の今月号に広告を載せるべきなのではないでしょうか。新しく家を建てる人の多くがこの雑誌を読みますし、彼らは夏に家族と水泳をすることを考えるでしょう。
Colin Sorenson [午後 3 時 33 分]
よさそうですね、Lisa。彼らに電話して 1 ページ丸々の広告掲載の費用を突き止めてくれますか。
Lisa Wang [午後 3 時 35 分]
もちろんいいですよ。
Donna Petrov [午後 3 時 38 分]
割引を提供する代わりに、無料アップグレードを提供するのはどうでしょうか。掃除する時間のない忙しい人には高級フィルターや自動清掃システムは魅力的かもしれません。
Harry Rollins [午後 3 時 42 分]
それもいい案ですね！その他には、水辺に設置するためのパラソルと 2 脚の椅子のセットを無料で提供することもできます。
Colin Sorenson [午後 3 時 45 分]
これらは全部よい案です。決定する前に、火曜日の朝に集まってそれについて話し合いましょう。
Donna Petrov [午後 3 時 46 分]
Harry と Lisa が空いているのは分かっています。私は Melville にいる顧客を訪問しなければなりません。水曜日はいかがでしょうか。
Colin Sorenson [午後 3 時 49 分]
きっとそれで大丈夫です。彼らは木曜日まではいます。

168 Where do the writers most likely work?

(A) At an advertising agency

(B) At a magazine publisher

(C) At a pool building company

(D) At a house cleaning company

書き手たちはどこに勤めていると考えられますか。

(A) 広告代理店

(B) 雑誌出版社

(C) プール建設会社

(D) 清掃代行会社

正解 **C**

設問に着目する問題

話し手たちは夏が近づいているので広告を出すことを相談している。広告を House and Garden に掲載するということや、A lot of new home builders read that magazine and they'll be thinking of swimming with their families over summer.「新しく家を建てる人の多くがこの雑誌を読みますし、彼らは夏に家族と水泳をすることを考える」という発言、さらには A deluxe filter or an automated cleaning system「高級フィルターや自動清掃システム」という語句からも、彼らは自宅用プールの施工会社と推測できる。(C) が正解。

169 What is Ms. Wang asked to do?

(A) Calculate the cost of production

(B) Purchase a copy of a magazine

(C) Attend a marketing conference

(D) Check the price of advertising

Wang さんは何をするよう求められていますか。

(A) 生産費用を計算する。

(D) 雑誌を 1 部購入する。

(C) マーケティング会議に出席する。

(D) 広告の価格を調べる。

正解 **D**

設問に着目する問題

Wang さんの、we should put an advertisement in this month's issue of House and Garden という広告掲載の提案発言を受けて、Sorenson さんは賛同の意を表し、続けて Can you call them and find out about the cost of placing a full-page advertisement?「彼らに電話して 1 ページ丸々の広告掲載の費用を突き止めてくれますか」と Wang さんに依頼している。find out about the cost を check the price と言い換えている (D) が正解。

170 At 3:42 P.M., what does Mr. Rollins mean when he writes, "That's an idea"?

(A) He doubts a plan will work.

(B) He likes the suggestion.

(C) He has heard the idea before.

(D) He needs more time to consider.

午後 3 時 42 分に Rollins さんが "That's an idea" と書く際、何を意図していますか。

(A) 彼は計画がうまくいくか疑っている。

(B) 彼は提案が気に入っている。

(C) 彼はその案を以前聞いたことがある。

(D) 彼はもっと考える時間が必要である。

正解 **B**

意図問題

That's an idea. はイディオムで「それも 1 つの考えだ」と賛同を表す表現。That はその前に発言している Petrov さんの「割引を提供する代わりに、無料アップグレードを提供する」ことを指している。Rollins さんは、直後に Otherwise, we could offer ～と自分の案を提案している。Rollins さんは、Petrov さんの提案もいい考えだと認めた上で意見を述べているという流れが読み取れる。正解は (B)。

171 When will the writers most likely meet?

(A) On Tuesday　　(B) On Wednesday

(C) On Thursday　　(D) On Friday

書き手たちはいつ集まると考えられますか。

(A) 火曜日　　(B) 水曜日

(C) 木曜日　　(D) 金曜日

正解 **B**

設問に着目する問題

Sorenson さんが Let's get together on Tuesday morning と、まず火曜日に集まることを提案すると、Petrov さんは、Melville へ出張という理由で、How's Wednesday? と、水曜日を提案する。それに対し、Sorenson さんは、I'm sure that'll be fine. と答えているので、水曜日に同意していることが分かる。正解は (B)。

Questions 172-175 refer to the following e-mail.

To:	Kent Walsh <kwalsh@freemontfarms.com>
From:	Stephanie Carter <scarter@verhovenproductions.com>
Date:	September 9
Subject:	123 Field's Road

[172] Dear Mr. Walsh,

[173] My name is Stephanie Carter and I am a producer for the video production company, Verhoven Productions. I got your e-mail address from the sign in front of your property at 123 Field's Road. [172] We are looking for locations to shoot a drama about the lives of some early 20th Century New England dairy farmers and one of our location scouts discovered your farm while driving through the area. — [1] — . She took some photographs from the road and I believe it will be a perfect setting. [174] I would like to ask whether or not you would object to our using the farm as a location for the drama.

— [2] — . A few members of the production team and I [173] are currently staying in the Grand Hotel in Bangor while we make preparations for filming. You can contact me at this e-mail address or by telephone at 090-555-8323. We would like to confirm the production locations by Friday, September 15 as [173] we will be returning to Philadelphia on September 16. Therefore, I would be most appreciative if you could contact us as soon as possible.

[175] I have brought the director and a production designer with me on this trip. — [3] — . We would be happy to visit you at your farm or get together in one of the meeting spaces in the hotel.

[173] The production is likely to take around three weeks from mid-February to early March. [174] We would like to use your barns for our interior and exterior shots. We can schedule production for mornings or afternoons depending on your work schedule. — [4] — . If you are not able to accommodate our request, we would appreciate an introduction to any of your neighbors who might be interested in cooperating with the production.

Sincerely,

Stephanie Carter
Verhoven Productions

問題 172-175 は次の E メールに関するものです。

宛先：Kent Walsh <kwalsh@freemontfarms.com>
送信者：Stephanie Carter <scarter@verhovenproductions.com>
日付：9 月 9 日
件名：Field's 通り 123 番地

Walsh 様

私は Stephanie Carter と申しまして、Verhoven プロダクションという映像制作会社のプロデューサーをしています。あなたの E メールアドレスを、Field's 通り 123 番地にあるあなたの土地の前の看板から知りました。私たちは 20 世紀初頭のニューイングランドの酪農家の生活についてのドラマを撮影する場所を探しており、場所探しをしていたスタッフの一人がその地域を車で通っていたときにあなたの農場を発見しました。彼女は道路から何枚か写真を撮り、私はそこが完璧な舞台になると思っています。ドラマの撮影場所としてその農場を私たちが使用することにあなたが反対かどうかをお尋ねしたいと思います。

制作チームの数人と私は撮影の準備をしながら、現在 Bangor の Grand ホテルに滞在中です。あなたはこの E メールアドレスを使うか、090-555-8323 までお電話いただくかで私に連絡を取ることができます。私たちは 9 月 16 日にフィラデルフィアに戻る予定ですので、9 月 15 日の金曜日までには制作場所を確定したいと思っています。ですので、できるだけ早くご連絡いただけますと幸いです。

監督とプロダクションデザイナーをこの出張に連れてきています。＊もし彼らにお尋ねになりたいことがあれば、私に知らせてください。喜んであなたの農場にお伺いするか、ホテルの会議場の 1 つでお会いします。

映画制作には 2 月中旬から 3 月初旬まで約 3 週間かかると思われます。あなたの納屋を屋内と屋外の撮影に使いたいと思います。あなたの仕事のご都合次第で、制作は午前か午後に予定することができます。私たちの依頼を受け入れられない場合は、映画制作協力に興味がありそうなご近所のどなたかにご紹介いただけますと幸いです。
よろしくお願いします。
Stephanie Carter
Verhoven プロダクション

語彙チェック

☐ shoot	～を撮影する		☐ object to ～	～に反対する
☐ dairy	酪農の		☐ barn	納屋
☐ scout	スカウト、偵察者		☐ accommodate	～を受け入れる、承諾する

172 Who most likely is Mr. Walsh?

(A) A dairy farmer

(B) An experienced filmmaker

(C) A real estate agent

(D) A movie director

Walsh さんとは誰だと考えられますか。

(A) 酪農家

(B) 経験豊富な映画制作者

(C) 不動産業者

(D) 映画監督

正解 A

設問に着目する問題

Walsh さんは E メールの受信者。送信者である Carter さんは、We are looking for locations to shoot a drama about the lives of some early 20th Century New England dairy farmers and one of our location scouts discovered your farm while driving through the area. と書いており、20 世紀初頭のニューイングランドの酪農家の生活についてのドラマの撮影場所を探していることが分かる。そして、Walsh さんの農場が完璧だということで、撮影の許可をお願いしている。つまり、彼は酪農をしていると推測できるので、(A) が正解。

173 What is NOT suggested about Ms. Carter?

(A) She has visited Mr. Walsh's property.

(B) She is an employee of Verhoven Productions.

(C) She works for a company in Philadelphia.

(D) She will return to Bangor in February.

Carter さんについて分からないことは何ですか。

(A) 彼女は Walsh さんの土地建物を訪れたことがある。

(B) 彼女は Verhoven プロダクションの従業員である。

(C) 彼女はフィラデルフィアの会社に勤めている。

(D) 彼女は 2 月に Bangor に戻ってくる。

正解 A

NOT 問題

Carter さんは E メールの冒頭で I am a producer for the video production company, Verhoven Productions と書いているので、(B) に一致。are currently staying in the Grand Hotel in Bangor とあり、Carter さんは現在 Bangor に滞在中だが、we will be returning to Philadelphia on September 16 とあるので、彼女の会社は Philadelphia にあると判断でき、(C) に一致。(D) は The production is likely to take around three weeks from mid-February to early March. We would like to use your barns とあり、彼女は 2 月中旬より Bangor で撮影を開始すると考えられるので、一致する。彼女が Walsh さんの農場を訪れたかどうかは言及がないので、(A) が正解。

174 What is Mr. Walsh asked to do?

(A) Visit Verhoven Productions' studios

(B) Supply some photographs of his land

(C) Allow a movie crew to use his property

(D) Reserve a meeting space at the Grand Hotel

Walsh さんは何をするよう求められていますか。

(A) Verhoven プロダクションのスタジオを訪れる。

(B) 彼の土地の写真を何枚か提供する。

(C) 映画スタッフに彼の所有地の使用を許可する。

(D) Grand ホテルの会議場を予約する。

正解 C

設問に着目する問題

Walsh さんに求められていることはいくつかあるが、映画の撮影地を探している Carter さんは、I would like to ask whether or not you would object to our using the farm as a location for the drama.「ドラマの撮影場所としてその農場を私たちが使用することにあなたが反対かどうかをお尋ねしたい」や、We would like to use your barns for our interior and exterior shots.「あなたの納屋を屋内と屋外の撮影に使いたい」と述べている。Walsh さんから彼の土地建物を撮影する許可を得たいと分かるので、(C) が正解。

175 In which of the positions marked [1], [2], [3], and [4] does the following sentence best belong?

"If there are any questions you would like to ask them, please let me know."

(A) [1]   (B) [2]   (C) [3]   (D) [4]

[1] , [2], [3], [4] と記載された箇所のうち、次の文が入るのに最もふさわしいのはどれですか。

「もし彼らにお尋ねになりたいことがあれば、私に知らせてください」

(A) [1]   (B) [2]   (C) [3]   (D) [4]

正解 C

文挿入問題

文挿入の問題では、挿入文中にある代名詞が何を指すか、文脈の流れ、または論理関係を示す挿入文中の副詞がヒントになる。この問題では、ask them の them が指す内容に注目する。挿入文を [3] に入れると、them は前文の the director and a production designer を指し、Carter さんが連れてきている監督とプロダクションデザイナーに質問があれば知らせてほしい、となり文意が通る。正解は (C)。

Questions 176-180 refer to the following receipt and e-mail.

Customer name: Freda Dali
Account number: 7834939
Date: December 3

NutriSpark

Quantity	176 Description	Price
1	BBN Facial Cleanser 250ml	$56.00
3	Coconut Oil Body Cream 500ml	$36.00
2	Dr. Swan's Body Wash	$30.00
1	Wood pin hairbrush	$54.00

Subtotal:	$176.00
NutriSpark Frequent Shopper's Discount (5%):	$8.80
[177]Delivery:	[177]$0.00
Amount paid:	**$167.20**

Thank you for choosing to shop at the NutriSpark Online Shopping. [177]Purchases totaling more than $100 automatically qualify for free delivery within the United States.
[179]Please take the time to write a review of the products after trying them out. Consistent and informative contributors to the reviews section are often rewarded with discounts or even free items from manufacturers.

To:	Freda Dali <fdali@novabird.com>
From:	Brendan Philips <bphilips@ysc.com>
Date:	December 21
Subject:	Thank you

Dear Ms. Dali,

[178]Yakkleman Skin Care has signed a deal with NutriSpark Online Shopping making them the only retailer with access to our products. In return for making this exclusive commitment to NutriSpark, Yakkleman has been afforded assistance with its marketing efforts. Your name and contact details were provided to us in accordance with the NutriSpark member's agreement.

[179]We would like to send you some free product samples in return for an honest review to be posted on the NutriSpark Web site. To ensure that shoppers get completely honest and reliable information, your reviews will be attributed to a username unknown to Yakkleman Skin Care. Reviews will be monitored by NutriSpark Online Shopping to ensure quality. You are under no obligation to write positive reviews of the free products you receive.

[180]If you are interested in taking part, please click the following link and register as a trusted reviewer with NutriSpark Online Shopping. You may then nominate Yakkleman Skin Care as a candidate for product reviews.

Trusted Reviewer Registration Page

Sincerely,

Brendan Philips
Yakkleman — Marketing Division

問題 **176-180** は次の領収書と E メールに関するものです。

お客様氏名:Freda Dali		
顧客番号:7834939	**NutriSpark**	
日付:12 月 3 日		

数量	銘柄	価格
1	BBN 洗顔料 250 ml	56.00 ドル
3	ココナッツオイルボディクリーム 500ml	36.00 ドル
2	Dr. Swan's ボディウォッシュ	30.00 ドル
1	木製ピンヘアブラシ	54.00 ドル
	小計:	176.00 ドル
	NutriSpark お得意様割引(5%):	8.80 ドル
	配送料:	0.00 ドル
	支払額:	**167.20 ドル**

お買い物に NutriSpark オンラインショッピングをお選びいただきありがとうございます。総額 100 ドル以上のご購入で合衆国内の配送は自動的に無料となります。

製品をお試しの後、時間を取ってレビューをお書きください。継続的かつ有益なレビューの寄稿者にはしばしば割引や、メーカーからの無料商品さえ提供されます。

宛先:Freda Dali <fdali@novabird.com>

送信者:Brendan Philips <bphilips@ysc.com>

日付:12 月 21 日

件名:ありがとうございました

Dali 様

Yakkleman スキンケア社は、NutriSpark オンラインショッピング社を当社の商品を扱える唯一の小売店とする契約に署名しました。この NutriSpark 社への独占契約をする代わりに、Yakkleman 社はマーケティング業務に関する支援を受けております。あなたのご氏名と連絡先の詳細は NutriSpark 社の会員規約に則って当社に提供されました。

NutriSpark 社のウェブサイトに率直なレビューを投稿していただくお礼に、当社から無料の製品サンプルをお送りしたいと思います。顧客が完全に率直で信頼できる情報を得るようにするために、あなたのレビューは Yakkleman スキンケア社が知らないユーザー名のものとされます。質を保証するために、レビューは NutriSpark オンラインショッピング社によって監視されます。あなたが受け取る無料製品に肯定的なレビューを書く義務はまったくありません。

もし参加することに興味がありましたら、以下のリンクをクリックして NutriSpark オンラインショッピング社の信頼できるレビュアーとして登録してください。その後、製品レビューの候補として Yakkleman スキンケア社を指定していただけます。

信頼できるレビュアー登録ページ

よろしくお願いします。

Brendan Philips

Yakkleman 社 ─ マーケティング部門

176

What is probably true about NutriSpark?

(A) It specializes in health and beauty products.

(B) It recently changed ownership.

(C) It does not accept payment by credit card.

(D) It promises same day delivery.

NutriSpark 社について正しいと思われることは何ですか。

(A) それは健康と美容の製品に特化している。

(B) それは最近所有者を変えた。

(C) それはクレジットカードでの支払いを受け付けない。

(D) それは即日配送を約束している。

正解 **A**

選択肢に着目する問題

NutriSpark の顧客への領収書内の商品名を見ると、Facial Cleanser、Body Cream、Body Wash、hairbrush など美容と健康に関する商品が並んでいる。specialize in ～で、「～を専門に扱う」という意味なので、(A) が正解。オーナーや支払い方法については言及がないので (B)、(C) は不適切。配送料金については述べられているが、即日配送に関する記述はないので、(D) も不適切。

177

How did Ms. Dali qualify for free delivery?

(A) By living outside the United States

(B) By becoming a NutriSpark frequent shopper

(C) By ordering during the month of December

(D) By spending more than a certain amount

Dali さんはどのようにして無料配送の資格を得ましたか。

(A) 合衆国外に住んでいることによって。

(B) NutriSpark 社のお得意様になることによって。

(C) 12 月中に注文することによって。

(D) 一定金額以上を費やすことによって。

正解 **D**

設問に着目する問題

領収書内の Delivery の価格は 0 ドルとなっており、欄外に Purchases totaling more than $100 automatically qualify for free delivery within the United States.「総額 100 ドル以上のご購入で合衆国内の配送は自動的に無料となる」と、配送無料の条件が記されている。購買価格の総額 100 ドルが送料無料になる最低金額と分かる。正解は (D)。

178

What is indicated about Yakkleman Skin Care?

(A) It has supplied products to Ms. Dali in the past.

(B) It has merged with NutriSpark Online Shopping.

(C) Its products are only available from NutriSpark.

(D) Its customers are automatically entered into a competition.

Yakkleman スキンケア社について何が示されていますか。

(A) それは過去に Dali さんに製品を提供したことがある。

(B) それは NutriSpark オンラインショッピング社と合併した。

(C) その製品は NutriSpark からのみ入手可能である。

(D) その顧客は自動的にコンペに参加させられる。

正解 **C**

選択肢に着目する問題

Yakkleman Skin Care は、E メールの送信者の会社である。この問題の正解の根拠は E メールの冒頭にある。Yakkleman Skin Care has signed a deal with NutriSpark Online Shopping making them the only retailer with access to our products.「Yakkleman スキンケア社は、NutriSpark オンラインショッピング社を当社の商品を扱える唯一の小売店とする契約に署名した」とあり、NutriSpark 社のみが Yakkleman の商品を販売できると分かる。正解は (C)。

☐ merge with ～　　　　　～と合併する

179 What is implied about Ms. Dali?

(A) She is an employee of NutriSpark Online Shopping.

(B) She has written reviews of products she purchased.

(C) She purchased a Yakkleman Skin Care product.

(D) She will pay a visit to the Yakkleman Skin Care headquarters.

Dali さんについて何が示唆されていますか。

(A) 彼女は NutriSpark オンラインショッピング社の従業員である。

(B) 彼女は購入した製品のレビューを書いたことがある。

(C) 彼女は Yakkleman スキンケア社の商品を購入した。

(D) 彼女は Yakkleman スキンケア社の本社を訪れる。

正解 **B**

選択肢に着目するクロス問題

領収書を見ると、商品の購入者の Dali さんは、商品のレビューを書くことを依頼されている。さらに Consistent and informative contributors to the reviews section are often rewarded with discounts or even free items from manufacturers.「継続的かつ有益なレビューの寄稿者にはしばしば割引や、メーカーからの無料商品さえ提供される」とある。E メールを見ると、We would like to send you some free product samples in return for an honest review to be posted on the NutriSpark Web site. とあり、無料サンプルが送られているので、Dali さんは consistent contributor「継続的に寄稿を行っている人」と判断できる。(B) が正解。

180 How is Ms. Dali directed to take up an offer?

(A) By sending an e-mail

(B) By purchasing a product

(C) By accessing a Web page

(D) By completing a survey

Dali さんはどのようにして申し出を受け入れるよう指示されていますか。

(A) E メールを送ることによって。

(B) 製品を購入することによって。

(C) ウェブページにアクセスすることによって。

(D) アンケート調査に記入することによって。

正解 **C**

設問に着目する問題

E メールで、レビューの報酬として無料サンプルを送るというオファーを Dali さんに出した Yakkleman は、If you are interested in taking part, please click the following link and register as a trusted reviewer with NutriSpark Online Shopping. と、興味がある場合はリンクをクリックしてレビュアーとして登録するよう指示している。E メール上のリンクをクリックしてウェブサイトに行き、登録をするというプロセスと判断できるので、(C) が正解。

語彙チェック

☐ subtotal	小計	☐ exclusive commitment	独占契約
☐ frequent shopper	得意客	☐ in accordance with ~	~に則り
☐ consistent	継続的な	☐ be attributed to ~	~によるものとなる
☐ informative	有益な	☐ under no obligation	義務がない
☐ contributor	寄稿者		

Questions 181-185 refer to the following job announcement and letter.

Bremerton Sun

| **Home** | **Advertising** | **Subscriptions** | **Archives** | **Jobs** | **Contact** |

Grand Design Architecture has the following positions available:

Structural Engineer

Our New Jersey office has a vacancy for a structural engineer. The position requires you to be available to both clients and the in-house architects to consult on the structural strength and sustainability of building designs. The successful applicant must have some experience in housing construction.

Marketing Manager

There is an opportunity for an experienced marketing manager at our Boston office. The role requires you to come up with innovative and effective strategies to attract new clients to the firm. Applicants must have a solid understanding of architecture and the building industry. The position is suited to someone with experience as a real estate agent, particularly in houses and apartments. You will regularly be required to attend marketing events on Saturdays and Sundays so you must be flexible when it comes to taking time off.

Preliminary interviews for both positions will be carried out using video conferencing software. However, the final interview will take place at our head office in Springfield.

March 23
Dear Ms. Kim,

I am very interested in working for Grand Design Architecture. In fact, the home I grew up in was designed by Grand Design Architecture and indeed that is what inspired me to study engineering in college. I studied engineering and architecture at Valiance University in Manchester. After graduating, I took a job working as a building inspector for the state government, where I learned a great deal about efficient home design. I think my education and experience make me highly suited to the structural engineer position.

Please find my résumé enclosed.

Sincerely,

Brad Durden

Brad Durden

Bremerton Sun

ホーム	広告	購読	アーカイブ	求人情報	連絡先

Grand Design 建築会社は以下の職種を募集しています:

構造設計者
ニュージャージー営業所では構造設計者の欠員があります。この職種では、構造上の強度と建築物設計の持続可能性に関して顧客と社内の建築家の両方の相談を受けられる必要があります。採用されるには住宅建設の経験がなくてはなりません。

マーケティングマネージャー
ボストン営業所に経験豊富なマーケティングマネージャーのチャンスがあります。この役割では、当社に新たな顧客を引き付けるための革新的かつ効果的な戦略を考案することを求められます。応募者は建築と建築業界に関するしっかりした理解がなくてはなりません。この職種は特に住宅やアパートを扱う不動産業者としての経験がある人に適しています。土日のマーケティングイベントに定期的に出席することが求められますので、休暇を取ることに関しては融通がきかなくてはなりません。

どちらの職種も予備面接はビデオ会議ソフトを用いて行われます。しかし、最終面接はスプリングフィールドにある本社で行われます。

3月23日
Kim 様

Grand Design 建築会社で働くことにたいへん興味を持っています。実は、私が育った家は Grand Design 建築会社に設計されたもので、実際そのために私は大学で工学を学ぼうという気になりました。私はマンチェスターの Valiance 大学で工学と建築学を学びました。卒業後、州政府の建築物検査官として職を得て働き、そこで効率的な住宅設計について多くを学びました。私の教育と経験をもって、私は構造設計者の職に非常に適していると考えております。

履歴書を同封いたしましたのでご確認ください。

よろしくお願いいたします。

Brad Durden（署名）
Brad Durden

181

What is a requirement for both of the positions?

(A) A background in residential property

(B) The possession of a driver's license

(C) Certification to use specialized equipment

(D) Experience in management

両方の職種の必要条件は何ですか。

(A) 住宅用物件業界での経歴

(B) 運転免許証の所有

(C) 特殊な設備の使用認定書

(D) 経営経験

正解 A

設問に着目する問題

Grand Design 建築会社が 2 つの職種において募集をしている。Structural Engineer においては、The successful applicant must have some experience in housing construction.「採用されるには住宅建設の経験がなくてはならない」、また Marketing Manager においては、The position is suited to someone with experience as a real estate agent, particularly in houses and apartments.「この職種は特に住宅やアパートを扱う不動産業者としての経験がある人に適している」という要件がある。ともに住宅に関わった経験が必要ということなので、それらを抽象的に background in residential property「住宅用物件業界での経歴」と言い表している (A) が正解。

☐ possession　　　　　　所有
☐ equipment　　　　　　設備

182

What is suggested about Grand Design Architecture?

(A) It generates publicity through television advertising.

(B) It was founded by a team of architects.

(C) It specializes in creating unusual buildings.

(D) It carries out promotional activities on weekends.

Grand Design 建築会社について何が分かりますか。

(A) それはテレビ広告を通して知名度を上げている。

(B) それは建築家のチームによって設立された。

(C) それは珍しい建物を建てることに特化している。

(D) それは週末に宣伝活動を行っている。

正解 D

選択肢に着目する問題

Grand Design 建築会社の募集しているマーケティングマネージャーの職種の説明の最後に、You will regularly be required to attend marketing events on Saturdays and Sundays so you must be flexible when it comes to taking time off.「土日のマーケティングイベントに定期的に出席することが求められますので、休暇を取ることに関しては融通がきかなくてはならない」とある。この会社は土日に営業活動を行っていることが分かる。marketing events を promotional activities と言い換えている (D) が正解。carry out 〜「〜を行う」。

☐ generate　　　　　　〜を生む
☐ publicity　　　　　　知名度

183

In the letter, the word "deal" in paragraph 1, line 5 is closest in meaning to

(A) arrangement

(B) amount

(C) selection

(D) distribution

手紙の第 1 段落・5 行目にある deal に最も意味が近いのは

(A) 取り決め

(B) 量

(C) 選択

(D) 配分

正解 B

同義語問題

deal を含む文は、大学卒業後、州政府の建築物検査官として働いたことで効率的な住宅設計について学んだという内容。その後に、それらの経験が自分を構造設計者として適格にしていると自分のアピールポイントを結んでいることから、a great deal は learned の目的語として、「たくさんのこと、相当量」という意味で使われていると判断できる。この deal に最も近いのは「量」という意味の amount。正解は (B)。

184 In his letter, what does Mr. Durden communicate to Ms. Kim?

(A) The motivation for his career choice

(B) The reason for his leaving his current position

(C) The kind of salary he expects to receive

(D) The date of an appointment

手紙で、Durden さんは Kim さんに何を伝えていますか。

(A) 彼の職業選択についての動機

(B) 彼が現在の職をやめる理由

(C) 彼が受け取ることを期待している給料の種類

(D) 面接日

正解 **A**

設問に着目する問題

Grand Design 建築会社に就職を希望する Durden さんは、同社の Kim さんに宛てた E メールの冒頭に、the home I grew up in was designed by Grand Design Architecture and indeed that is what inspired me to study engineering in college と書いており、自分の育った家が就職を希望している会社の設計であり、そのことが建築を志すきっかけとなったと伝えている。それを、motivation for his career choice と言い表している (A) が正解。

185 Where would Mr. Durden prefer to work?

(A) In Springfield

(B) In Boston

(C) In New Jersey

(D) In Manchester

Durden さんはどこで働きたいですか。

(A) Springfield

(B) Boston

(C) New Jersey

(D) Manchester

正解 **C**

設問に着目するクロス問題

手紙の最後にある I think my education and experience make me highly suited to the structural engineer position. から、Durden さんは構造設計者としての職を希望していることが分かる。求人票を見てみると、Structural Engineer「構造設計者」の詳細に、Our New Jersey office has a vacancy for a structural engineer. とあり、構造設計者はニュージャージー営業所勤務となると判断できる。したがって、Durden さんはニュージャージーで勤務することを希望していると分かる。正解は (C)。

語彙チェック

subscription	購読	solid	しっかりした、固形の
archive	保存記録、アーカイブ	flexible	柔軟な
in-house	社内の	preliminary	予備の
consult	相談する	indeed	いかにも、実に
sustainability	持続可能性	inspire	～を動機づける、その気にさせる
innovative	革新的な	inspector	検査官

Questions 186-190 refer to the following conditions, e-mail, and notice.

Rasmussen Science Fiction Writers' Guild
Conditions of Membership

The Rasmussen Science Fiction Writers' Guild is based in Chicago, Illinois. It is an organization created by like-minded writers for [186] the purpose of sharing story ideas, supporting and fostering new talent and providing career advice to people who make their living from creative writing specifically in the science fiction genre.

Applicants for membership in the Rasmussen Science Fiction Writers' Guild (RSFWG) must satisfy the following conditions for consideration.

Applicants must :
- have had a science fiction story published in one of the magazines listed on the RSFWG Web site at www.rasmussensfwg.org/acceptedmagazines and [188] have had a novel or short story published by one of the publishers listed with the North American Publishing Association www.napa.com.
- make the major portion of their personal income from the publication and sale of fictional works.
- live in the United States of America.
- be over the age of 21.
- be contactable by both e-mail and telephone.

[187] Applications will be reviewed by the chairperson of the guild, Mr. Lee Davies and the members of the steering committee.

To:	Maurine Spencer <mspencer@spencerwriting.com>
[187] From:	Lee Davies <ldavies@rasmussensfwg.org>
Subject:	Application for membership
Date:	February 12

Dear Ms. Spencer,

I regret to inform you that your application to the Rasmussen Science Fiction Writers' Guild has been unsuccessful at this time. Your application appears to be incomplete so you may well still qualify. [188] Before resubmitting your application, please refer to the following Web site www.napa.com. [189] I hope that you will manage to register in time for our annual meeting, which will be held in your hometown this year. If you have any questions, please do not hesitate to contact the secretary, Vince Hammond at vhammond@rasmussensfwg.org.

Sincerely,

Lee Davies

問題 **186-190** は次の条件書、E メール、お知らせに関するものです。

Rasmussen SF 作家組合

入会条件

Rasmussen SF 作家組合はイリノイ州シカゴに本拠を置く。それは、同じ志向の作家たちによって作られた組織で、物語のアイデアを共有し、新しい才能を支援・育成し、特に SF ジャンルでの創作で生計を立てる人々に職業アドバイスを提供することを目的としている。

Rasmussen SF 作家組合（RSFWG）への入会志願者は審議のために以下の条件を満たさなければならない。

志願者の条件：

・RSFWG のウェブサイト www.rasmussensfwg.org/acceptedmagazines 上にリストアップされている雑誌のうち 1 つに SF 作品を発表したことがあり、北米出版協会の www.napa.com 上にリストアップされている出版社のうち 1 社から小説もしくは短編小説を出版したことがある。
・個人所得の大部分をフィクション作品の出版と販売で得ている。
・アメリカ合衆国在住である。
・年齢が 21 歳を超えている。
・E メールと電話の両方で連絡が取れる。

申し込みは組合議長の Lee Davies 氏と運営委員会のメンバーによって検討される。

宛先：Maurine Spencer <mspencer@spencerwriting.com>
送信者：Lee Davies <ldavies@rasmussensfwg.org>
件名：入会申し込み
日付：2 月 12 日

Spencer 様

残念ながら Rasmussen SF 作家組合へのあなたの入会申し込みは、現時点ではうまくいっておりません。申込書が不完全なようですので、まだ入会資格を得られる可能性はあります。申込書を再提出される前に、以下のウェブサイト www.napa.com をご参照ください。私たちの年次会議は今年はあなたのお住まいの町で開催される予定ですので、それに間に合うように登録できることを願います。何かご質問があれば、ご遠慮なく当方の秘書 Vince Hammond 宛てに vhammond@rasmussensfwg.org までご連絡ください。

よろしくお願いします。

Lee Davies

Annual Meeting of the Rasmussen Science Fiction Writers' Guild In Boulder, Colorado

[189] This year's annual gathering of the Rasmussen Science Fiction Writers' Guild will be held at the Hillview Inn in Boulder, Colorado. The event takes place over two days — April 23 and 24.

There will be presentations from some industry professionals as well as networking opportunities for writers.

In addition, several major literary agents will have booths where members can discuss subjects such as writing contracts, publicity, and industry standards. [190] Register in advance by calling the organizing committee at 773-555-9078.

Rasmussen SF 作家組合年次会議

ボルダー、コロラド

今年の Rasmussen SF 作家組合の年次会合はコロラド州ボルダーの Hillview Inn にて開催されます。イベントは 4 月 23 日と 24 日の 2 日間です。

作家のネットワーク作りの機会だけでなく、業界専門家によるプレゼンテーションもあります。

加えて、執筆契約、宣伝、業界規範といったテーマについて議論できるブースをいくつかの主要な著作権エージェントが出します。組織委員会に 773-555-9078 まで電話をしてあらかじめご登録ください。

What is NOT an objective of the Rasmussen Science Fiction Writers' Guild?

Rasmussen SF 作家組合の目的ではないものは何ですか。

(A) Encouraging inexperienced writers

(A) 未熟な作家を応援すること。

(B) Conducting survey research for publishing

(B) 出版のためのアンケート調査を行うこと。

(C) Exchanging thoughts about story writing

(C) 物語創作について意見を交換すること。

(D) Suggesting ways to succeed professionally

(D) プロとして成功する方法を提案すること。

正解 B

NOT 問題

Rasmussen SF 作家組合については、条件書の中に詳細が述べられている。正解の根拠は条件書の冒頭にある。(A) は supporting and fostering new talent と一致する。動詞 foster は「〜を育成する」という意味。(C) は sharing story ideas と一致する。(D) は providing career advice to people who make their living from creative writing と一致する。アンケート調査に関しては言及がないので、(B) が正解。

☐ inexperienced   経験の浅い

From whom did Ms. Spencer receive an e-mail?

Spencer さんは誰から E メールを受け取りましたか。

(A) The president of an association

(A) 組合長

(B) The secretary of a guild

(B) 組合の秘書

(C) An editor from a publishing company

(C) 出版社の編集者

(D) A retired science fiction writer

(D) 引退した SF 作家

正解 A

設問に着目するクロス問題

Spencer さんが受信した E メールの送信者は Lee Davies とある。条件書の最後を見ると、Applications will be reviewed by the chairperson of the guild, Mr. Lee Davies「申し込みは組合議長の Lee Davies 氏によって検討される」とあり、Davies さんは作家組合の議長と分かる。それを、president of an association「組合長」と表現している (A) が正解。

Why most likely was Ms. Spencer's application unsuccessful?

Spencer さんの申し込みがうまくいかなかったのはなぜだと考えられますか。

(A) Her age has not reached the minimum requirement.

(A) 彼女の年齢が最低限の条件に満たないから。

(B) She has not read the guild's code of conduct.

(B) 彼女は組合の行動規範を読まなかったから。

(C) She is employed full time in another profession.

(C) 彼女は別の職業でフルタイムで雇われているから。

(D) She did not provide information on her previous publications.

(D) 彼女は以前の出版物に関しての情報を提供しなかったから。

正解 D

設問に着目するクロス問題

入会申し込みを出した Spencer さんへ宛てられた E メールの冒頭に、入会申し込みが認められなかったことが述べられている。続いて、Your application appears to be incomplete so you may well still qualify. Before resubmitting your application, please refer to the following Web site www.napa.com. と、申込書は不十分であるが、認められる可能性があるので、もう一度 www.napa.com を確認するよう指示されている。条件書を見ると、have had a novel or short story published by one of the publishers listed with the North American Publishing Association www.napa.com. とあるので、Spencer さんは出版物の情報を提供しなかったのではと推測できる。正解は (D)。

☐ requirement   必要条件
☐ code of conduct   行動規範
☐ profession   職業

189 What is implied about Ms. Spencer?

(A) She is from Boulder, Colorado.

(B) She will give a presentation at the annual meeting.

(C) She is planning on visiting Chicago.

(D) She was admitted into RSFWG.

Spencer さんについて何が示唆されていますか。

(A) 彼女はコロラド州ボルダー出身である。

(B) 彼女は年次会議でプレゼンテーションを行う。

(C) 彼女はシカゴを訪れる予定である。

(D) 彼女は RSFWG に入会を許可された。

正解
A

☐
☐
☐

選択肢に着目するクロス問題

Spencer さん宛ての E メールに、I hope that you will manage to register in time for our annual meeting, which will be held in your hometown this year.「私たちの年次会議は今年はあなたのお住まいの町で開催される予定ですので、それに間に合うように登録できることを願う」と述べられている。そこで、年次会議のお知らせを見ると、冒頭に、開催場所が at the Hillview Inn in Boulder, Colorado とある。したがって、Spencer さんはコロラド州ボルダーの出身であると分かる。正解は (A)。

190 How should interested people register for the annual meeting?

(A) By e-mail

(B) By telephone

(C) By letter

(D) By text message

興味のある人は年次会議にどのようにして登録すべきですか。

(A) E メールで。

(B) 電話で。

(C) 手紙で。

(D) テキストメッセージで。

正解
B

☐
☐
☐

設問に着目する問題

年次会議のお知らせの中に正解の根拠がある。年次会議の内容など詳細が述べられた後、最後に、Register in advance by calling the organizing committee at 773-555-9078.「組織委員会に 773-555-9078 まで電話をしてあらかじめご登録ください」と指示がある。(B) が正解。

Questions 191-195 refer to the following advertisement, e-mail, and review.

Introducing the Resoluxe line of video projectors!

Resoluxe H78	Resoluxe Y65
Designed for the home cinema, this projector is an excellent balance of quality, function, and value for money. The H78 won this year's home cinema design award at the Paris Technology Expo. $730	The Y65 has the brightest lamp of the entire Resoluxe range. This projector can be used in well-lit rooms or even outdoors. Picture resolution is also second to none. This is truly the choice of professionals. $3,500
Resoluxe X45	Resoluxe T67
A perfect choice for classrooms and conference centers. This projector can automatically detect a whiteboard or blackboard and adjust its colors and light intensity to match. $2,040	This tiny portable projector is perfect for projecting photographs or advertisements in dimly lit spaces. $198

To:	Mark Blinks <mblinks@lawsonuniforms.com>
From:	Sarah Miller <smiller@lawsonuniforms.com>
Subject:	Convention
Date:	September 18

Mark,

I would like you to represent the company at the Uniform and Workwear Convention at the Springfield Arena on October 14. I remember you mentioning that you might take a vacation next month. You were still undecided. If you decide to take your vacation during the week of the convention, let me know and I will send Rose Wang instead.

If you end up going, you will be required to take some product samples to display at the booth. I have recently had a commercial produced and I would like you to play that for the people who come to the booth. This means that you will need to get a projector. I recommend that you purchase one online. From personal experience, I can tell you that they are quite heavy so you should try to find a portable model.

Regards,

Sarah

問題 **191-195** は次の広告、E メール、レビューに関するものです。

Resoluxe 製映像プロジェクターのご紹介！

Resoluxe H78	**Resoluxe Y65**
ホームシアター用に設計されたこのプロジェクターは品質、機能、コストパフォーマンスのバランスが非常に優れています。H78 はパリ技術博覧会において今年のホームシアターデザイン賞を受賞しました。730 ドル	Y65 は全 Resoluxe 製品の中で最も明るいランプを持っています。このプロジェクターは明るい室内や、屋外でさえ使用可能です。画像解像度も他に引けを取りません。これはまさに専門家の選択する品です。3,500 ドル
Resoluxe X45	**Resoluxe T67**
教室や会議センターにはうってつけの製品です。このプロジェクターは自動的にホワイトボードや黒板を検知し、色彩と光の強度が合うように調節します。2,040 ドル	この小さな持ち運び用プロジェクターは、薄暗い場所で写真や広告を映し出すのにうってつけです。198 ドル

宛先：Mark Blinks <mblinks@lawsonuniforms.com>

送信者：Sarah Miller <smiller@lawsonuniforms.com>

件名：大会

日付：9 月 18 日

Mark

10 月 14 日のスプリングフィールドアリーナでの制服と作業着会議で、あなたに会社の代表を務めてほしいと思います。来月休暇を取るかもしれないと言っていたのを覚えています。まだあなたは決めていませんでした。会議の週に休暇を取ると決めていたらお知らせください、代わりに Rose Wang を送ります。

もし行くことになったら、ブースで展示するための製品サンプルをいくつか持って行く必要があります。最近コマーシャルを製作してもらったので、それをブースに来る人々のために上映してもらいたいと思います。つまり、あなたはプロジェクターを入手する必要があるということです。オンラインで購入することをお薦めします。私の個人的な経験から言いますと、プロジェクターはとても重いので、持ち運び用モデルを見つけるようにしたほうがいいです。

よろしくお願いします。

Sarah

Product Reviews

[194]Reviewer: Rose Wang (Corporate Customer) Date: October 14
Rating: ★★★★☆

We needed a projector to display presentation slides at a convention booth. I was very impressed with the speed of delivery.[194] I ordered the projector on October 12 and it arrived on October 13, which was in time for the event on October 14. I did not read the advertisement carefully enough.[192] The room I was in was far too bright for the projector to work effectively. In a more suitable venue, I am sure that the projector would have performed adequately.[195] Based on the quality of this item, I will probably purchase more Resoluxe products in the future.

製品レビュー

レビュアー：Rose Wang（法人顧客）日付：10月14日

評価：★★★★☆

私たちはコンベンションのブースでプレゼンテーションのスライドを見せるためにプロジェクターが必要でした。私は配送の速さに感激しました。10月12日にプロジェクターを注文して10月13日に届き、10月14日のイベントに間に合いました。私は広告をあまりしっかり読んでいませんでした。私がいた部屋はあまりにも明る過ぎて、プロジェクターは効果的に作動しませんでした。もっと適切な場所であれば、プロジェクターはきっと適切に機能したでしょう。この製品の品質を踏まえれば、たぶん私は今後もっと多くのResoluxe製品を購入するでしょう。

191 What is implied about the Resoluxe Y65?

(A) It comes with a 12-month warranty.

(B) It has received an award for its design.

(C) It has the highest image quality available.

(D) It is the company's best-selling model.

Resoluxe Y65 について何が示唆されていますか。

(A) それは 12 か月の保証付きである。

(B) それはデザインで賞を受賞した。

(C) それは購入可能な中で最高の画像品質である。

(D) それは会社の最もよく売れるモデルである。

正解 C

選択肢に着目する問題

この問題の根拠は、広告の Y65 についての記述内にある。Picture resolution is also second to none.「画像解像度も他に引けを取らない」とある。resolution には「解像度」という意味があり、高いほど分解能が高く優れている。second to none は「何物にも劣らない、最高な」という意味。highest image quality が得られると言い換えている (C) が正解。

☐ warranty　　　　　　　　　保証

---

192 Which projector did Lawson Uniforms most likely buy?

(A) Resoluxe H78

(B) Resoluxe Y65

(C) Resoluxe X45

(D) Resoluxe T67

Lawson 制服社はどのプロジェクターを買ったと考えられますか。

(A) Resoluxe H78

(B) Resoluxe Y65

(C) Resoluxe X45

(D) Resoluxe T67

正解 D

設問に着目するクロス問題

製品レビューのレビュアーである Rose Wang は、E メールアドレスから Lawson 制服社の社員と判断でき、Mark さんが都合が悪い場合に出席を依頼されていると分かる。彼女は The room I was in was far too bright for the projector to work effectively.「私がいた部屋はあまりにも明る過ぎて、プロジェクターは効果的に作動しなかった」と書いており、彼女の買ったものは明るい所には不向きだったことが分かる。また、E メールの最後で Sarah さんが try to find a portable model と、持ち運びに便利な軽いものを勧めていることもヒントになる。正解は (D)。

---

193 What has Sarah Miller recently done?

(A) Tested several Resoluxe products

(B) Commissioned a promotional video

(C) Visited a convention venue

(D) Written a spending report

Sarah Miller さんは最近何をしましたか。

(A) いくつかの Resoluxe 製品を試した。

(B) 販売促進用映像の制作を発注した。

(C) 会議の会場を訪れた。

(D) 支出報告書を書いた。

正解 B

設問に着目する問題

Miller さんは、彼女の E メールの中で、I have recently had a commercial produced「最近コマーシャルを製作してもらった」と書いている。それを Mark さんに会場で上映してもらうことを考えて、彼にプロジェクターの購入を薦めている。動詞 commission には「～を依頼する、発注する」という意味がある。正解は (B)。

☐ spending　　　　　　　　　支出、出費

194 What is implied about Mr. Blinks?

(A) He took a vacation in October.

(B) He forgot to take the projector.

(C) He agreed to replace Ms. Wang.

(D) He recommended Resoluxe brand.

Blinks さんについて何が示唆されていますか。

(A) 彼は 10 月に休暇を取った。

(B) 彼はプロジェクターを持って行くのを忘れた。

(C) 彼は Wang さんに取って代わることに同意した。

(D) 彼は Resoluxe ブランドを推薦した。

正解 A

選択肢に着目するクロス問題

E メールの受信者である Blinks さんは Sarah さんから、If you decide to take your vacation during the week of the convention, let me know and I will send Rose Wang instead. 「会議の週に休暇を取ると決めていたらお知らせください、代わりに Rose Wang を送る」と伝えられている。そこで、レビューを見ると、Wang さんが会場でプロジェクターを使用した感想を述べているので、Wang さんがコンベンションに出席し、Blinks さんは 10 月には休暇を取ったと判断できる。正解は (A)。

195 In the review, the phrase, "Based on" in paragraph 1, line 6 is closest in meaning to

(A) Located in

(B) Conditioned for

(C) Founded on

(D) Judging from

レビューの第 1 段落・6 行目にある Based on に最も意味が近いのは

(A) ～に位置して

(B) ～向けに調整されて

(C) ～に基づいて

(D) ～から判断して

正解 D

同義語問題

Based on を含む文では、「将来的にも Resoluxe 社製品をおそらく購入するだろう」ということが述べられている。文頭の Based on the quality of this item は、「この製品の品質に基づけば」と、その後の文の根拠を表していると判断できる。最も意味が近いのは (D)。

Questions 196-200 refer to the following card, letter, and e-mail.

---

[196]Welcome to the
Boatman's Arms Hotel.

[196]The management and staff hope you have a great time during your stay and would be more than happy to assist in any way they can. If you need anything, please do not hesitate to contact the concierge desk on Ext. 772.

[197]To celebrate our 50th anniversary, a complimentary nightly concert is being held in the hotel's main ballroom each evening. Entertainment will include well-known singers and comedians such as Holly Fields and Reg Sumner.[198] On Saturday, May 29 and Sunday, May 30, a golf tournament is being held on the Royal Wings Golf Course attached to the hotel. There are still some spots available for hotel guests so please contact the Golf Clubhouse on Ext. 623 to register.[198] There is $5,000 in prize money up for grabs and you can register for the price of a standard round of 18 holes.

Sincerely,

Ying Pin Lo

Ying Pin Lo
Manager

June 1

To whom it may concern:
I am writing to commend the staff of the Boatman's Arms who made my stay in Charleston such a pleasure. I was originally planning to stay there from May 28 to 29 to purchase some land for a new business I am launching. Unfortunately, the negotiations fell through, and I was feeling rather disappointed. My interactions with[198] the staff there were cheerful and put me in a more positive state of mind, and I decided to stay one more night to attend the event in the hotel's facility. I hardly expected to walk away from the trip thousands of dollars better off, but[198] thanks to the auspicious timing of my visit, I ended up making money. By chance, I met a local business person in the lobby and spent both evenings discussing other potential locations for my business.

Considering the excellent[200] service and wonderful experiences I had at the Boatman's Arms Hotel, I can assure you that I intend to stay there whenever I am back in Charleston.

Sincerely,

Matthew Klinger

Matthew Klinger
MishMash Home Decor

Boatman's Arms ホテルへようこそ。

経営陣とスタッフはあなたがご滞在中すばらしい時間を過ごされるよう願い、できる限りの方法で喜んでお手伝いさせていただきます。何かご入用の際は、内線 772 番のコンシェルジュデスクまでご遠慮なくご連絡ください。

当ホテルの 50 周年を祝うため、毎夕ホテルの大舞踏室にて、無料の夜間コンサートを開催しております。催しには Holly Fields や Reg Sumner などといった有名歌手やコメディアンも登場します。5 月 29 日の土曜日と 5 月 30 日の日曜日には、ホテル付属の Royal Wings ゴルフコースにてゴルフ大会が開催されます。宿泊のお客様にはまだ空きがございますので、登録には内線 623 番のゴルフクラブハウスまでご連絡ください。賞金 5,000 ドルが用意されており、18 ホールのスタンダードラウンドの価格でご登録いただけます。

どうぞよろしくお願いいたします。

Ying Pin Lo（署名）

Ying Pin Lo
支配人

---

6 月 1 日

関係者各位
私のチャールストン滞在を非常に楽しいものにしてくれた Boatman's Arms のスタッフを称賛するため、これを書いています。私はもともとは始めようとしている新事業のための土地を購入するために 5 月 28 日から 29 日の週末に町に滞在する予定でした。残念ながら交渉は失敗に終わり、私は非常に落胆しておりました。そこでのスタッフとの交流は楽しいもので、私をより前向きな気持ちにさせてくれました。ホテルの施設で行われるイベントに参加するため、もう一晩滞在することに決めました。何千ドルも入手して出張を終えることになるとはほとんど期待しておりませんでしたが、幸運なタイミングで訪問したおかげで、最終的にはお金を稼ぐことができました。偶然、私は地元の実業家とロビーで会って、2 晩とも、私の事業のために利用できる可能性のある他の場所について議論して過ごしました。

私が Boatman's Arms ホテルで体験した優れたサービスとすばらしい経験を考慮し、チャールストンに行くときはいつでも、必ずそちらに滞在するつもりです。

よろしくお願いします。

Matthew Klinger（署名）

Matthew Klinger
MishMash 内装社

To:	Matthew Klinger <mklinger@mishmash.com>
From:	Rhonda Montgomery <rmontgomery@charlestoncoc.com>
Subject:	Our meeting
Date:	June 2

Dear Mr. Klinger,

As I mentioned during our impromptu meeting on the evening of May 29, I am a member of the Charleston Chamber of Commerce, and as such, I am involved in supporting new businesses moving into the area. Having spoken with a number of other members, I have learned of a few properties you may be interested in. None of them have been listed with real estate agents yet. So, you will have to negotiate directly with the owners. I would be glad to help facilitate that communication if you so wish.

We discussed meeting again on June 5 so that I could take you around the properties. I will pick you up at your hotel in the morning so please let me know where you will be staying. It is not the busy season so I am sure you will be able to find vacancies at most hotels.

Let me know if you need to change our arrangements.

Sincerely,

Rhonda Montgomery
Chairperson — Charleston Chamber of Commerce

宛先：Matthew Klinger <mklinger@mishmash.com>
送信者：Rhonda Montgomery <rmontgomery@charlestoncoc.com>
件名：私たちの会議
日付：6月2日

Klinger 様

5月29日夕方の即席会議で申し上げた通り、私はチャールストン商工会議所のメンバーであり、そういうものとして、当地に参入してくる新事業を支援することに関わっております。他の多くのメンバーと話して、あなたが興味を持ちそうな数か所の土地を知りました。どれも不動産業者にはまだ登録されていません。ですので、あなたは所有者と直接交渉しなければなりません。ご希望であれば、その連絡を進行するお手伝いを喜んでさせていただきます。

6月5日にそれらの土地を案内するためにまたお会いしましょうと話していました。朝、ご滞在のホテルにお迎えに上がりますので、どこにご宿泊されるかお知らせください。繁忙期ではありませんので、きっとほとんどのホテルで空きを見つけられるでしょう。

予定を変更する必要があったらお知らせください。

よろしくお願いします。

Rhonda Montgomery
会頭 – チャールストン商工会議所

語彙チェック

☐ happy to *do*	喜んで～する		☐ interaction	交流
☐ assist	手伝う		☐ positive state of mind	ポジティブな精神状態
☐ do not hesitate to *do*	遠慮なく～する		☐ better off	よりたっぷりある
☐ Ext.	内線番号		☐ auspicious	幸先のよい
☐ complimentary	無料の		☐ end up *doing*	結局～することになる
☐ attached	付属した		☐ by chance	偶然
☐ up for grabs	誰もが手に届く		☐ potential	可能性のある
☐ to whom it may concern	関係各位		☐ intend to *do*	～するつもりである
☐ commend	～を称賛する		☐ impromptu	即興の、緊急の
☐ launch	～を開始する		☐ be involved in ～	～に関わる
☐ negotiation	交渉		☐ facilitate	～を容易にする、円滑に進める
☐ fall through	失敗に終わる			

For whom is the card intended?

(A) A health inspector

(B) A hotel patron

(C) A customer service trainee

(D) A financial advisor

カードは誰に向けたものですか。

(A) 健康審査官

(B) ホテルの顧客

(C) 顧客サービス実習生

(D) 財務顧問

正解 B

設問に着目する問題

カードの表題に Welcome to the Boatman's Arms Hotel. とあり、ホテルからのウェルカムカードと分かる。続いて、staff hope you have a great time during your stay and would be more than happy to assist や、If you need anything, please do not hesitate to contact the concierge desk on Ext. 772.「何かご入用の際は、内線 772 番のコンシェルジュデスクまでご遠慮なくご連絡ください」とあり、客室に置かれたカードと判断できる。patron「得意客、ひいき客」を使ってホテル客を言い表している (B) が正解。

What is being offered for free?

(A) Admission to a performance

(B) Entry into a golf competition

(C) Tours of Charleston

(D) Club membership

無料で提供されているものは何ですか。

(A) 演奏会への入場

(B) ゴルフコンペへの参加

(C) チャールストンのツアー

(D) クラブ会員の地位

正解 A

設問に着目する問題

カードの中盤にホテル 50 周年についての記述がある。To celebrate our 50th anniversary, a complimentary nightly concert is being held in the hotel's main ballroom「当ホテルの 50 周年を祝うため、ホテルの大舞踏室にて無料の夜間コンサートを開催している」と、イベントの情報が記載されている。complimentary は「無料の」という意味がある。このようなイベントへの参加が無料であるということで、(A) が正解。admission は「入場」。

What is implied about Mr. Klinger?

(A) He attended one of the nightly concerts.

(B) He was able to negotiate a price reduction.

(C) He took part in the sporting competition.

(D) He has joined a frequent guest program.

Klinger さんについて何が示唆されていますか。

(A) 彼は夜間コンサートの 1 つに出席した。

(B) 彼は交渉して値下げを決めることができた。

(C) 彼はスポーツ競技に参加した。

(D) 彼は常連客用プログラムに参加した。

正解 C

選択肢に着目する問題

カードから 5 月 29 日と 30 日にホテルのゴルフコースでコンペがあり、$5,000 in prize money と、5 千ドルの賞金があると記されている。また、Klinger さんはホテル宛ての手紙に、I decided to stay one more night to attend the event in the hotel's facility「ホテルの施設で行われるイベントに参加するため、もう一晩滞在することに決めた」や、thanks to the auspicious timing of my visit, I ended up making money「幸運なタイミングで訪問したおかげで、最終的にはお金を稼ぐことができた」と書いている。Klinger さんは 30 日のゴルフコンペで賞金を獲得したと想像できるので、(C) が正解。

reduction	削減、値下げ	
frequent	頻繁な	

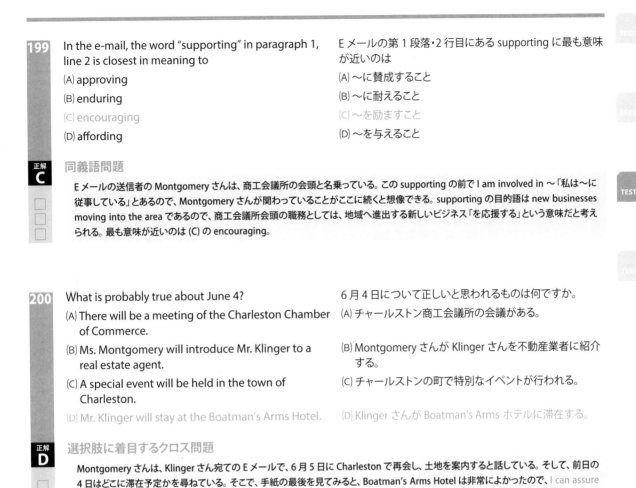

199 In the e-mail, the word "supporting" in paragraph 1, line 2 is closest in meaning to

(A) approving

(B) enduring

(C) encouraging

(D) affording

E メールの第 1 段落・2 行目にある supporting に最も意味が近いのは

(A) 〜に賛成すること

(B) 〜に耐えること

(C) 〜を励ますこと

(D) 〜を与えること

正解 C

同義語問題

E メールの送信者の Montgomery さんは、商工会議所の会頭と名乗っている。この supporting の前で I am involved in 〜「私は〜に従事している」とあるので、Montgomery さんが関わっていることがここに続くと想像できる。supporting の目的語は new businesses moving into the area であるので、商工会議所会頭の職務としては、地域へ進出する新しいビジネス「を応援する」という意味だと考えられる。最も意味が近いのは (C) の encouraging。

200 What is probably true about June 4?

(A) There will be a meeting of the Charleston Chamber of Commerce.

(B) Ms. Montgomery will introduce Mr. Klinger to a real estate agent.

(C) A special event will be held in the town of Charleston.

(D) Mr. Klinger will stay at the Boatman's Arms Hotel.

6 月 4 日について正しいと思われるものは何ですか。

(A) チャールストン商工会議所の会議がある。

(B) Montgomery さんが Klinger さんを不動産業者に紹介する。

(C) チャールストンの町で特別なイベントが行われる。

(D) Klinger さんが Boatman's Arms ホテルに滞在する。

正解 D

選択肢に着目するクロス問題

Montgomery さんは、Klinger さん宛ての E メールで、6 月 5 日に Charleston で再会し、土地を案内すると話している。そして、前日の 4 日はどこに滞在予定かを尋ねている。そこで、手紙の最後を見てみると、Boatman's Arms Hotel は非常によかったので、I can assure you that I intend to stay there whenever I am back in Charleston「チャールストンに行くときはいつでも、必ずそちらに滞在するつもりだ」と Klinger さんは書いている。したがって、(D) が正解と判断できる。

Day 37

【TEST 3 Questions 147-175】　2/5回目

Day 37は、Day 27〜31で解いたシングルパッセージ10題をもう一度まとめて解く日です。別冊TEST 3の147番〜175番（別冊P51〜61）を解きましょう。制限時間は29分です。解き終わったら、解説はDay 27〜31の解説ページ（本冊P110〜129）を見て確認してください。

Day 38

【TEST 3 Questions 176-200】　2/5回目

Day 38は、Day 32〜36で解いたマルチプルパッセージ5題をもう一度まとめて解く日です。別冊TEST 3の176番〜200番（別冊P62〜71）を解きましょう。制限時間は25分です。解き終わったら、解説はDay 32〜36の解説ページ（本冊P130〜155）を見て確認してください。

Day 39

【TEST 3 Questions 147-200】　3/5回目

Day 39は、Day 27〜36で解いた問題をまとめて解く日です。別冊TEST 3の147番〜200番（別冊P51〜71）を解きましょう。制限時間は54分です。解き終わったら、解説はDay 27〜36の解説ページ（本冊P110〜155）を見て確認してください。

TEST 4

解答&解説

正解一覧

問題番号	正解	問題番号	正解
147	A	176	A
148	D	177	D
149	B	178	B
150	C	179	C
151	C	180	C
152	D	181	B
153	B	182	D
154	C	183	A
155	B	184	A
156	A	185	B
157	C	186	A
158	D	187	D
159	A	188	B
160	D	189	A
161	A	190	C
162	A	191	C
163	C	192	D
164	A	193	B
165	B	194	A
166	C	195	D
167	B	196	B
168	C	197	A
169	B	198	C
170	D	199	C
171	B	200	D
172	A		
173	C		
174	A		
175	D		

Questions 147-148 refer to the following notice.

Important Notice

[148]HBM Fitness Club on Sutter Street prides itself on the quality of its equipment, the cleanliness of the facilities, and [148]its ability to stay open 24-hours a day. Twice a year, however, [148]we need to close between the hours of 12:00 midnight and 6:00 A.M. for upgrades to the amenities and maintenance work to be carried out on the security system.[148] The next closure will occur on Saturday, October 27. The facilities will be available again from 6:00 A.M. on Sunday morning.[147]We sincerely regret this disruption to your workout schedule. Please keep in mind, the HBM Fitness Club in Hampton will be available during these hours and that your membership entitles you to the use of that location as well.

問題 **147-148** は次のお知らせに関するものです。

重要なお知らせ

Sutter 通りの HBM フィットネスクラブは設備の質、施設の清潔さ、24 時間営業できる能力を誇っています。しかし、年に 2 回、設備のアップグレードと防犯システムのメンテナンス作業のために深夜 12 時から午前 6 時まで閉鎖する必要があります。次回の閉鎖日は 10 月 27 日（土）です。日曜日の朝 6 時に施設は再開します。お客様のトレーニングスケジュールを中断させてしまい、たいへん申し訳ありません。なお、ハンプトンの HBM フィットネスクラブは上記の時間帯も利用可能であり、会員の皆さまはそちらの施設もお使いいただけます。

147 For whom is the notice most likely intended?

(A) Gym members

(B) Vehicle owners

(C) Security personnel

(D) Event organizers

お知らせは誰に向けられていると考えられますか。

(A) ジム会員

(B) 車の所有者

(C) 警備員

(D) イベント主催者

正解 **A**

設問に着目する問題

冒頭から、このお知らせはフィットネスクラブからのものであり、年 2 回のメンテナンスのための閉鎖について述べられている。そして後半で、We sincerely regret this disruption to your workout schedule.「お客様のトレーニングスケジュールを中断させてしまい、たいへん申し訳ない」と謝罪していることから、お知らせは、ジムの利用者に対してのものと判断できる。したがって、正解は (A)。

☐ personnel　　　　　　　　　職員
☐ organizer　　　　　　　　　主催者

148 According to the notice, what will be unavailable on October 28?

(A) Network connections

(B) Membership information

(C) Public transportation

(D) 24-hour access

お知らせによると、10 月 28 日には利用不可能なものは何ですか。

(A) ネットワーク接続

(B) 会員情報

(C) 公共交通機関

(D) 24 時間利用

正解 **D**

設問に着目する問題

冒頭の HBM Fitness Club on Sutter Street prides itself on 〜 its ability to stay open 24-hours a day.「Sutter 通りの HBM フィットネスクラブは〜24 時間営業できる能力を誇っている」より、このジムの誇りの 1 つに 24 時間営業ということが挙げられている。しかし、we need to close between the hours of 12:00 midnight and 6:00 A.M. と The next closure will occur on Saturday, October 27. The facilities will be available again from 6:00 A.M. on Sunday morning. から、年 2 回は夜間閉鎖され、次回は 10 月 27 日深夜より 28 日午前 6 時まで閉鎖されるということが分かるので、(D) が正解。ネットワーク接続、会員情報、交通機関についてはまったく言及がない。

☐ connection　　　　　　　　接続

語彙チェック
☐ pride *oneself* on 〜　　　　〜を誇る、自慢する
☐ equipment　　　　　　　　設備
☐ cleanliness　　　　　　　　清潔さ
☐ amenity　　　　　　　　　設備、施設
☐ closure　　　　　　　　　閉鎖
☐ disruption　　　　　　　　中断
☐ entitle *A* to *B*　　　　　　*A* に *B* の権利を与える

Questions 149-150 refer to the following text-message chain.

JACK VOORHEES [8:50 A.M.]
¹⁴⁹I'm going to apply for a bigger budget for the landscaping project.

MARY WANG [8:51 A.M.]
I'm sure they'll just tell you to get estimates from more companies.

JACK VOORHEES [8:53 A.M.]
I know. The problem is that there are no other companies that can do the work by the December deadline.

MARY WANG [8:53 A.M.]
Did you try searching online?

JACK VOORHEES [8:54 A.M.]
That was the first place I looked. There is a company that I haven't called, but their reviews weren't very good.

MARY WANG [8:59 A.M.]
Best to steer clear, then. We don't want any complications or poor workmanship.

JACK VOORHEES [9:02 A.M.]
Right. I'll let you know how it goes. ¹⁵⁰If they say "no," we'll have to save money by scrapping the plans for a fountain.

MARY WANG [9:03 A.M.]
I hope it doesn't come to that. ¹⁵⁰I think one would look great there.

問題 **149-150** は次のテキストメッセージのやりとりに関するものです。

JACK VOORHEES　　[午前 8 時 50 分]
造園プロジェクトのためにもっと予算を増やしてもらうよう申し込むつもりだ。

MARY WANG　　[午前 8 時 51 分]
きっと、もっと多くの会社から見積もりをもらうように言われるだけよ。

JACK VOORHEES　　[午前 8 時 53 分]
分かってる。問題は、12 月の締め切りまでにその仕事ができる会社が他にないってことだよ。

MARY WANG　　[午前 8 時 53 分]
オンラインで検索してみたの？

JACK VOORHEES　　[午前 8 時 54 分]
そこは僕が最初に見たところだよ。電話をしなかったところが 1 社あるけど、彼らの評価はあまりよくなかった。

MARY WANG　　[午前 8 時 59 分]
じゃあ避けるのが一番ね。厄介ごとや技術の低い仕事はいらないから。

JACK VOORHEES　　[午前 9 時 2 分]
その通り。どんなふうに進んでいるか君に知らせるよ。もし「ダメだ」と言われたら、噴水の計画をやめにしてお金を節約しないといけなくなるな。

MARY WANG　　[午前 9 時 3 分]
そうならないといいわね。噴水がそこにあったら素敵な眺めになると思うの。

149 What is the text-message chain mostly about?

(A) An advertising campaign

(B) A project budget

(C) A news story

(D) A building relocation

テキストメッセージのやりとりは主に何についてですか。

(A) 広告キャンペーン

(B) プロジェクトの予算

(C) ニュース記事

(D) 建物の移転

正解 **B**

設問に着目する問題

Voorhees さんが I'm going to apply for a bigger budget for the landscaping project. と、造園プロジェクトの予算の増額を申請すると発言すると、Wang さんはより多くの会社の見積もりを手に入れるように言われるだけだろうと悲観的な返答をしている。また、適当な会社が見つからないと Voorhees さんが言うと、慎重になるべきだと Wang さんが意見している。その後も Voorhees さんは申請について、I'll let you know how it goes. と、申請の進捗を Wang さんに知らせていくと言っている。2 人は造園プロジェクトの予算について話し合っているので、正解は (B)。

☐ relocation　　　　　　　　移転

150 At 9:03 A.M., what does Ms. Wang mean when she writes, "I hope it doesn't come to that"?

(A) She thinks that a fountain is affordable for the company.

(B) She cannot support Mr. Voorhees' request.

(C) She does not want to compromise on the plans.

(D) She would like to postpone a project.

午前 9 時 3 分に Wang さんが "I hope it doesn't come to that" と書く際、何を意図していますか。

(A) 彼女は噴水は会社が入手可能だと思っている。

(B) 彼女は Voorhees さんの依頼を支持できない。

(C) 彼女は計画について妥協したくない。

(D) 彼女はプロジェクトを延期したい。

正解 **C**

意図問題

Voorhees さんはこの発言の直前に、If they say "no," we'll have to save money by scrapping the plans for a fountain. と、申請が通らなかったら、造園プロジェクトの噴水をやめて節約する必要があると発言している。また、Wang さんは、直後に I think one would look great there. と書き、one「＝噴水」があったら素敵なのにと残念がっている。Wang さんはこの発言によって、当初のプロジェクトの予定を変更したくないことを伝えていると判断できるので、動詞 compromise「〜を妥協する」を使って表現している (C) が正解。

語彙チェック

☐ landscaping	造園
☐ steer clear	問題を避ける、関わらない
☐ complication	厄介な問題
☐ scrap	〜を廃止する
☐ fountain	噴水

Questions 151-152 refer to the following e-mail.

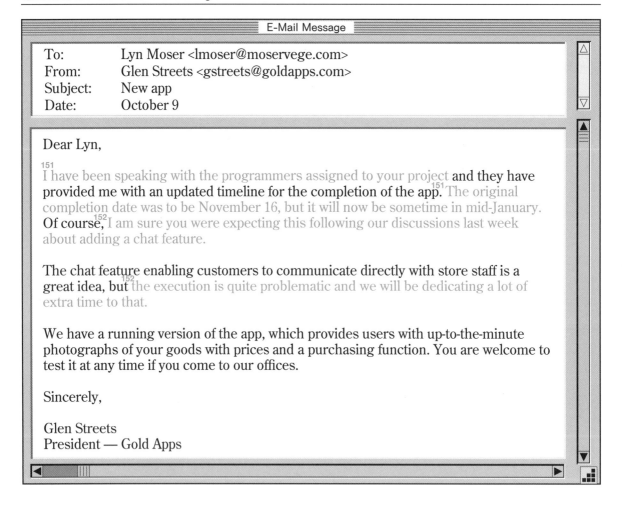

```
┌─────────────────── E-Mail Message ───────────────────┐
│                                                        │
│  To:        Lyn Moser <lmoser@moservege.com>          │
│  From:      Glen Streets <gstreets@goldapps.com>      │
│  Subject:   New app                                    │
│  Date:      October 9                                  │
│                                                        │
└────────────────────────────────────────────────────────┘
```

Dear Lyn,

[151] I have been speaking with the programmers assigned to your project **and they have provided me with an updated timeline for the completion of the app.** [151] The original completion date was to be November 16, but it will now be sometime in mid-January. Of course, [152] I am sure you were expecting this following our discussions last week about adding a chat feature.

The chat feature enabling customers to communicate directly with store staff is a great idea, but [152] the execution is quite problematic and we will be dedicating a lot of extra time to that.

We have a running version of the app, which provides users with up-to-the-minute photographs of your goods with prices and a purchasing function. You are welcome to test it at any time if you come to our offices.

Sincerely,

Glen Streets
President — Gold Apps

問題 **151-152** は次の E メールに関するものです。

宛先：Lyn Moser <lmoser@moservege.com>
送信者：Glen Streets <gstreets@goldapps.com>
件名：新しいアプリケーション
日付：10 月 9 日

Lyn 様

貴社のプロジェクト担当のプログラマーと話をしていて、アプリケーション完成までの最新の予定表を受け取りました。当初の完成予定日は 11 月 16 日でしたが、今や 1 月半ばごろになりそうです。もちろん、チャット機能を追加することについての先週の話し合いの後、こうなることはきっと予想されていたと思います。

顧客が店のスタッフと直接交信できるようにするチャット機能はすばらしい案なのですが、実行には多々問題があり、私たちはそれに多くの追加の時間を割くことになるでしょう。

そのアプリケーションの現行バージョンがあり、それは貴社の商品の最新の写真と価格、また購入機能をユーザーに提供します。当社のオフィスにいらっしゃればいつでもそれをご自由にお試しいただけます。

よろしくお願いします。

Glen Streets
社長 — Gold アプリケーション社

151 What is the purpose of the e-mail?

(A) To explain the cancellation of a project

(B) To request payment for some services

(C) To provide an updated project schedule

(D) To describe the process of creating an app

E メールの目的は何ですか。

(A) プロジェクトの中止について説明すること。

(B) 一部のサービスの支払いを依頼すること。

(C) 最新のプロジェクトスケジュールを提供すること。

(D) アプリケーション制作の工程を説明すること。

正解 C

設問に着目する問題

E メールの目的が何かということが問われている。E メールや、手紙などの文書の目的は、冒頭付近に書かれていることが多いが、この E メールでも同様。アプリ開発会社の社長から、顧客に宛てられた E メールだということは、I have been speaking with the programmers assigned to your project から判断できる。続けて、The original completion date was to be November 16, but it will now be sometime in mid-January.「当初の完成予定日は 11 月 16 日だったが、今や 1 月半ばごろになりそうだ」とあるので、正解は (C)。

152 What has caused the delay in the development of the app?

(A) An unexpected software update

(B) Changes in government regulations

(C) Usage of copyrighted material

(D) An additional request from the client

何がアプリケーションの開発の遅れを引き起こしましたか。

(A) 予想外のソフトウェア更新

(B) 政府の規制の変更

(C) 著作権のある作品の使用

(D) 顧客からの追加依頼

正解 D

設問に着目する問題

完成日の遅れを伝えた後、I am sure you were expecting this following our discussions last week about adding a chat feature. と、チャット機能追加の話し合いで、遅れも予想できたはずだと述べ、また、the execution is quite problematic and we will be dedicating a lot of extra time to that「(チャット機能追加の)実行には多々問題があり、私たちはそれに多く追加の時間を割くことになる」と、遅れの原因は機能の追加であるとはっきりと説明している。正解は (D)。

regulations	規則、規定
copyrighted	版権のある、著作権を取得している

TEST 1

TEST 2

TEST 3

TEST 4

語彙チェック

assign A to B	A を B に割り当てる
completion	完成
feature	機能
enable A to do	A が〜できるようにする
execution	実行
problematic	問題のある
dedicate	〜をささげる
running	現行の
up-to-the-minute	最新の

Questions 153-154 refer to the following advertisement.

Volunteer at Porpoise Point!

Every year, [153] groups of concerned citizens gather at the lighthouse on Porpoise Point to carry out a general cleanup of the area after the busy tourist season. We all benefit from the boost to the economy the tourists bring, and it is upon all of us to do our part to help return the environment to an acceptable condition after they leave. [153] Porpoise Point is a protected environmental reserve so we must do our best to remove all trash and signs of human use where possible.

After the cleanup, popular local band Dukes of the Dunes will be providing a free concert. Furthermore, [154] Harper's Steak and Seafood has promised a free hamburger and drink to every registered volunteer.

Learn more at www.porpoisepoint.gov/annualcleanup.

問題 **153-154** は次の広告に関するものです。

Porpoise 岬でのボランティア募集！

毎年、関心のある市民の団体が Porpoise 岬の灯台に集まり、忙しい観光シーズン後に地域の大掃除をします。私たちは皆、観光客がもたらす経済促進の恩恵を受けており、彼らが去った後に環境を許容できる状態に戻す手伝いをする役割を果たすのは私たちの責任です。Porpoise 岬は環境保護区なので、可能な場所ではすべてのゴミと人間の使用の痕跡を除去するべく最善を尽くさなければなりません。

掃除の後、地元の人気バンド Dukes of the Dunes が無料のコンサートを行います。さらに、Harper's ステーキアンドシーフードが登録ボランティア全員に無料のハンバーガーとドリンクを提供すると約束してくれました。

詳細については www.porpoisepoint.gov/annualcleanup にアクセスしてください。

153 Why are volunteers needed?

(A) To guide tourists around Porpoise Point

(B) To remove trash from a protected area

(C) To help plan an outdoor concert

(D) To deliver refreshments at a sporting event

ボランティアはなぜ必要とされていますか。

(A) 観光客に Porpoise 岬の案内をするため。

(B) 保護区からゴミを撤去するため。

(C) 野外コンサートを企画するのを手伝うため。

(D) スポーツイベントで軽食を配達するため。

正解 B

設問に着目する問題

冒頭には、groups of concerned citizens gather at the lighthouse on Porpoise Point to carry out a general cleanup of the area after the busy tourist season とあり、観光シーズン後に岬のエリアの大掃除をする人たちがいることが分かる。さらに、Porpoise Point is a protected environmental reserve so we must do our best to remove all trash and signs of human use 「Porpoise 岬は環境保護区なので、すべてのゴミと人間の使用の痕跡を除去するべく最善を尽くさなければならない」とあり、人間が汚した自然を掃除しなければならないと述べているので、正解は (B)。

☐ refreshments　　　　　　　　軽食

---

154 What is mentioned about Harper's Steak and Seafood?

(A) Its employees will all be volunteering.

(B) It is run inside the lighthouse.

(C) It will be providing free food for participants.

(D) Its menu was changed at the end of summer.

Harper's ステーキアンドシーフードについて何が述べられていますか。

(A) その従業員は全員ボランティアを行う。

(B) それは灯台内部で経営されている。

(C) それは参加者に無料の食事を提供する。

(D) そのメニューは夏の終わりに変更された。

正解 C

選択肢に着目する問題

ボランティアの後に無料コンサートが開催されることが述べられ、さらに、Harper's Steak and Seafood has promised a free hamburger and drink to every registered volunteer 「Harper's ステーキアンドシーフードが登録ボランティア全員に無料のハンバーガーとドリンクを提供すると約束している」とある。volunteer を participant と言い換えている (C) が正解。

語彙チェック

☐ point　　　　　　　　岬
☐ concerned　　　　　　関心を持っている
☐ lighthouse　　　　　　灯台
☐ benefit　　　　　　　利益を得る
☐ boost to ～　　　　　～への後押し
☐ acceptable　　　　　　許容できる
☐ reserve　　　　　　　保護区

Questions 155-157 refer to the following article.

Get Fit Quick

The Dundee area has a wide variety of activities available for people looking for something to do after work or on the weekend. However, it has been mentioned in the past that when it comes to healthy endeavors the region is sorely lacking.

That is until now. [155,156] Ben and Joe Harper have recently founded the Dundee Fitness and Fun Foundation (DFFF) to coordinate the activities of a number of local health and fitness enthusiasts and encourage more people to try out healthier lifestyles and activities. [156] They did this in response to an observation that the only physical pastime popular in the area was ten pin bowling at Double P Lanes — something that while fun, has few health benefits.

The DFFF now publishes a monthly newsletter and helps coordinate more than 10 events a week. These include [157] bushwalks, bicycle tours, indoor and outdoor climbing events as well as a number of [157] sporting competitions for people of various ages. If you are interested in joining, contact Ben Harper at bh@dundeefff.org.

問題 **155-157** は次の記事に関するものです。

すぐに健康になろう

Dundee 地区には、仕事の後や週末にすることを探している人々が利用できる多種多様なアクティビティがある。しかし、過去には、この地域は健康によい活動に関してははなはだ不足していると言われてきた。

それもここまでの話である。Ben Harper と Joe Harper は最近、地域の多数の健康マニアによる活動を調整し、より健康的なライフスタイルや活動を実践してみるようより多くの人に奨励するために、Dundee フィットネス娯楽財団（DFFF）を設立した。この地域で人気の唯一の身体を使う娯楽が Double P Lanes のボウリングだけであり、それは楽しくはあるけれども健康にはほとんど利点がないという観察結果に基づいて、彼らはこれを行った。

DFFF は現在、月報を発行し、週に 10 以上のイベントをまとめている。これらにはハイキング、自転車ツアー、屋内外のクライミングイベント、また様々な年齢の人向けのスポーツ競技がたくさん含まれている。参加に興味があれば、Ben Harper に bh@dundeefff.org までご連絡を。

155

Where would the article most likely be found?

(A) In a business news magazine

(B) In an entertainment guide

(C) In an investment magazine

(D) In a museum newsletter

記事はどこに掲載されていると考えられますか。

(A) ビジネスニュース雑誌

(B) 娯楽ガイド誌

(C) 投資雑誌

(D) 美術館の館報

正解 **B**

設問に着目する問題

the Dundee Fitness and Fun Foundation (DFFF) というフィットネスと娯楽の財団が、今まで健康に関する活動が少なかった Dundee 地区に設立されたことを伝える記事である。この地域の健康と娯楽について地域の人に知らせる内容なので、(B) が適切。

☐ investment　　　　　　　　　　投資

156

What is implied about Double P Lanes?

(A) It has a longer history than DFFF.

(B) It is sponsored by the local government.

(C) It is owned by Ben and Joe Harper.

(D) It is no longer open for business.

Double P Lanes について何が示唆されていますか。

(A) それは DFFF より長い歴史を持つ。

(B) それは地方自治体の後援を受けている。

(C) それは Ben Harper と Joe Harper に所有されている。

(D) それはもう営業していない。

正解 **A**

選択肢に着目する問題

Ben and Joe Harper have recently founded the Dundee Fitness and Fun Foundation (DFFF)「Ben Harper と Joe Harper は最近、Dundee フィットネス娯楽財団 (DFFF) を設立した」とあり、それを受けて They did this in response to an observation that the only physical pastime popular in the area was ten pin bowling at Double P Lanes「この地域で人気の唯一の身体を使う娯楽が Double P Lanes のボウリングだけであるという観察結果に基づいて、彼らはこれを行った」と述べられている。Double P Lanes だけでは住民の健康によくないという観点から DFFF が設立したことが分かるので、(A) が正解。

157

What kind of event is DFFF NOT associated with?

(A) Athletic contests

(B) Hiking

(C) Cooking classes

(D) Cycling trips

DFFF が関係していないのはどのようなイベントですか。

(A) スポーツコンテスト

(B) ハイキング

(C) 料理教室

(D) サイクリング旅行

正解 **C**

NOT 問題

DFFF の活動内容については、後半に述べられている。The DFFF now～helps coordinate more than 10 events a week.「DFFF は現在、～週に 10 以上のイベントをまとめている」とあり、その後 These include ～に続けて、そのイベントの種類が挙げられている。(A) は sporting competitions と一致する。(B) は bushwalks と一致する。(D) は bicycle tours と一致する。(C) についてはまったく言及がないので、正解は (C)。

語彙チェック

☐ get fit	健康になる、身体を鍛える	☐ enthusiast	熱心な人
☐ when it comes to ～	～のことになると	☐ in response to ～	～に応えて
☐ endeavor	試み、企て	☐ observation	観察、観察結果
☐ sorely	非常に	☐ pastime	娯楽
☐ lacking	不足している	☐ while	～ではあるものの、とはいえ
☐ coordinate	～を調整する	☐ bushwalk	ハイキング、ピクニック

Questions 158-160 refer to the following flyer.

The Wagon Train
The Authentic Taste of the West

The Wagon Train has been serving meals based on the recipes of the European settlers to America for more than 40 years. In order to serve more hungry Orlando residents than ever before, [158] we have recently transferred to Shop 45 in the Bronson Hotel Building on Hounslow Road.

We still have the same hugely popular menu and rustic interior, which have made the restaurant a success [159] since it was founded by Davida Coleman. Ms. Coleman has handed over the duties of head chef to her grandson and now spends most of her time planning [160] her Saturday afternoon cooking class, which she runs in the restaurant's huge, modern kitchen. It is so large, in fact, that the restaurant can continue to operate while the class is in session. Indeed, that day of the week is the busiest for the restaurant as [160] it hosts live performances from local musicians and usually remains open past midnight.

Make a reservation for your next night out by calling 732-555-4899.

問題 **158-160** は次のチラシに関するものです。

The Wagon Train
西部の本物の味覚

The Wagon Train は 40 年以上にわたって、アメリカへのヨーロッパ人入植者のレシピに基づいて食事を提供してきました。今まで以上に多くのお腹をすかせたオーランドの住民に食事を提供するために、私たちは最近、Hounslow 通りの Bronson ホテル内の Shop 45 に移転しました。

私たちは今でも変わらない大人気メニューと素朴な内装を保持しており、それらのおかげでこのレストランは Davida Coleman によって設立されて以来ずっと成功をおさめてきました。Coleman さんは料理長としての務めを孫に引き継いで、今は、ほとんどの時間を彼女が当店の大きくて現代的なキッチンで開講している土曜日午後の料理教室の計画を立てて過ごしています。実際、キッチンは非常に大きいため、料理教室の授業中でもレストランは営業できます。地元のミュージシャンによる生演奏を主催し、たいてい深夜過ぎまで開店しているので、実はその曜日が週で最も多忙な日となっています。

次の夜のおでかけに、732-555-4899 に電話して予約をしてください。

158

What is a purpose of the flyer?

(A) To announce the launch of a new menu

(B) To encourage people to attend a special event

(C) To provide information about an investment opportunity

(D) To inform customers of a changed location for a business

チラシの目的は何ですか。

(A) 新メニューの発売を告知すること。

(B) 人々に特別イベントに出席するよう促すこと。

(C) 投資の機会についての情報を提供すること。

(D) 変更した店舗の場所を顧客に知らせること。

正解 **D**

設問に着目する問題

様々な文書の目的は、冒頭付近に書かれていることが多く、この問題の正解の根拠も、冒頭近くに登場している。40 年の歴史のあるこのレストランは発展拡大のため、we have recently transferred to Shop 45 in the Bronson Hotel Building on Hounslow Road と知らせているが、それがこのチラシの目的と判断できる。transfer を changed location for a business と言い表している (D) が正解。

☐ launch　　　　　　開始　　　　　☐ investment　　　　投資

159

What is stated about Ms. Coleman?

(A) She established The Wagon Train.

(B) She works as the head chef.

(C) She lives above the restaurant.

(D) She has appeared on television.

Coleman さんについて述べられていることは何ですか。

(A) 彼女は The Wagon Train を設立した。

(B) 彼女は料理長として働いている。

(C) 彼女はレストランの上に住んでいる。

(D) 彼女はテレビに出演したことがある。

正解 **A**

選択肢に着目する問題

Coleman さんは since it was founded by Davida Coleman「それは Davida Coleman によって設立されて以来」で登場する。この it は前にある the restaurant、つまり The Wagon Train を指すので、彼女がそのレストランの創業者と分かる。found を establish と言い換えている (A) が正解。なお、続いて Ms. Coleman has handed over the duties of head chef to her grandson とあり、かつて彼女は料理長であったが今は孫に引き継いでいるため、(B) は不適切。

160

What is NOT indicated about Saturdays?

(A) Entertainment is provided for diners.

(B) Cooking classes are available.

(C) The restaurant operates until late.

(D) Discount meals are on offer.

土曜日について示されていないことは何ですか。

(A) 客のために催し物が提供されている。

(B) 料理教室が開講されている。

(C) レストランは遅くまで営業している。

(D) 割引の食事が提供されている。

正解 **D**

NOT 問題

移転後のレストランの営業について、チラシの後半で説明されている。it hosts live performances from local musicians とあり (A) は一致する。live performance を entertainment と言い換えている。(B) は her Saturday afternoon cooking class と一致する。(C) は usually remains open past midnight と一致する。discount については言及がないので、(D) が正解。

☐ diner　　　　　食事をする人、(飲食店の) 客　　　☐ operate　　　　　操業する

語彙チェック

☐ authentic　　　本物の　　　　　　☐ hand over　　　　〜を引き継ぐ
☐ settler　　　　　入植者　　　　　　☐ run　　　　　　　　〜を運営する
☐ hugely　　　　　とても　　　　　　☐ in session　　　　授業中で、開催中で
☐ rustic　　　　　素朴な　　　　　　☐ indeed　　　　　　確かに、いかにも

Questions 161-163 refer to the following Web page.

https://www.blueflowos.com

BlueFlow Online Shopping

— [1] — . November 11 is the date of our yearly sale and items in every category will be sold at between 30 and 50 percent off.

[161] Preorder now and save! All items being sold as part of the November 11 sale are marked with a purple star. — [2] —. [161] Every year, most of the items sell out before the closing time. So that you don't miss out, we have made it possible to preorder.

By choosing the preorder option, you will be charged 10 percent now, and the balance will be charged automatically on November 11.

[163] Please note that November 11 sale items will not be shipped until the sale is completed. — [3] — . Also, the 10-percent deposit cannot be refunded even if you choose not to go through with the purchase. — [4] — . Naturally, [162] if you make the purchase and then find any defect in the product, you will receive a refund of the full purchase price.

問題 **161-163** は次のウェブページに関するものです。

https://www.blueflowos.com

BlueFlow オンラインショッピング

11 月 11 日は年に一度のセールの日であり、全部門の商品を 30% から 50% 割引で販売します。

事前注文をしてお金を節約しましょう！ 11 月 11 日のセールで売り出されるすべての商品に紫の星のマークがついています。毎年ほとんどの商品が終了時刻の前に売り切れてしまいます。あなたがチャンスを逃さないように、事前注文ができるようにいたしました。

事前注文のオプションを選ぶと、その時点で代金の 10% が請求され、差額は 11 月 11 日に自動的に請求されます。

11 月 11 日のセール品はセールが終わるまで配送されないということにご注意ください。＊ ですので、緊急で商品が必要な場合、事前注文オプションを選択しないようにご注意ください。また、10% の頭金は、購入を取りやめにすることを選択されたとしても返金できません。もちろん、ご購入後に製品に何らかの欠陥を見つけられた場合は、ご購入金額は全額返金いたします。

161 Why should customers order before November 11?

(A) Their products are likely to be out of stock quickly.

(B) They can take advantage of even larger discounts.

(C) They will receive free shipping on their orders.

(D) They can receive a free bonus item.

顧客はなぜ 11 月 11 日以前に注文すべきですか。

(A) 彼らの商品はすぐに売り切れる可能性が高いから。

(B) 彼らはさらに大幅な割引を得られるから。

(C) 彼らは注文品を無料配送してもらえるから。

(D) 彼らは無料のプレゼント商品をもらえるから。

正解 **A**

設問に着目する問題

11 月 11 日に開始されるオンラインショッピングのセールの案内で、Preorder now and save! とあり、読者はプレオーダーをするよう勧められている。続いて、Every year, most of the items sell out before the closing time.「毎年ほとんどの商品が終了時刻の前に売り切れてしまう」と、その理由が述べられている。正解は (A)。out of stock「在庫切れの」。

162 What is indicated about the deposit?

(A) It will only be refunded if the product is flawed.

(B) It will be donated to a worthy cause.

(C) It will be used for future product development.

(D) It is a flat rate for all products.

頭金について何が示されていますか。

(A) それは商品が欠陥であった場合にのみ返金される。

(B) それは立派な目的のために寄付される。

(C) それは将来の製品開発のために利用される。

(D) それは全商品一律料金である。

正解 **A**

選択肢に着目する問題

the deposit は、事前注文の際に引き落とされる価格の 10%分を指している。if you make the purchase and then find any defect in the product, you will receive a refund of the full purchase price「ご購入後に製品に何らかの欠陥を見つけられた場合は、ご購入金額は全額返金する」とある。全額返金には、頭金も含まれると判断できるので、(A) が正解。

☐ flat rate　　　　　　　　　均一料金

163 In which of the positions marked [1], [2], [3], and [4] does the following sentence best belong?

"Therefore, if you need an item urgently, you should be careful not to select the preorder option."

(A) [1]　　(B) [2]　　(C) [3]　　(D) [4]

[1] , [2], [3], [4] と記載された箇所のうち、次の文が入るのに最もふさわしいのはどれですか。

「ですので、緊急で商品が必要な場合、事前注文オプションを選択しないようにご注意ください」

(A) [1]　　(B) [2]　　(C) [3]　　(D) [4]

正解 **C**

文挿入問題

挿入文の文頭の Therefore は「それ故に」と前後の論理関係を説明する副詞。よって、空所の前の文の内容が挿入文の理由となる。挿入文を [3] に入れると、前文の Please note that November 11 sale items will not be shipped until the sale is completed.「11 月 11 日のセール品はセールが終わるまで配送されないということにご注意ください」が、挿入文の if you need an item urgently, you should be careful not to select the preorder option「緊急で商品が必要な場合、事前注文オプションを選択しないようにご注意ください」の理由となり文意が合う。(C) が正解。

語彙チェック			
☐ preorder	事前注文をする、事前注文	☐ deposit	頭金
☐ miss out	見逃す	☐ defect	欠陥
☐ complete	〜を終える		

Questions 164-167 refer to the following letter.

Centenary Tower Office Suites
101 Ocean View Parade
Miami, FL 33132

March 23

Ms. Helen Carter
Fielding Accounting Agency
Post Office Box 1204
Miami, FL 33132

Dear Ms. Carter,

It is my sincere pleasure to welcome you and your staff to Centenary Tower Office Suites, Miami's most distinguished business address. I hope that you will take some time to make your employees aware of the building management authority's rules concerning the use of the facilities and conduct within the building and on its grounds.

The building has some amenities which are available for all tenants to use. To ensure that these shared assets are used fairly by all tenants, there are some guidelines which we must all follow.

Parking in the underground garage is limited to one car per tenant unless other arrangements are agreed to at the time of signing the lease. Any cars parked in spaces allocated to other tenants will be towed away at the owner's expense. The first-floor meeting room is available to each tenant for a total of 48 hours per year. There is a similar arrangement for use of the rooftop barbecue area and equipment on the 25th floor. It is necessary to make reservations for both online at www.centenarytoweros.com/amenres.

Building management is available between the hours of 9:00 A.M. and 5:00 P.M. Monday through Friday. Should you need assistance after hours, please call the emergency hotline at 555-9393. Please do not call this line to discuss matters regarding the lease or to discuss matters related to business.

Thank you for choosing Centenary Tower Office Suites. We hope your business will continue to prosper at its new address.

Sincerely,

Philip Gould

Philip Gould
Building Manager — Centenary Tower Office Suites

問題 **164-167** は次の手紙に関するものです。

Centenary タワーオフィススイート
Ocean View Parade 101 番地
マイアミ、FL 33132

3 月 23 日

Helen Carter 様
Fielding 会計事務所
私書箱 1204 号
マイアミ、FL 33132

Carter 様

マイアミの最も著名なビジネス街である Centenary タワーオフィススイートにあなたとあなたのスタッフをお迎えできることを心から喜んでおります。施設使用と建物内部および敷地内での行動に関する建物管理上のルールについて、従業員にご注意いただく時間を取っていただければと思います。

建物内には入居者全員が利用できる快適な設備がいくつかあります。入居者全員が公平にこれらの共有財産を利用できることを保証するために、私たち全員が従わなければならない指針がいくつかあります。

地下ガレージでの駐車は、賃貸借契約の際に他の取り決めで合意していない限り、1 テナントあたり 1 台に制限されています。他のテナントに割り当てられた場所に駐車されたいかなる車も、所有者負担でレッカー移動します。1 階会議室は各テナントが年に合計 48 時間利用できます。屋上のバーベキューエリアと 25 階の設備についても同様の取り決めがあります。どちらも www.centenarytoweros.com/amenres にてオンラインで予約する必要があります。

月曜日から金曜日までの午前 9 時から午後 5 時までの間は、建物管理者が対応可能です。万一その時間帯以降に支援が必要なら、555-9393 まで緊急直通電話をかけてください。賃貸契約に関する事や事業に関する事について話し合うためにこの電話番号にかけることはなさらないでください。

Centenary タワーオフィススイートをお選びいただきありがとうございます。あなたの事業が新しい場所でも成功し続けることを願っております。よろしくお願いします。

Philip Gould（署名）
Philip Gould
建物管理者 — Centenary タワーオフィススイート

語彙チェック

☐ distinguished　　　著名な

☐ tow away　　　〜をレッカー移動する

164

What is the purpose of the letter?

(A) To provide information to new tenants

(B) To inform a tenant about a renewal of the lease

(C) To ask for some financial advice

(D) To advertise office suites available for rental

手紙の目的は何ですか。

(A) 新しいテナントに情報提供すること。

(B) 賃貸契約の更新についてテナントに知らせること。

(C) 財政上の助言を求めること。

(D) 貸出可能なオフィススイートを宣伝すること。

正解 A

設問に着目する問題

手紙の目的は冒頭付近に書かれていることが多く、この問題の正解の根拠も、冒頭近くにある。手紙は Centenary タワーオフィススイートのビル管理者から Carter さんに宛てられており、冒頭に It is my sincere pleasure to welcome you and your staff to Centenary Tower Office Suites とあり、Carter さんとその会社を歓迎している。その後も I hope that you will take some time to make your employees aware of the building management authority's rules concerning the use of the facilities and conduct within the building and on its grounds と、ビル内施設のルールや注意事項を知ってほしいという内容が述べられているので、(A) が正解。

165

What is indicated about Centenary Tower Office Suites?

(A) It is reasonably priced.

(B) It is very prestigious.

(C) It is located near a park.

(D) It has reached maximum occupancy.

Centenary タワーオフィススイートについて何が示されていますか。

(A) それは手頃な値段である。

(B) それは非常に有名である。

(C) それは公園の近くに位置している。

(D) それは満室に達している。

正解 B

選択肢に着目する問題

冒頭に Centenary Tower Office Suites, Miami's most distinguished business address とある。この distinguished は「際立った、著名な、すばらしい」という意味の形容詞。これを、prestigious「名声のある、一流の」と言い換えている (B) が正解。(A) の価格、(C) の公園近くという立地、また (D) の occupancy「占有率」については言及はない。

166

What is NOT a part of the building's amenities?

(A) An underground parking garage

(B) A first-floor meeting room

(C) A spa and gym

(D) An open-air barbecue area

建物の設備に含まれていないものは何ですか。

(A) 地下駐車場

(B) 1 階会議室

(C) スパとジム

(D) 屋外バーベキューエリア

正解 C

NOT 問題

amenity は「設備、施設」という意味。建物の設備の中にないものが問われている。(A) は the underground garage と一致する。(B) は The first-floor meeting room is available と一致する。(D) は the rooftop barbecue area と一致する。rooftop が open-air と言い換えられている。スパとジムについては言及がないので、(C) が正解。

167

According to the letter, what should people avoid doing?

(A) Parking vehicles in the space in front of the building's front door

(B) Using the emergency line to discuss the rental agreement

(C) Inviting guests to tenant-only events

(D) Eating lunch in the building's lobby

手紙によると、人々がするのを避けるべきことは何ですか。

(A) 建物の正面玄関の前の場所に駐車すること。

(B) 賃貸契約について話し合うために緊急電話回線を利用すること。

(C) テナント専用イベントに客を招くこと。

(D) 建物のロビーで昼食を食べること。

正解 B

選択肢に着目する問題

中盤以降にビル内で従うべき指針がいくつか述べられていて、テナントがすべきでないことは、「地下駐車場の割り当て以外の場所への駐車」と「緊急用の直通電話を緊急時以外に使用すること」が読み取れる。(B) が正解。

Questions 168-171 refer to the following online chat discussion.

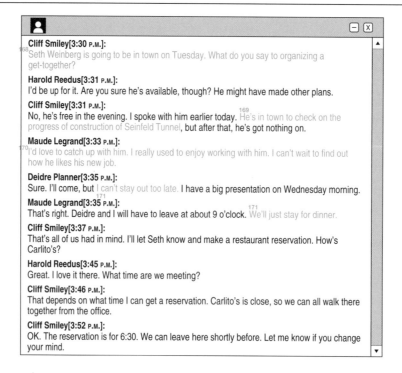

Cliff Smiley[3:30 P.M.]:
[168]Seth Weinberg is going to be in town on Tuesday. What do you say to organizing a get-together?

Harold Reedus[3:31 P.M.]:
I'd be up for it. Are you sure he's available, though? He might have made other plans.

Cliff Smiley[3:31 P.M.]:
No, he's free in the evening. I spoke with him earlier today. [169]He's in town to check on the progress of construction of Seinfeld Tunnel, but after that, he's got nothing on.

Maude Legrand[3:33 P.M.]:
[170]I'd love to catch up with him. I really used to enjoy working with him. I can't wait to find out how he likes his new job.

Deidre Planner[3:35 P.M.]:
Sure. I'll come, but I can't stay out too late. I have a big presentation on Wednesday morning.

Maude Legrand[3:35 P.M.]:
That's right. Deidre and I will have to leave at about 9 o'clock. [171]We'll just stay for dinner.

Cliff Smiley[3:37 P.M.]:
That's all of us had in mind. I'll let Seth know and make a restaurant reservation. How's Carlito's?

Harold Reedus[3:45 P.M.]:
Great. I love it there. What time are we meeting?

Cliff Smiley[3:46 P.M.]:
That depends on what time I can get a reservation. Carlito's is close, so we can all walk there together from the office.

Cliff Smiley[3:52 P.M.]:
OK. The reservation is for 6:30. We can leave here shortly before. Let me know if you change your mind.

問題 **168-171** は次のオンラインチャットの話し合いに関するものです。

Cliff Smiley [午後 3 時 30 分]:

Seth Weinberg が火曜日に町に来るんだ。みんなで集まることを企画するのはどうかな？

Harold Reedus [午後 3 時 31 分]:

僕は賛成だ。でも、彼は本当に来られるのかい？　彼には他の予定があるかもしれないよ。

Cliff Smiley [午後 3 時 31 分]:

いいや、彼は夕方は空いているよ。今日さっき彼と話したんだ。彼は Seinfeld トンネル建設の進行状況を確認するために町に滞在するのだけれど、その後は何もないみたいだよ。

Maude Legrand [午後 3 時 33 分]:

彼の近況をぜひ聞きたいなあ。彼と一緒に働くのは本当に楽しかった。彼の新しい仕事がどんな感じか聞くのが待ちきれないわ。

Deidre Planner [午後 3 時 35 分]:

ええ。私は行くけど、あまり遅くまでは残れないの。水曜日の午前中に大きなプレゼンテーションをするから。

Maude Legrand [午後 3 時 35 分]:

そうなのよ。Deidre と私は 9 時ごろに出るわ。私たちはディナーだけにする。

Cliff Smiley [午後 3 時 37 分]:

僕らみんなそのつもりだよ。僕が Seth に知らせてレストランの予約を取ろう。Carlito's はどうかな？

Harold Reedus [午後 3 時 45 分]:

いいね。あそこは大好きだよ。何時に集まろうか？

Cliff Smiley [午後 3 時 46 分]:

何時に予約が取れるかによるね。Carlito's は近いから、僕らみんな一緒に、オフィスから歩いて行けるよ。

Cliff Smiley [午後 3 時 52 分]:

よし。予約は 6 時 30 分だ。その少し前にここを出ればいい。気が変わったら知らせてね。

語彙チェック

☐ organize	〜を企画する	☐ check on 〜	〜を点検する
☐ get-together	集まり	☐ progress	進行状況
☐ up for 〜	〜に乗り気で	☐ catch up with 〜	〜の近況を知る、に追いつく

168

Why did Mr. Smiley start the online chat?

(A) To introduce a new colleague
(B) To request an extension of a deadline
(C) To suggest a gathering
(D) To announce the signing of a contract

Smiley さんはなぜオンラインチャットを始めましたか。

(A) 新しい同僚を紹介するため。
(B) 締め切りの延長を依頼するため。
(C) 集まりを提案するため。
(D) 契約書の署名を告知するため。

正解 C

設問に着目する問題

正解の根拠は Smiley さんの最初の発言にある。Seth Weinberg is going to be in town on Tuesday. What do you say to organizing a get-together? と、Seth Weinberg という人物が来るので集まらないかと呼び掛けている。What do you say to 〜は「〜はいかがですか」と、提案をしたり、人の意向を尋ねたりするときに使える言い回し。正解は (C)。

☐ extension　　　　　　　　　　　延長

169

What is the purpose of Mr. Weinberg's trip?

(A) To take a vacation
(B) To inspect a construction project
(C) To purchase a property
(D) To interview a job applicant

Weinberg さんの旅行の目的は何ですか。

(A) 休暇を取ること。
(B) 建設プロジェクトを視察すること。
(C) 不動産を購入すること。
(D) 求職者と面接すること。

正解 B

設問に着目する問題

Weinberg さんが町に来るということで、みんなで集まることを提案した Smiley さんは、さらに彼について、He's in town to check on the progress of construction of Seinfeld Tunnel「彼は Seinfeld トンネル建設の進行状況を確認するために町に滞在する」と書いているので、(B) が正解と判断できる。

170

Who most likely is Mr. Weinberg?

(A) A prospective client
(B) A potential supplier
(C) A financial consultant
(D) A previous co-worker

Weinberg さんとは誰だと考えられますか。

(A) 見込み客
(B) 潜在的な納入業者
(C) 財務顧問
(D) 以前の同僚

正解 D

設問に着目する問題

Legrand さんの発言に正解の根拠がある。Weinberg さんについて Legrand さんは、I'd love to catch up with him. I really used to enjoy working with him. I can't wait to find out how he likes his new job.「彼の近況をぜひ聞きたい。彼と一緒に働くのは本当に楽しかった。彼の新しい仕事がどんな感じか聞くのが待ちきれない」と書いている。catch up with 〜は「〜の近況について知る」というイディオム。過去に一緒に働いていたということなので、(D) が正解と分かる。

☐ prospective　　　　見込みのある　　　☐ potential　　　　潜在的な、可能性がある

171

At 3:37 P.M., what does Mr. Smiley mean when he writes, "That's all of us had in mind"?

(A) All of the writers have to give a presentation on Wednesday.
(B) All of the writers were planning to leave after having dinner together.
(C) Some of the writers will meet Mr. Carlito before Tuesday.
(D) One of the writers will leave earlier than the others.

午後 3 時 37 分に Smiley さんが "That's all of us had in mind" と書く際、何を意図していますか。

(A) 書き手は全員水曜日にプレゼンテーションをしなければならない。
(B) 書き手の全員が一緒に夕食を取った後に帰るつもりでいた。
(C) 書き手の何人かは火曜日より前に Carlito さんに会う。
(D) 書き手のうち 1 人は他の人たちより早く出る。

正解 B

意図問題

夜の会食の話が決まりつつあるが、Planner さんと Legrand さんは、それぞれ I can't stay out too late や、We'll just stay for dinner. と書いて長居はできないことを告げている。それに対する応答が Smiley さんの That's all of us had in mind.「僕らみんなそのつもりだ」である。つまり、みんな長居はせずに、夕食後は帰るつもりだという気持ちで書いていると想像できる。正解は (B)。

Questions 172-175 refer to the following article.

Bradford Inquirer — Business Profile: Salinger Surfwear

Two years ago, Salinger Surfwear was nearly out of business. It had some loyal customers, but sales were far too low to sustain the company for more than a half year. As the situation became more and more apparent, several of the company's leaders left for more promising positions. These included chief designer, Carrie Heart, and head of marketing, Steve Pinochet. They were replaced by Dean Manos and Helen Frente respectively. — [1] — .

Neither Mr. Manos nor Ms. Frente had any experience in leading as both had graduated from university just one year earlier. — [2] — . Nevertheless, their energy, enthusiasm, courage, and newly acquired skills made them the perfect team to turn the company's fortunes around. Within four months, sales were at a 10-year high, and the company was having trouble filling the orders coming from both here and overseas.

The main reason for the success has been attributed to an idea that came from the new head of marketing. They sent junior employees out to film young surfers and skateboarders in the area. — [3] — . The videos included interviews and the participants were offered free clothes in return for their time. The videos were posted online and became an overnight hit, and the clothing, which had been newly designed by Mr. Manos, drew more and more attention as days and weeks passed. Slowly but surely, sales improved.

This week, the brand opened its first store at Atlantic Fair Shopping Center. — [4] — . Sales have been so high that the staff has been having trouble stocking the shelves with enough merchandise.

問題 **172-175** は次の記事に関するものです。

Bradford Inquirer 新聞―企業紹介：Salinger サーフウェア

2 年前、Salinger サーフウェアは廃業寸前だった。いくらかの常連客はいたものの、売り上げはあまりにも低調で、会社を半年以上持たせることはできないくらいだった。状況がだんだん明らかになるにつれて、何人かの会社の指導者たちがさらに将来性のある職を求めて去って行った。その中にはチーフデザイナーの Carrie Heart とマーケティング部主任の Steve Pinochet も含まれていた。それぞれ Dean Manos と Helen Frente が彼らの後任となった。

Manos 氏も Frente 氏も、大学をその 1 年前に卒業したばかりだったので、指導の経験はなかった。にもかかわらず、彼らのエネルギー、情熱、勇気、そして新しく得た技能によって、彼らは会社の命運をひっくり返す完璧なチームとなった。4 か月のうちに、売り上げは 10 年間の最高額に達し、会社は国内外からの注文に応じるのに苦労するようになっていた。

この成功の主な理由は新しいマーケティング主任が出したアイデアのおかげであった。彼らはその地域の若いサーファーやスケートボーダーの映像を撮影するよう準社員を送り出した。映像はインタビューを含み、参加者は時間を提供した見返りに無料のウェアを提供された。映像はオンライン上に掲載されて一夜にしてヒットし、Manos 氏に新たにデザインされたウェアは日や週を追うごとにますます注目を集めていった。少しずつ、しかし確実に、売り上げは改善していった。

今週、そのブランドは Atlantic Fair ショッピングセンターに初の店舗を出店した。＊ 店員によると、大忙しの数日間だった。売り上げは非常に好調なので、スタッフは十分な数量の商品を棚に供給するのに苦労している。

語彙チェック

profile	紹介、側面	courage	勇気
loyal customer	常連客	acquired	獲得した
sustain	～を持続させる	fortune	運、富
apparent	明らかな	fill an order	注文に応じる
promising	将来性のある	be attributed to ～	～に帰する、のせいである
respectively	それぞれ	post	～を掲載する
leading	指導	draw attention	注目を集める
nevertheless	しかしながら	merchandise	商品
enthusiasm	情熱		

172 What is the purpose of the article?

(A) To explain how employee changes affected a company's earnings

(B) To describe a company's new clothing designs

(C) To report an expected change in a company's leadership

(D) To announce the launch of a new product line

記事の目的は何ですか。

(A) 従業員の入れ替わりがどのように会社の収入に影響したかを説明すること。

(B) 会社の新しい服のデザインを説明すること。

(C) 予定されている会社の指導者層の交代を報じること。

(D) 新しい製品ラインナップの発売を告知すること。

正解 A

設問に着目する問題

新聞の見出しから、ある企業についての記事と分かる。売り上げが非常に悪く、会社の主要人物も離れていき、部門トップが刷新される。そして、デザイナーとマーケティングに経験の浅い新しい主任が採用されたことが述べられている。続いて、Nevertheless, their energy, enthusiasm, courage, and newly acquired skills made them the perfect team to turn the company's fortunes around. Within four months, sales were at a 10-year high とあり、新しいスタッフのおかげで会社の売り上げが急上昇したことが述べられている。(A) が正解。

173 What is true about Salinger Surfwear?

(A) It was founded by Carrie Heart.

(B) It sells its merchandise online.

(C) It has international customers.

(D) It has its merchandise produced locally.

Salinger サーフウェアについて正しいことは何ですか。

(A) それは Carrie Heart によって設立された。

(B) それは商品をオンラインで売っている。

(C) それは海外の顧客を持っている。

(D) それは地元で商品を生産してもらっている。

正解 C

選択肢に着目する問題

売り上げが持ち直して、10 年間で最高額に達したと述べられている。続いて、the company was having trouble filling the orders coming from both here and overseas と述べられているので、海外にも販売していることが分かる。正解は (C)。

174 Who suggested starting an online video channel?

(A) Helen Frente

(B) Carrie Heart

(C) Steve Pinochet

(D) Dean Manos

オンライン映像チャンネルを始めることを提案したのは誰ですか。

(A) Helen Frente

(B) Carrie Heart

(C) Steve Pinochet

(D) Dean Manos

正解 A

設問に着目する問題

1 文書内のクロス問題。第 3 の段落に The main reason for the success has been attributed to an idea that came from the new head of marketing. とあり、事業成功のカギとして、サーファーの映像をオンラインに投稿したことが挙げられており、その提案は the new head of marketing からされていると分かる。第 1 段落に会社を離れたのは chief designer と head of marketing で They were replaced by Dean Manos and Helen Frente respectively.「それぞれ Dean Manos と Helen Frente が彼らの後任となった」とあるので、(A) が正解。

175 In which of the positions marked [1], [2], [3], and [4] does the following sentence best belong?

"According to its sales assistants, it has been a hectic few days."

(A) [1]　(B) [2]　(C) [3]　(D) [4]

[1] , [2], [3], [4] と記載された箇所のうち、次の文が入るのに最もふさわしいのはどれですか。

「店員によると、大忙しの数日間だった」

(A) [1]　(B) [2]　(C) [3]　(D) [4]

正解 D

文挿入問題

挿入文中の its sales assistants「店員」に注目する。空所 [4] の前文では、the brand opened its first store at Atlantic Fair Shopping Center と、初めての店舗が開店したことが述べられている。挿入文を [4] に入れると、its sales assistants はその初店舗の店員を指すことになる。また、hectic「とても忙しい」という店の様子も、[4] の後ろの文の、売り上げが多く商品棚への供給が大変だったという内容に自然とつながる。正解は (D)。

Questions 176-180 refer to the following e-mail and form.

To:	Colin Freeman <cfreeman@hhmachinery.com>
From:	Rhonda Jones <rjones@hhmachinery.com>
Date:	September 27
Subject:	Update
[178] Attachment:	📎 VBIblank

Hi Colin,

At the end of last week, I was shown the revenue reports for the last six months. [176] I was very pleased to find that your branch has beaten its previous best and has become HH Machinery Rental's most profitable location. I put this down to the efforts of you and your excellent staff. I have a couple of requests for the Verisdale branch. First, I would like you to accept a visit from the managers of some of the other branches. [177] Please show them around and explain what you have been doing to achieve such excellent results.

Second, I understand that you are currently understocked on some kinds of machinery. I am planning to have surplus items transported from other offices around the state. [179] It is also possible that you have some inventory that you do not need. If so, please let me know and I will consider distributing it to where it can do the most good. You can send me that information by filling in the required details in the attached spreadsheet. [178]

Sincerely,

Rhonda Jones
General Manager — HH Machinery Rental

Inventory Tracking Form — HH Machinery Rental

Item	Quantity	Origin	Destination	Date of Arrival (Estimated)
Frontend loader	2	Stanthorpe	Verisdale	October 10
Cherry picker	1	Camden	Verisdale	October 12
[179] Backhoe	1	Verisdale	Camden	October 19
Skid-steer loader	3	Camden	Stanthorpe	October 21

Unfortunately rental of power tools has been very limited across all of our locations. This is most likely because of the recent drop in the purchase price of such items as cheap imports have flooded the market. The products we have are excellent quality and the resale value is likely to be high. [180] The company's entire inventory of these items will be sold to Brady's Used Machinery at the end of the year. All store managers will be instructed to send their entire stock to Brady's Used Machinery's head office in Brisbane by December 10.

問題 **176-180** は次の E メールと用紙に関するものです。

受信者：Colin Freeman <cfreeman@hhmachinery.com>
送信者：Rhonda Jones <rjones@hhmachinery.com>
日付：9 月 27 日
件名：更新
添付：VBIblank

こんにちは Colin

先週末に、最近 6 か月の収益報告書を拝見しました。あなたの支店がこれまでの最高額を超えて HH 機械レンタルの中で最も利益を出したと知って私はとてもうれしかったです。これはあなたとあなたの優秀なスタッフたちの努力によるものだと思います。Verisdale 支店にいくつか依頼したいことがあります。まず、他のいくつかの支店の部長たちの訪問を受け入れてほしいです。彼らの案内をして、このような優れた結果を達成するためにあなた方がしてきたことを説明してください。

2 つ目に、あなたのところでいくつかの種類の機械の在庫が現在不足しているのは分かっています。州内の他の営業所から余っている品物を運送してもらうつもりです。あなたのところに必要ない在庫品がある可能性もあります。もしそうであれば知らせてください、そうすれば最も有効に使われる場所にそれを分配することを考えます。添付した表計算シートに必要な詳細を記入することで、その情報を私に送ることができます。

よろしくお願いします。

Rhonda Jones
総支配人 — HH 機械レンタル

在庫追跡用紙 — HH 機械レンタル				
品目	数量	発送元	発送先	到着日 （予定）
フロントエンドローダー	2	Stanthorpe	Verisdale	10 月 10 日
移動クレーン	1	Camden	Verisdale	10 月 12 日
バックホウ	1	Verisdale	Camden	10 月 19 日
スキッドステアローダー	3	Camden	Stanthorpe	10 月 21 日

残念ながら、我が社のすべての営業所において電動器具のレンタルは非常に少ないです。これは、安価な輸入品が市場に出回ったことでこの種の品物の購入価格が最近下落しているためだと考えられます。我が社の製品は品質が優れており、再販価格はおそらく高いでしょう。我が社のこれらの品物の全在庫は、年末に Brady's 中古機械社に売却される予定です。全支店長はそれらすべての在庫を Brady's 中古機械社のブリスベン本社に 12 月 10 日までに送付するよう指示があります。

176 What is one purpose of the e-mail?

(A) To commend employees

(B) To recommend a procedure

(C) To announce a new policy

(D) To suggest an advertising strategy

E メールの 1 つの目的は何ですか。

(A) 従業員をほめること。

(B) 手続きを推薦すること。

(C) 新しい方針を告知すること。

(D) 広告戦略を提案すること。

正解 A

設問に着目する問題

HH 機械レンタル社の総支配人は、まず、過去 6 か月の収益報告の結果、Freeman さんの支店が 1 位になったことへの喜びを伝え、続けて、I put this down to the efforts of you and your excellent staff.「これはあなたとあなたの優秀なスタッフたちの努力によるものだと思う」と、Freeman さんとスタッフをねぎらっている。これが目的の 1 つと判断できる。put down A to B ～は「A を B のせいにする」というイディオム。put down to the efforts of you を、commend「～をほめる」という語で言い表している (A) が正解。

177 What is Mr. Freeman required to do?

(A) Reduce department spending

(B) Attend a weekend workshop

(C) Review a product design

(D) Share ideas with other branches

Freeman さんは何をするよう求められていますか。

(A) 部署の支出を減らす。

(B) 週末のワークショップに出席する。

(C) 製品デザインを論評する。

(D) 他の支店とアイデアを共有する。

正解 D

設問に着目する問題

よい成績を上げた支店の支店長である Freeman さんは、総支配人から、他の支店の店長たちに対し、Please ～ explain what you have been doing to achieve such excellent results「～このような優れた結果を達成するためにあなた方がしてきたことを説明してください」と依頼されている。これを言い換えた (D) が正解。

☐ spending　　　　　　　　支出

178 What is the attachment included with the e-mail?

(A) A product catalog

(B) A spreadsheet

(C) A photograph

(D) A revenue report

E メールに付いていた添付物は何ですか。

(A) 製品カタログ

(B) 表計算シート

(C) 写真

(D) 収益報告書

正解 B

設問に着目する問題

E メールの最後に You can send me that information by filling in the required details in the attached spreadsheet.「添付した表計算シートに必要な詳細を記入することで、その情報を私に送ることができる」と記されている。spreadsheet を添付したということなので、(B) が正解。

179 What is most likely true about the backhoe?

(A) It was in need of some repairs.

(B) It was purchased a long time ago.

(C) It is not needed by Mr. Freeman.

(D) It is not in working order.

バックホウについて正しいと考えられるものは何ですか。

(A) それは修理を必要としていた。

(B) それはずっと以前に購入された。

(C) それは Freeman さんには必要ではない。

(D) それは正常に作動していない。

正解 **C**

選択肢に着目するクロス問題

用紙の品目に backhoe とあり、Verisdale 支店から発送され Camden 支店に到着すると読み取れる。E メールの 2 番目の用件で、支店間の在庫機械の転送について述べられている。It is also possible that you have some inventory that you do not need. If so, please let me know and I will consider distributing it to where it can do the most good. とあり、余剰のものがあれば他店で活用するために分配されると分かる。Verisdale の支店長は Freeman さんなので、正解は (C) となる。

☐ in need of ～　　　　　　　～を必要としている

180 What does the company intend to do with its power tools?

(A) Offer discount rental rates

(B) Advertise in an industry publication

(C) Sell them to a second-hand store

(D) Export them to another country

電動器具について会社は何をするつもりですか。

(A) 割引レンタル料を提案する。

(B) 業界の出版物で宣伝する。

(C) 中古品店に売却する。

(D) 外国に輸出する。

正解 **C**

設問に着目する問題

用紙の下段には power tools についての記述がある。The company's entire inventory of these items will be sold to Brady's Used Machinery at the end of the year.「我が社のこれらの品物の全在庫は、年末に Brady's 中古機械社に売却される予定だ」とあるので、second-hand store に売却するという (C) が正解。

語彙チェック

☐ revenue	収益	☐ inventory	在庫品
☐ beat	～を打ち負かす	☐ spreadsheet	集計表、表計算シート
☐ put down A to B	A を B のせいにする	☐ tracking	追跡すること
☐ understocked	供給不足の	☐ flood	～にあふれる
☐ machinery	機械	☐ resale	再販売
☐ surplus	余分の、余った		

Questions 181-185 refer to the following article and flyer.

Rosemont — On July 21 and 22, Rosemont will once again be hosting the Rosemont Country Music Festival. Every year since its inception some 40 years ago, the festival has grown. The first festival occupied only one stage and we hosted only five musical acts. This year we will have more than 100 artists performing on seven different stages. The main stage is, as it has always been, the one in Kingsmith Square on William Street. Workers have already begun assembling the stands for audience seating. This year, the city council has requested seating for more than 5,000 people. Acts that will be performing there include The Harry Wonder 5, The Heartbreakers, and Vavoom. So that we do not have a repeat of last year's unfortunate cancellations, a shelter is being erected over the stands and the stage itself.

Festival organizers have been encouraging local bands to enter a song contest as part of the festival. Traditionally, the contest has been held on the second day of the festival. Organizers say they will have to hold the event over two days if there are more entrants than last time. That may or may not happen, as last year saw a record number of entrants. The contest will be held at The Old Rosemont Hall on Sparrow Street. The event is sponsored by Radio 6TG, which will be supplying the $4,000 prize money for the winner.

To register for the competition, check the performance schedule, or find out anything more you need to know about the festival, visit the official Web site at www.rosemontcmf.org.

The Rosemont City Council Presents
The Annual Rosemont Country Music Festival
July 21 and 22

Enjoy the free performances at the main stage in Kingsmith Square from 11:00 A.M. to 7:00 P.M. on both days.

Register to take part in any one of 20 workshops by professional country music singers.

You can purchase tickets for performances at the other six stages from the usual ticket sellers. Ticket prices vary and specific information is only available from the respective promoters. Bands include Lumberjacks, Cloudplay, The Heartbreakers, and The Dudley Brothers.

The 21st Rosemont Residents' Song Competition is being held as part of the festival and this year the competition will be held over both days. Its results will be announced on July 22 on the main stage.

www.rosemontcmf.org.

問題 **181-185** は次の記事とチラシに関するものです。

Rosemont ― 7 月 21 日と 22 日に、Rosemont は再び、Rosemont カントリーミュージックフェスティバルを主催する。約 40 年前のスタート以来毎年、フェスティバルは大きくなってきた。最初のフェスティバルは 1 つしかステージを使わず、音楽出演団体も 5 つしかなかった。今年は、7 つの異なるステージで 100 以上のアーティストが演奏する予定である。メインステージはいつも通り、William 通りの Kingsmith Square のステージである。作業員がすでに観客席用にスタンドを組み立て始めている。今年は、市議会が 5,000 人超収容の座席を依頼した。そこで演奏する予定の団体は The Harry Wonder 5、The Heartbreakers、Vavoom などである。昨年の不運な中止を繰り返さないために、スタンドとステージ自体の上に雨除けが建設中だ。

フェスティバル主催者は地元のバンドに、フェスティバルの一環である歌唱コンテストに参加するよう促してきた。伝統的に、このコンテストはフェスティバルの 2 日目に行われてきた。前回よりも参加者が多ければ、このイベントは 2 日間にまたがって開催しなければならないだろうと主催者側は言う。昨年の参加者は今までの最高数を記録したため、それは起こるかもしれないし起こらないかもしれない。コンテストはSparrow 通りの Old Rosemont ホールで開催される。イベントはラジオ 6TG の後援を受けており、優勝者には局が 4,000 ドルの賞金を授与する。

コンテストに参加登録したり、演奏予定表の確認をしたり、フェスティバルについてもっと知る必要があれば、公式ウェブサイト www.rosemontcmf.org にアクセスしてください。

Rosemont 市議会提供
毎年恒例 Rosemont カントリーミュージックフェスティバル
7 月 21 日・22 日

両日ともに、午前 11 時から午後 7 時まで、Kingsmith Square のメインステージにて、無料の音楽演奏を楽しんでください。

プロのカントリーミュージック歌手による 20 の講習会に参加するには登録をお願いします。

他の 6 つのステージでの演奏会チケットは通常のチケット販売者から購入可能です。チケット価格は様々で、具体的な情報はそれぞれのプロモーターからしか入手できません。バンドは Lumberjacks、Cloudplay、The Heartbreakers、The Dudley Brothers などが出演します。

フェスティバルの一環として第 21 回 Rosemont 市民歌唱コンテストが開催されますが、今年はコンテストは両日にわたって開催されます。コンテスト結果は 7 月 22 日にメインステージにて発表されます。

www.rosemontcmf.org

What is indicated about the Rosemont Country Music Festival?

(A) Tickets are available online.

(B) It was first held at Kingsmith Square.

(C) It is expected to draw fewer people than before.

(D) Performers are all from the Rosemont area.

Rosemont カントリーミュージックフェスティバルについて何が示されていますか。

(A) チケットはオンラインで入手可能である。

(B) それは最初 Kingsmith Square で開催された。

(C) それは以前より集客数が減ると予想されている。

(D) 演奏者は全員が Rosemont 地域出身である。

正解 B

選択肢に着目する問題

記事の冒頭でミュージックフェスティバルが 40 年間成長を続けてきたことが述べられ、続いて、開催会場について言及されている。The main stage is, as it has always been, the one in Kingsmith Square on William Street. 「メインステージはいつも通り、William 通りの Kingsmith Square のステージだ」とあり、第 1 回目も Kingsmith Square で行われたと判断できるので、正解は (B)。

☐ draw　　　　　　　　　〜を引き寄せる

What is most likely true about last year's festival?

(A) Tickets were available from the Web site.

(B) It was held in another town.

(C) The preparations went over budget.

(D) There was some inclement weather.

昨年のフェスティバルについて正しいと考えられることは何ですか。

(A) チケットはウェブサイトから入手可能だった。

(B) それは別の町で開催された。

(C) 準備が予算オーバーした。

(D) 天気が荒れた。

正解 D

選択肢に着目する問題

昨年のフェスティバルについては、記事の中頃に So that we do not have a repeat of last year's unfortunate cancellations, a shelter is being erected over the stands and the stage itself. 「昨年の不運な中止を繰り返さないために、スタンドとステージ自体の上に雨除けが建設中だ」という記述がある。今年は雨除けを作るということは、昨年は雨で中止になったと想像できる。inclement weather「荒天」という語で表現している (D) が正解。

According to the article, how can people get more information about the festival?

(A) By accessing the festival Web site

(B) By calling the organizers

(C) By subscribing to a newsletter

(D) By listening to a radio program

記事によると、どのようにしてフェスティバルについてさらなる情報を得られますか。

(A) フェスティバルのウェブサイトにアクセスすることによって。

(B) 主催者に電話をかけることによって。

(C) 会報を定期購読することによって。

(D) ラジオ番組を聞くことによって。

正解 A

設問に着目する問題

記事や案内、お知らせなどの文書では、さらなる詳細の問い合わせ方法を文書の最後に記すことが多く、この問題も正解の根拠は記事の最後にある。(To) find out anything more you need to know about the festival, visit the official Web site at www.rosemontcmf.org 「フェスティバルについてもっと知る必要があれば、公式ウェブサイト www.rosemontcmf.org にアクセスしてください」とあるので、(A) が正解。visit the official Web site が access the festival Web site と言い換えられている。

☐ subscribe to 〜　　　　　　　　〜を定期購読する

184 Which band will provide both free and ticketed performances?

(A) The Heartbreakers

(B) Lumberjacks

(C) The Harry Wonder 5

(D) Cloudplay

無料公演と有料公演の両方を行うのはどのバンドですか。

(A) The Heartbreakers

(B) Lumberjacks

(C) The Harry Wonder 5

(D) Cloudplay

正解 A

設問に着目するクロス問題

無料公演についてはチラシの冒頭に、Enjoy the free performances at the main stage in Kingsmith Square とある。また、記事の中盤にメインステージで行われる公演について、Acts that will be performing there include The Harry Wonder 5, The Heartbreakers, and Vavoom. とあり、無料公演をするバンド名が挙げられている。有料公演については、チラシの中盤に You can purchase tickets for performances at the other six stages とあり、Lumberjacks, Cloudplay, The Heartbreakers, and The Dudley Brothers の 4 つのバンド名が挙げられている。無料、有料の両方の公演を行うのは The Heartbreakers と分かるので、正解は (A)。

185 What is implied about the 21st Rosemont Residents' Song Competition?

(A) All performances will be given on the main stage.

(B) It has received a record number of applicants.

(C) Its venue was changed after the article was published.

(D) There is a registration fee for participants.

第 21 回 Rosemont 市民歌唱コンテストについて何が示唆されていますか。

(A) すべての演奏がメインステージで行われる。

(B) それは最高応募者数を記録した。

(C) その開催場所は記事が発行された後に変更された。

(D) 参加者には登録料が課せられる。

正解 B

選択肢に着目するクロス問題

チラシには、this year the competition will be held over both days とあり、歌唱コンテストは 21 日と 22 日の両日行われることになったと分かる。そこで記事を見ると、恒例では歌唱コンテストは 2 日目に行われるとあるが、昨年より参加者が多ければ両日行われる予定と記されている。また、last year saw a record number of entrants「昨年の参加者は今までの最高数を記録した」とある。これらのことから、今年の参加者が昨年を超え、今までの最高数となったと判断できる。正解は (B)。

☐ venue　　　　　　　　　開催場所、会場

語彙チェック

☐ inception	始まり、開始	☐ erect	～を立てる、設置する
☐ act	出し物、芸人	☐ traditionally	伝統的に
☐ assemble	～を組み立てる	☐ entrant	参加者
☐ city council	市議会	☐ vary	変わる、変化する
☐ unfortunate	不運な	☐ respective	それぞれの

Questions 186-190 refer to the following e-mail, article, and schedule.

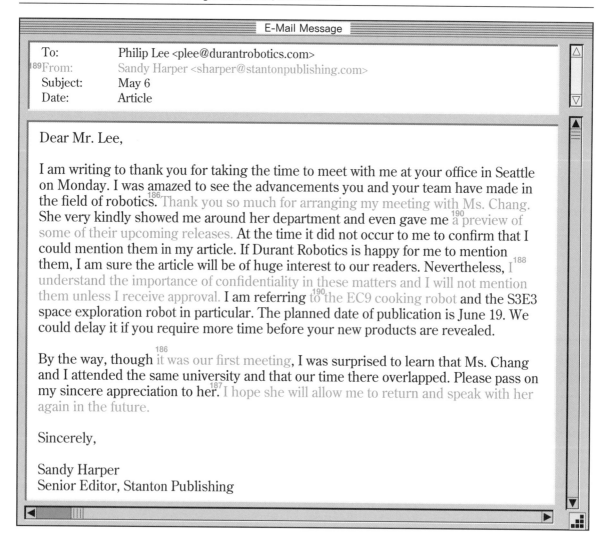

E-Mail Message

To: Philip Lee <plee@durantrobotics.com>
From: Sandy Harper <sharper@stantonpublishing.com>
Subject: May 6
Date: Article

Dear Mr. Lee,

I am writing to thank you for taking the time to meet with me at your office in Seattle on Monday. I was amazed to see the advancements you and your team have made in the field of robotics. Thank you so much for arranging my meeting with Ms. Chang. She very kindly showed me around her department and even gave me a preview of some of their upcoming releases. At the time it did not occur to me to confirm that I could mention them in my article. If Durant Robotics is happy for me to mention them, I am sure the article will be of huge interest to our readers. Nevertheless, I understand the importance of confidentiality in these matters and I will not mention them unless I receive approval. I am referring to the EC9 cooking robot and the S3E3 space exploration robot in particular. The planned date of publication is June 19. We could delay it if you require more time before your new products are revealed.

By the way, though it was our first meeting, I was surprised to learn that Ms. Chang and I attended the same university and that our time there overlapped. Please pass on my sincere appreciation to her. I hope she will allow me to return and speak with her again in the future.

Sincerely,

Sandy Harper
Senior Editor, Stanton Publishing

Durant Robotics Opens New Facility

By Sandy Harper
June 19

Durant Robotics is one of the most exciting companies in the robotics industry and their new facility in Bathurst is an architectural wonder. The head of design, Ms. Luisa Chang, is heading up a team of some of the world's most talented robotics engineers with a view to developing the next generation of robots, which will likely touch most of our daily lives. The facility employs some 300 people in its various departments including research, design, engineering, marketing, and production.

Durant Robotics' CEO, Philip Lee, stated that he expected the company to start mass producing robots for purchase by the general public within the two years. With this goal in mind, they are planning a new production facility in nearby Redmond. Work on that project should start early next year and they will be employing staff for the factory in late February.

問題 **186-190** は次の E メール、記事、予定表に関するものです。

宛先：Philip Lee <plee@durantrobotics.com>
送信者：Sandy Harper <sharper@stantonpublishing.com>
日付：5 月 6 日
件名：記事

Lee 様

月曜日にシアトルのあなたの事務所で私と会う時間を取っていただいたお礼を申し上げたくこれを書いています。ロボット工学の分野においてあなたとあなたのチームがなさってきた進歩を見て驚きました。Chang さんと私の面会を手配していただき本当にありがとうございます。彼女は親切にも彼女の部署を案内してくださり、今度発売の製品のいくつかの内見までさせてくださいました。そのときは、私の記事でそれらに言及してよいということを確認するなどということは思いつきませんでした。もし Durant ロボット社が私がそれらに言及することを喜んでくださるのでしたら、その記事は間違いなく私たちの読者にとって非常に興味深いものになるでしょう。しかし、こうした問題における機密性の重要さは理解しておりますので、同意いただかない限り記事で言及することはいたしません。特に EC9 料理ロボットと S3E3 宇宙探査ロボットに言及するつもりです。発行予定日は 6 月 19 日です。あなたの新製品が公になる前にもっと時間が必要であるなら、遅らせることもできます。

ところで、私たちは初めて会ったのですが、Chang さんと私は同じ大学に通っていて、在学期間が重なっていたと知って驚きました。彼女に私の心からの感謝をお伝えください。将来、再訪してまたお話しすることを彼女が許してくださればと願っています。

よろしくお願いします。

Sandy Harper
副編集長、Stanton 出版

Durant ロボット社、新施設を開設
Sandy Harper
6 月 19 日

Durant ロボット社はロボット工学業界で最も面白い会社の 1 つであり、そのバサーストの新施設は建築上の驚異である。設計リーダーの Luisa Chang 氏は私たちの日常生活のほとんどに関わるだろう次世代ロボットを開発することを目指して、世界で最も才能豊かなロボット工学エンジニアたち数人のチームを率いている。その施設は調査、デザイン、工学、マーケティング、生産を含む様々な部署でおよそ 300 名を雇う。

Durant ロボット社の最高経営責任者の Philip Lee 氏は、当社が 2 年以内に一般大衆が購入できるロボットの大量生産を始めることを期待していると述べた。この目標を胸に、彼らは新しい生産施設をレドモンドの近くに建設予定である。そのプロジェクトの作業は来年初めに始まり、2 月下旬にその工場のスタッフを雇う予定である。

From the desk of Luisa Chang

August

Sunday	Monday	Tuesday	Wednesday	Thursday	Friday	Saturday
12	13 Day off	14 2 P.M. Departmental meeting	15 Orientation for new staff members	16 [190] EC9 Product Launch	17 Freemantle Robotics Conference	18 Meeting with Tim Rice at HTO

| Luisa Chang の机から | | | | | | |

8月

日	月	火	水	木	金	土
12	13 休み	14 午後2時 部署会議	15 新スタッフのオリエンテーション	16 EC9　商品発売	17 Freemantle ロボット工学会議	18 HTO にて Tim Rice と面会

語彙チェック

☐ be amazed to *do*	～して驚く	☐ reveal	～を公開する
☐ advancement	進歩	☐ pass on ～	～を伝える
☐ robotics	ロボット工学	☐ sincere	心からの
☐ upcoming	来たる、次回の	☐ appreciation	感謝
☐ release	発売、公開作品	☐ facility	施設
☐ confidentiality	機密性	☐ architectural	建築の
☐ approval	許可	☐ wonder	驚異、奇跡
☐ refer to ～	～に言及する	☐ head up ～	～を率いる
☐ exploration	探査、探検	☐ with a view to ～	～を目指して
☐ delay	～を遅らせる		

What is one purpose of the e-mail?

(A) To express gratitude for an introduction

(B) To announce the launch of a new publication

(C) To request an introduction to a supplier

(D) To congratulate a colleague on a promotion

E メールの 1 つの目的は何ですか。

(A) 紹介してもらったことへの謝意を表すこと。

(B) 新しい出版物の発売を告知すること。

(C) 供給業者への紹介を依頼すること。

(D) 同僚の昇進を祝うこと。

正解 A

設問と選択肢に着目する問題

E メールの送信者である Harper さんは、冒頭で Lee さんが面会してくれたことに謝意を表し、次に、Thank you so much for arranging my meeting with Ms. Chang. と、Chang さんとの面会を手配してくれたことにも謝意を表している。その後、Chang さんとの面会について it was our first meeting と書いており、Chang さんを Lee さんが紹介してくれて初めて会ったと判断できる。(A) が正解。

187

What does Ms. Harper hope to do in the future?

(A) Take a position at Durant Robotics

(B) Bring forward the date of publication

(C) Purchase products from Durant Robotics

(D) Have another interview with Ms. Chang

Harper さんは将来何をすることを願っていますか。

(A) Durant ロボット社に就職する。

(B) 発行日を繰り上げる。

(C) Durant ロボット社の製品を購入する。

(D) Chang さんともう一度面会する。

正解 D

設問に着目する問題

E メールの最後で Harper さんは、Chang さんと通っていた大学が同じだったことを述べ、彼女によろしく伝えてほしいと Lee さんに頼んでいる。さらに I hope she will allow me to return and speak with her again in the future.「将来、再訪してまたお話することを彼女が許してくだされば願っている」と書いていることから、(D) が正解と判断できる。

188

What is suggested about Ms. Harper?

(A) She decided to delay the date of publication.

(B) She was asked not to write about certain technologies.

(C) She received assistance from her editor.

(D) She wrote the article as a freelance writer.

Harper さんについて何が分かりますか。

(A) 彼女は発行日を遅らせることに決めた。

(B) 彼女はある科学技術について書かないよう頼まれた。

(C) 彼女は編集者の力を借りた。

(D) 彼女はフリーランスのライターとして記事を書いた。

正解 B

選択肢に着目するクロス問題

E メールで、出版社の Harper さんは、I understand the importance of confidentiality in these matters and I will not mention them unless I receive approval.「こうした問題における機密性の重要さは理解しておりますので、同意いただかない限り記事で言及することはしない」と述べ、具体的には EC9 料理ロボットと S3E3 宇宙探査ロボットについてと説明している。記事の内容を見ると、売り出し予定のロボットについては一切述べられていないので、同意が得られなかったと判断できる。正解は (B)。

189 To whom did Ms. Harper send her e-mail?

(A) A company president

(B) A customer service officer

(C) A product designer

(D) A journalist

Harper さんは誰に E メールを送りましたか。

(A) 会社の社長

(B) 顧客サービス担当者

(C) 製品デザイナー

(D) ジャーナリスト

設問に着目するクロス問題

E メールの受信者は Philip Lee さんである。記事の中に、Durant Robotics' CEO, Philip Lee とあるので、Lee さんは、Durant ロボット社の CEO であることが分かる。正解は (A)。

190 What will Ms. Chang do on August 16?

(A) Demonstrate a flying robot for a client

(B) Take a follow-up meeting with a journalist

(C) Introduce a cooking robot to the market

(D) Make a presentation at an industry convention

Chang さんは 8 月 16 日に何をしますか。

(A) 顧客に空飛ぶロボットの実物宣伝をする。

(B) ジャーナリストと再度面会する。

(C) 料理ロボットを市場に披露する。

(D) 業界の大会でプレゼンテーションを行う。

設問に着目するクロス問題

Chang さんの 1 週間の予定表を見ると 8 月 16 日に、EC9 Product Launch「EC9　商品発売」とある。EC9 に関しては、E メールの中に、近日発表される新製品として、the EC9 cooking robot と述べられている。そのことを、introduce ～ to the market「市場に～を披露する」と言い表している (C) が正解。

Questions 191-195 refer to the following advertisement, e-mail, and review.

Maxwell Adventures

We have an amazing holiday adventure package for the travelers looking for something new, and it's for as little as $600. This is amazing value for a week unlike anything you've ever experienced. [191]Your first and last night will be enjoyed in Spandau Valley's only first-class hotel. The remaining five nights will be spent in the Canadian wilderness with a highly trained survival expert. You will learn to [191]fish for salmon in a pristine mountain stream, build a camp in uninhabited forests, and climb mountains to [191]take in breathtaking views of the Burroughs Range and beyond.

[193]For an additional $130, you can purchase airfare from anywhere in Canada to Bania, which is only a short train journey to the beautiful Spandau Valley.

To learn more or to reserve a [194]spot, check out the Maxwell Adventures Web site at www.maxwelladventures.com.

E-mail	
From:	Clementine Day <cday@novastar.com>
To:	Jim Maxwell <jm@maxwelladventures.com>
Subject:	Spandau Valley
Date:	August 12

I would like to commend Maxwell Adventures for putting together this excellent package. [193]They managed to get me an airplane ticket, even though I asked them to get it at the last minute. Moreover, the tour was excellent. If this is the standard for Maxwell Adventures, I would love to purchase another package for next year. Naturally, I would like to do something different from what I just did. [195]Perhaps a river rafting tour would be an interesting option for your company to offer. I promise I will be among the first people to make a reservation should you decide to offer such a package.

[192]I'm planning on advising some friends to take part so I was wondering if you have any special discount offers they could take advantage of.

Thanks,
Clementine Day

問題 **191-195** は次の広告、E メール、レビューに関するものです。

Maxwell Adventures 社

当社は新しいものを探している旅行者のためにすばらしい休暇の冒険パッケージ旅行を提供しており、お値段はたったの 600 ドルです。今までにご経験なさったものとは違い、1 週間にしては驚くべき価格です。初日と最終日のご宿泊は Spandau 渓谷唯一のファーストクラスホテルでお楽しみいただけます。残り 5 晩はカナダの原野にて、非常によく訓練されたサバイバルの専門家と一緒にお過ごしいただけます。山の清流での鮭釣りや人の住まない森でのキャンプ設営の方法、そして山を登って Burroughs 山脈とその向こうの息を飲むような景色を眺める方法を学ぶことができます。

130 ドルの追加料金を払うと、カナダの任意の地点から、美しい Spandau 渓谷まで電車ですぐの Bania への航空運賃を購入できます。

さらなる情報の入手やご予約には、Maxwell Adventures 社のウェブサイト www.maxwelladventures.com をご確認ください。

送信者：Clementine Day <cday@novastar.com>
宛先：Jim Maxwell <jm@maxwelladventures.com>
件名：Spandau 渓谷
日付：8 月 12 日

この優れたパッケージ旅行を企画した Maxwell Adventures 社をほめたいと思います。直前にお願いしたのにもかかわらず、なんとか航空券を用意してくれました。さらに、ツアーはすばらしかったです。もしこれが Maxwell Adventures 社の標準なのだとしたら、来年もぜひ別のパッケージ旅行を購入したいです。当然ながら、今年体験したのとは違うことがしたいです。もしかしたら、川下りツアーは提供したら面白い選択肢となるかもしれません。万が一そのようなパッケージ旅行を提供することを決められたなら、予約をする最初の客の一人となることをお約束します。

何人か友達に参加するようアドバイスするつもりなのですが、彼らが利用できる特別割引があるでしょうか。

よろしくお願いします。
Clementine Day

Reviews of Maxwell Adventures
Rating: ★★★★☆ Wonderful!
By: Clementine Day

I had a great time on this tour. Maxwell Adventures is a great little tour company run by some very professional and knowledgeable people.[195] I recently took part in a rafting trip down the Dawson River and it was one of the most enjoyable experiences of my life. This is a new tour and I was invited to take part as a rehearsal for the guides and organizers. The only shortcoming was that the accommodation was not as nice as that of their other tour.

Maxwell Adventures 社のレビュー
評価: ★★★★☆　すばらしい!
レビュアー:　Clementine Day
私はこのツアーですばらしいときを過ごしました。Maxwell Adventures 社はプロの、博識な人々が運営している、小規模ながらすばらしいツアー会社です。私は最近、Dawson 川での川下りツアーに参加しましたが、それは人生で最も楽しい経験の 1 つでした。これは新しいツアーで、私はガイドと主催者の予行演習として参加するよう招待されました。唯一の欠点は、宿泊施設が同社の他のツアーほどよくはなかったということです。

語彙チェック

☐	remaining	残りの	☐ commend	～をほめる
☐	wilderness	荒野、手つかずの自然	☐ take advantage of ～	～をうまく活用する
☐	pristine	汚れのない	☐ run	～を運営する
☐	uninhabited	無人の	☐ rehearsal	リハーサル
☐	breathtaking	息を飲む	☐ shortcoming	欠点
☐	airfare	航空運賃	☐ accommodation	宿泊施設

What is NOT mentioned as an attraction of the Spandau Valley?

(A) A pure river

(B) Luxury accommodation

(C) Traditional architecture

(D) Stunning scenery

Spandau 渓谷の魅力として述べられていないものは何ですか。

(A) 澄んだ川

(B) 高級宿泊施設

(C) 伝統的な建築

(D) すばらしい景色

正解 C

NOT 問題

広告で宣伝されているのが Spandau 渓谷のツアーである。fish for salmon in a pristine mountain stream とあり、そこにある川が鮭釣りができるほどの pristine「手つかずの」川と述べられているので、(A) はそれに一致する。(B) は be enjoyed in Spandau Valley's only first-class hotel と一致する。また、登山では take in breathtaking views of the Burroughs Range and beyond とあるので、(D) が一致する。建築物については言及がないので、(C) が正解。

☐ stunning　　　　　　　　　　　すばらしい、美しい

What is one purpose of the e-mail?

(A) To commend a specific employee

(B) To reserve a seat on a vehicle

(C) To explain the reason for a delay

(D) To inquire about special prices

E メールの 1 つの目的は何ですか。

(A) 特定の従業員をほめること。

(B) 乗り物の座席を予約すること。

(C) 遅延の理由を説明すること。

(D) 特別価格について尋ねること。

正解 D

選択肢に着目する問題

E メールの目的は複数あるので、選択肢を 1 つ 1 つ検討する必要がある。冒頭で旅行会社を賛辞しているが、特定の従業員をほめてはいないので、(A) は不適切。乗り物の予約や、遅延に関する記述はないので、(B) と (C) も不適切。メールの最後に I'm planning on advising some friends to take part so I was wondering if you have any special discount offers they could take advantage of. とあり、紹介する友人たちが利用できる特別割引があるかどうかを尋ねているので、(D) が正解。

What is suggested about Ms. Day?

(A) She had taken part in the tour before.

(B) She paid a supplemental fee.

(C) She viewed the advertisement on television.

(D) She lives near the town of Bania.

Day さんについて何が分かりますか。

(A) 彼女は以前にもツアーに参加したことがある。

(B) 彼女は追加料金を支払った。

(C) 彼女はテレビで広告を見た。

(D) 彼女は Bania の町の近くに住んでいる。

正解 B

選択肢に着目するクロス問題

Day さんは E メールで、They managed to get me an airplane ticket, even though I asked them to get it in the last minutes. と述べており、旅行会社から航空券も購入したことが分かる。また、広告を見ると、For an additional $130, you can purchase airfare from anywhere in Canada to Bania「130 ドルの追加料金を払うと、カナダの任意の地点から Bania への航空運賃を購入できる」と説明がある。したがって、彼女は航空券代として 130 ドルを追加で支払ったと考えられるので、(B) が正解。additional を supplemental「追加の」と言い換えている。

194

In the advertisement, the word "spot" in paragraph 3, line 1 is closest in meaning to

(A) seat

(B) mark

(C) deal

(D) cause

広告の第 3 段落・1 行目にある spot に最も意味が近いのは

(A) 席

(B) しみ

(C) 取り引き

(D) 原因

正解 A

同義語問題

spot を含む文はツアー会社のツアーの広告の最後の文で、「ツアーの詳細や予約をするためにはウェブサイトを確認ください」ということが述べられている。spot には「場所」という意味があるが、reserve a spot「場所を予約する」、つまり「予約席を確保する」ということを表していると判断できるので、最も意味が近いのは、(A) の seat「（予約）席」。

195

What is most likely true about Maxwell Adventures?

(A) It has been mentioned in a television documentary.

(B) It employs people who speak different languages.

(C) It offers tours outside Canada.

(D) It adopted Ms. Day's idea.

Maxwell Adventures 社について正しいと考えられることは何ですか。

(A) それはテレビのドキュメンタリーで言及された。

(B) それは様々な言語を話す人々を雇っている。

(C) それはカナダ国外のツアーを提供している。

(D) それは Day さんの案を採用した。

正解 D

選択肢に着目するクロス問題

Day さんは、E メールの送信者であり、かつレビューの執筆者。E メールでは Maxwell Adventures 社がよかったことと同時に、Perhaps a river rafting tour would be an interesting option for your company to offer. I promise I will be among the first people to make a reservation should you decide to offer such a package. と、川下りツアーの企画を希望していることが分かる。また、彼女はレビューで I recently took part in a rafting trip down the Dawson River と書いており、彼女の希望した川下りツアーが実現したと判断できる。正解は (D)。

Questions 196-200 refer to the following e-mail, schedule, and Web site.

From:	Igor Popov <ipopov@goldburgassociates.com>
To:	Sally Winger <swinger@donaldadvertisinggroup.com>
Subject:	Sheffield Advertising Awards
Date:	March 13

Dear Ms. Winger,

196It is my great pleasure to inform you that your company is one of those nominated for this year's Sheffield Advertising Awards. It is very important to the organizers that all nominees be in attendance at the ceremony. To remain in contention for a prize, a member of the staff of Donald Advertising must attend the event. While we would prefer it if a member of the team involved in the production attended, any member of the staff may accept the prize.197In both cases, it is expected that award recipients will give a short acceptance speech. Please reply to this e-mail with the name of the person who will be attending the event by March 23. Otherwise, the nomination will be198 passed on to the creators of another of the qualifying advertisements.

Please visit the Sheffield Advertising Awards Web site at www.sheffieldaa.com to purchase tickets. 200Due to the modest size of the Hanson Convention Center, you are limited to two representatives for each nomination. Each ticket costs $120. The awards ceremony includes a number of speeches as well as entertainment from local artists. This year we will be entertained by local comedian, Jerry Wiseacre.199

Best regards,
Igor Popov

Sheffield Advertising Awards Ceremony
Hanson Convention Center, June 12, 6:00 P.M.
(Tentative Schedule as of March 20)

Time	Presentation	Speaker (s)	Award Recipient
6:00	Dinner		N/A
7:00	Award for Greatest Sales Influence	Barry Day and Tina Sales	To be announced
7:15	Award for Best Use of Music	Valerie Chang	To be announced
7:30	Award for Best Special Effects	Jose Ramirez	To be announced
7:45	199Entertainment — The Comedy of Holly Durant	Holly Durant	N/A
8:15	Award for Best Direction	Cloe Tanaka	To be announced
8:30	Keynote Speech: Truth in Advertising	Tim Clement, BTR Consultants	N/A

送信者：Igor Popov <ipopov@goldburgassociates.com>
宛先：Sally Winger <swinger@donaldadvertisinggroup.com>
件名：Sheffield 広告賞
日付：3 月 13 日

Winger 様

貴社が今年の Sheffield 広告賞にノミネートされた会社の 1 つとなっていることを喜んでお知らせいたします。主催者にとっては、すべてのノミネートされた会社が式典に出席することが非常に大切です。受賞の対象であり続けるには、Donald 広告社のスタッフの一人がイベントに出席しなければなりません。制作に関わるチームのメンバーにご出席いただける方がよいのですが、スタッフのどなたが賞を受け取ってもかまいません。どちらの場合でも、受賞者が短い受賞のスピーチをすることが期待されています。3 月 23 日までに、イベントに出席される方のご氏名を添えてこの E メールにご返信ください。そうされない場合、ノミネートは資格のある別の広告の制作者に移ることになります。

チケット購入のために、Sheffield 広告賞のウェブサイト www.sheffieldaa.com にアクセスしてください。Hanson 会議センターはあまり広くありませんので、1 つのノミネートについて 2 人の代表者までに限らせていただきます。チケットは 1 枚 120 ドルです。授賞式は地元アーティストによる余興とともに多くのスピーチを含みます。今年は地元のコメディアン Jerry Wiseacre が出演します。

よろしくお願いします。
Igor Popov

Sheffield 広告賞授賞式
Hanson 会議センター、6 月 12 日、午後 6 時
（3 月 20 日現在の暫定予定表）

時刻	発表	発表者	受賞者
6:00	夕食会		なし
7:00	最優秀販売促進賞	Barry Day、Tina Sales	未発表
7:15	最優秀音楽賞	Valerie Chang	未発表
7:30	最優秀特殊効果賞	Jose Ramirez	未発表
7:45	余興 — Holly Durant の喜劇	Holly Durant	なし
8:15	最優秀監督賞	Cloe Tanaka	未発表
8:30	基調講演：広告の真実	Tim Clement、BTR Consultants	なし

Sheffield Advertising Awards
— Reservations Page —

Name of Ticket Holder	Company	Preferred Table	Price
[200]Sally Winger	Donald Advertising	Table B	$120.00
Ralph Xenedes	Donald Advertising	Table B	$120.00
Jill Forbes	Donald Advertising	Table B	$120.00
Tobe Salinger	Donald Advertising	Table B	$120.00
		TOTAL	$480.00

PURCHASE

https://www.sheffieldaa.com/reservations

Sheffield 広告賞
―予約ページ―

チケット所有者名	会社名	希望のテーブル	価格
Sally Winger	Donald 広告社	テーブル B	120.00 ドル
Ralph Xenedes	Donald 広告社	テーブル B	120.00 ドル
Jill Forbes	Donald 広告社	テーブル B	120.00 ドル
Tobe Salinger	Donald 広告社	テーブル B	120.00 ドル
		合計	480.00 ドル

購入

What is a purpose of the e-mail?

(A) To request permission to host a ceremony

(B) To notify an award nominee

(C) To assign duties to an organizer

(D) To propose a change to competition guidelines

Ｅメールの目的は何ですか。

(A) 式典を主催する許可を申請すること。

(B) 授賞候補者に通知すること。

(C) 主催者に仕事を割り当てること。

(D) コンテストのガイドラインの変更を提案すること。

正解 B

設問と選択肢に着目する問題

質問文で What is a purpose ～と尋ねているので、Ｅメールの目的は複数あると判断できる。したがって、選択肢を１つずつ検討する必要がある。冒頭に、It is my great pleasure to inform you that your company is one of those nominated for this year's Sheffield Advertising Awards.「貴社が今年の Sheffield 広告賞にノミネートされた会社の１つとなっていることを喜んでお知らせいたします」とあるので、(B) が正解。nominee は「候補に指名された人」という意味。(A)、(C)、(D) については言及がない。

☐ assign A to B　　　　　　　　　　A を B に割り当てる

According to the e-mail, what is true about award recipients?

(A) They must prepare an acceptance message.

(B) They must be those who were directly involved in its production.

(C) They are chosen by the organizing committee.

(D) They can only be nominated in one category.

Ｅメールによると、賞の受取人について正しいことは何ですか。

(A) 受賞メッセージを準備しなければならない。

(B) その制作に直接関わった人でなければならない。

(C) 組織委員会によって選ばれる。

(D) １つのカテゴリーでしかノミネートされることができない。

正解 A

選択肢に着目する問題

賞を受け取る際のことは、Ｅメールに In both cases, it is expected that award recipients will give a short acceptance speech.「どちらの場合でも、受賞者が短い受賞のスピーチをすることが期待されている」とあることから正解は (A)。

In the e-mail, the phrase "passed on" in paragraph 1, line 7 is closest in meaning to

(A) rejected

(B) affirmed

(C) transferred

(D) revealed

Ｅメールの第 1 段落・7 行目にある passed on に最も意味が近いのは

(A) 拒絶される

(B) 断言される

(C) 移動される

(D) 明らかにされる

正解 C

同義語問題

passed on を含む文の前では、授賞式出席者の氏名を返信するように促している。そうでない場合は the nomination will be passed on to the creators of another of the qualifying advertisements とあるので、資格のある他の広告制作者に候補が「移される」という意味だと考えられる。最も意味が近いのは (C) の transferred。

199 What is suggested about the awards ceremony?

(A) The audience was too large for the original venue.

(B) A number of nominations were changed.

(C) A change was made to the entertainment.

(D) An award was presented by the previous winner.

授賞式について何が分かりますか。

(A) 観客がもともとの開催場所には多過ぎた。

(B) 多くのノミネートに変更があった。

(C) 余興に変更があった。

(D) 賞は前回の受賞者によって授与される。

正解 **C**

選択肢に着目するクロス問題

受賞候補を伝える 3 月 13 日付けの E メールの最後で、授賞式での余興について述べられている。This year we will be entertained by local comedian, Jerry Wiseacre. とあり、コメディアンの Jerry Wiseacre が出演することが分かるが、3 月 20 日現在の予定表では、余興の出演者は Holly Durant と変更されている。したがって、正解は (C)。

200 What is most likely true about Donald Advertising?

(A) It has won awards at the event in previous years.

(B) It was asked to organize next year's event.

(C) It is known for its use of special effects.

(D) It was nominated for multiple awards.

Donald 広告社について正しいと考えられることは何ですか。

(A) それは以前の年にそのイベントで賞を勝ち取った。

(B) それは来年のイベントを主催するよう求められた。

(C) それは特殊効果の使用で知られている。

(D) それは複数の賞でノミネートされた。

正解 **D**

選択肢に着目するクロス問題

E メールには、受賞のためには、チケットを購入して授賞式に出席することが必要と述べられており、さらに Due to the modest size of the Hanson Convention Center, you are limited to two representatives for each nomination. 「Hanson 会議センターはあまり広くありませんので、1 つのノミネートについて 2 人の代表者までに限られる」とある。ウェブサイトの予約ページには、Donald 広告社の 4 人の予約が示されているので、同社は 2 件以上のノミネートを受けていると判断できる。正解は (D)。

Day 50

【TEST 4 Questions 147-175】　2/5回目

Day 50は、Day 40～44で解いたシングルパッセージ10題をもう一度まとめて解く日です。別冊TEST 4の147番～175番（別冊P75～85）を解きましょう。制限時間は29分です。解き終わったら、解説はDay 40～44の解説ページ（本冊P158～177）を見て確認してください。

Day 51

【TEST 4 Questions 176-200】　2/5回目

Day 51は、Day 45～49で解いたマルチプルパッセージ5題をもう一度まとめて解く日です。別冊TEST 4の176番～200番（別冊P86～95）を解きましょう。制限時間は25分です。解き終わったら、解説はDay 45～49の解説ページ（本冊P178～203）を見て確認してください。

Day 52

【TEST 4 Questions 147-200】　3/5回目

Day 52は、Day 50～51で解いた問題をまとめて解く日です。別冊TEST 4の147番～200番（別冊P75～95）を解きましょう。制限時間は54分です。解き終わったら、解説はDay 40～49の解説ページ（本冊P158～203）を見て確認してください。

Day 53〜60

Day 53〜60は最後の総仕上げです。1日に1模試分のPart 7の問題を解いてください。学習の進め方については別冊P96をご覧ください。

Day 53 【TEST 1 Questions 147-200】　4/5回目
問題：別冊P3〜23　　　解説：本冊P14〜59

Day 54 【TEST 2 Questions 147-200】　4/5回目
問題：別冊P27〜47　　　解説：本冊P62〜107

Day 55 【TEST 3 Questions 147-200】　4/5回目
問題：別冊P51〜71　　　解説：本冊P110〜155

Day 56 【TEST 4 Questions 147-200】　4/5回目
問題：別冊P75〜95　　　解説：本冊P158〜203

Day 57 【TEST 1 Questions 147-200】　5/5回目
問題：別冊P3〜23　　　解説：本冊P14〜59

Day 58 【TEST 2 Questions 147-200】　5/5回目
問題：別冊P27〜47　　　解説：本冊P62〜107

Day 59 【TEST 3 Questions 147-200】　5/5回目
問題：別冊P51〜71　　　解説：本冊P110〜155

Day 60 【TEST 4 Questions 147-200】　5/5回目
問題：別冊P75〜95　　　解説：本冊P158〜203

990点獲得
Part 7 専用マークシート
（コピーしてお使いください）

本書では、4模試分のPart 7の問題を5回ずつ解くため、
5回分のPart 7専用マークシートを用意しました。
本番さながらにマークシートを使って問題を解くようにしましょう。

TEST ☐

1回目

Part 7

No.	ANSWER A B C D	No.	ANSWER A B C D	No.	ANSWER A B C D	No.	ANSWER A B C D	No.	ANSWER A B C D
151	Ⓐ Ⓑ Ⓒ Ⓓ	161	Ⓐ Ⓑ Ⓒ Ⓓ	171	Ⓐ Ⓑ Ⓒ Ⓓ	181	Ⓐ Ⓑ Ⓒ Ⓓ	191	Ⓐ Ⓑ Ⓒ Ⓓ
152	Ⓐ Ⓑ Ⓒ Ⓓ	162	Ⓐ Ⓑ Ⓒ Ⓓ	172	Ⓐ Ⓑ Ⓒ Ⓓ	182	Ⓐ Ⓑ Ⓒ Ⓓ	192	Ⓐ Ⓑ Ⓒ Ⓓ
153	Ⓐ Ⓑ Ⓒ Ⓓ	163	Ⓐ Ⓑ Ⓒ Ⓓ	173	Ⓐ Ⓑ Ⓒ Ⓓ	183	Ⓐ Ⓑ Ⓒ Ⓓ	193	Ⓐ Ⓑ Ⓒ Ⓓ
154	Ⓐ Ⓑ Ⓒ Ⓓ	164	Ⓐ Ⓑ Ⓒ Ⓓ	174	Ⓐ Ⓑ Ⓒ Ⓓ	184	Ⓐ Ⓑ Ⓒ Ⓓ	194	Ⓐ Ⓑ Ⓒ Ⓓ
155	Ⓐ Ⓑ Ⓒ Ⓓ	165	Ⓐ Ⓑ Ⓒ Ⓓ	175	Ⓐ Ⓑ Ⓒ Ⓓ	185	Ⓐ Ⓑ Ⓒ Ⓓ	195	Ⓐ Ⓑ Ⓒ Ⓓ
156	Ⓐ Ⓑ Ⓒ Ⓓ	166	Ⓐ Ⓑ Ⓒ Ⓓ	176	Ⓐ Ⓑ Ⓒ Ⓓ	186	Ⓐ Ⓑ Ⓒ Ⓓ	196	Ⓐ Ⓑ Ⓒ Ⓓ
157	Ⓐ Ⓑ Ⓒ Ⓓ	167	Ⓐ Ⓑ Ⓒ Ⓓ	177	Ⓐ Ⓑ Ⓒ Ⓓ	187	Ⓐ Ⓑ Ⓒ Ⓓ	197	Ⓐ Ⓑ Ⓒ Ⓓ
158	Ⓐ Ⓑ Ⓒ Ⓓ	168	Ⓐ Ⓑ Ⓒ Ⓓ	178	Ⓐ Ⓑ Ⓒ Ⓓ	188	Ⓐ Ⓑ Ⓒ Ⓓ	198	Ⓐ Ⓑ Ⓒ Ⓓ
159	Ⓐ Ⓑ Ⓒ Ⓓ	169	Ⓐ Ⓑ Ⓒ Ⓓ	179	Ⓐ Ⓑ Ⓒ Ⓓ	189	Ⓐ Ⓑ Ⓒ Ⓓ	199	Ⓐ Ⓑ Ⓒ Ⓓ
160	Ⓐ Ⓑ Ⓒ Ⓓ	170	Ⓐ Ⓑ Ⓒ Ⓓ	180	Ⓐ Ⓑ Ⓒ Ⓓ	190	Ⓐ Ⓑ Ⓒ Ⓓ	200	Ⓐ Ⓑ Ⓒ Ⓓ

147	Ⓐ Ⓑ Ⓒ Ⓓ
148	Ⓐ Ⓑ Ⓒ Ⓓ
149	Ⓐ Ⓑ Ⓒ Ⓓ
150	Ⓐ Ⓑ Ⓒ Ⓓ

2回目

Part 7

No.	ANSWER A B C D	No.	ANSWER A B C D	No.	ANSWER A B C D	No.	ANSWER A B C D	No.	ANSWER A B C D
151	Ⓐ Ⓑ Ⓒ Ⓓ	161	Ⓐ Ⓑ Ⓒ Ⓓ	171	Ⓐ Ⓑ Ⓒ Ⓓ	181	Ⓐ Ⓑ Ⓒ Ⓓ	191	Ⓐ Ⓑ Ⓒ Ⓓ
152	Ⓐ Ⓑ Ⓒ Ⓓ	162	Ⓐ Ⓑ Ⓒ Ⓓ	172	Ⓐ Ⓑ Ⓒ Ⓓ	182	Ⓐ Ⓑ Ⓒ Ⓓ	192	Ⓐ Ⓑ Ⓒ Ⓓ
153	Ⓐ Ⓑ Ⓒ Ⓓ	163	Ⓐ Ⓑ Ⓒ Ⓓ	173	Ⓐ Ⓑ Ⓒ Ⓓ	183	Ⓐ Ⓑ Ⓒ Ⓓ	193	Ⓐ Ⓑ Ⓒ Ⓓ
154	Ⓐ Ⓑ Ⓒ Ⓓ	164	Ⓐ Ⓑ Ⓒ Ⓓ	174	Ⓐ Ⓑ Ⓒ Ⓓ	184	Ⓐ Ⓑ Ⓒ Ⓓ	194	Ⓐ Ⓑ Ⓒ Ⓓ
155	Ⓐ Ⓑ Ⓒ Ⓓ	165	Ⓐ Ⓑ Ⓒ Ⓓ	175	Ⓐ Ⓑ Ⓒ Ⓓ	185	Ⓐ Ⓑ Ⓒ Ⓓ	195	Ⓐ Ⓑ Ⓒ Ⓓ
156	Ⓐ Ⓑ Ⓒ Ⓓ	166	Ⓐ Ⓑ Ⓒ Ⓓ	176	Ⓐ Ⓑ Ⓒ Ⓓ	186	Ⓐ Ⓑ Ⓒ Ⓓ	196	Ⓐ Ⓑ Ⓒ Ⓓ
157	Ⓐ Ⓑ Ⓒ Ⓓ	167	Ⓐ Ⓑ Ⓒ Ⓓ	177	Ⓐ Ⓑ Ⓒ Ⓓ	187	Ⓐ Ⓑ Ⓒ Ⓓ	197	Ⓐ Ⓑ Ⓒ Ⓓ
158	Ⓐ Ⓑ Ⓒ Ⓓ	168	Ⓐ Ⓑ Ⓒ Ⓓ	178	Ⓐ Ⓑ Ⓒ Ⓓ	188	Ⓐ Ⓑ Ⓒ Ⓓ	198	Ⓐ Ⓑ Ⓒ Ⓓ
159	Ⓐ Ⓑ Ⓒ Ⓓ	169	Ⓐ Ⓑ Ⓒ Ⓓ	179	Ⓐ Ⓑ Ⓒ Ⓓ	189	Ⓐ Ⓑ Ⓒ Ⓓ	199	Ⓐ Ⓑ Ⓒ Ⓓ
160	Ⓐ Ⓑ Ⓒ Ⓓ	170	Ⓐ Ⓑ Ⓒ Ⓓ	180	Ⓐ Ⓑ Ⓒ Ⓓ	190	Ⓐ Ⓑ Ⓒ Ⓓ	200	Ⓐ Ⓑ Ⓒ Ⓓ

147	Ⓐ Ⓑ Ⓒ Ⓓ
148	Ⓐ Ⓑ Ⓒ Ⓓ
149	Ⓐ Ⓑ Ⓒ Ⓓ
150	Ⓐ Ⓑ Ⓒ Ⓓ

3回目

Part 7

No.	ANSWER A B C D	No.	ANSWER A B C D	No.	ANSWER A B C D	No.	ANSWER A B C D	No.	ANSWER A B C D
		151	Ⓐ Ⓑ Ⓒ Ⓓ	161	Ⓐ Ⓑ Ⓒ Ⓓ	171	Ⓐ Ⓑ Ⓒ Ⓓ	181	Ⓐ Ⓑ Ⓒ Ⓓ	191	Ⓐ Ⓑ Ⓒ Ⓓ
		152	Ⓐ Ⓑ Ⓒ Ⓓ	162	Ⓐ Ⓑ Ⓒ Ⓓ	172	Ⓐ Ⓑ Ⓒ Ⓓ	182	Ⓐ Ⓑ Ⓒ Ⓓ	192	Ⓐ Ⓑ Ⓒ Ⓓ
		153	Ⓐ Ⓑ Ⓒ Ⓓ	163	Ⓐ Ⓑ Ⓒ Ⓓ	173	Ⓐ Ⓑ Ⓒ Ⓓ	183	Ⓐ Ⓑ Ⓒ Ⓓ	193	Ⓐ Ⓑ Ⓒ Ⓓ
		154	Ⓐ Ⓑ Ⓒ Ⓓ	164	Ⓐ Ⓑ Ⓒ Ⓓ	174	Ⓐ Ⓑ Ⓒ Ⓓ	184	Ⓐ Ⓑ Ⓒ Ⓓ	194	Ⓐ Ⓑ Ⓒ Ⓓ
		155	Ⓐ Ⓑ Ⓒ Ⓓ	165	Ⓐ Ⓑ Ⓒ Ⓓ	175	Ⓐ Ⓑ Ⓒ Ⓓ	185	Ⓐ Ⓑ Ⓒ Ⓓ	195	Ⓐ Ⓑ Ⓒ Ⓓ
		156	Ⓐ Ⓑ Ⓒ Ⓓ	166	Ⓐ Ⓑ Ⓒ Ⓓ	176	Ⓐ Ⓑ Ⓒ Ⓓ	186	Ⓐ Ⓑ Ⓒ Ⓓ	196	Ⓐ Ⓑ Ⓒ Ⓓ
147	Ⓐ Ⓑ Ⓒ Ⓓ	157	Ⓐ Ⓑ Ⓒ Ⓓ	167	Ⓐ Ⓑ Ⓒ Ⓓ	177	Ⓐ Ⓑ Ⓒ Ⓓ	187	Ⓐ Ⓑ Ⓒ Ⓓ	197	Ⓐ Ⓑ Ⓒ Ⓓ
148	Ⓐ Ⓑ Ⓒ Ⓓ	158	Ⓐ Ⓑ Ⓒ Ⓓ	168	Ⓐ Ⓑ Ⓒ Ⓓ	178	Ⓐ Ⓑ Ⓒ Ⓓ	188	Ⓐ Ⓑ Ⓒ Ⓓ	198	Ⓐ Ⓑ Ⓒ Ⓓ
149	Ⓐ Ⓑ Ⓒ Ⓓ	159	Ⓐ Ⓑ Ⓒ Ⓓ	169	Ⓐ Ⓑ Ⓒ Ⓓ	179	Ⓐ Ⓑ Ⓒ Ⓓ	189	Ⓐ Ⓑ Ⓒ Ⓓ	199	Ⓐ Ⓑ Ⓒ Ⓓ
150	Ⓐ Ⓑ Ⓒ Ⓓ	160	Ⓐ Ⓑ Ⓒ Ⓓ	170	Ⓐ Ⓑ Ⓒ Ⓓ	180	Ⓐ Ⓑ Ⓒ Ⓓ	190	Ⓐ Ⓑ Ⓒ Ⓓ	200	Ⓐ Ⓑ Ⓒ Ⓓ

4回目

Part 7

No.	ANSWER A B C D	No.	ANSWER A B C D	No.	ANSWER A B C D	No.	ANSWER A B C D	No.	ANSWER A B C D
		151	Ⓐ Ⓑ Ⓒ Ⓓ	161	Ⓐ Ⓑ Ⓒ Ⓓ	171	Ⓐ Ⓑ Ⓒ Ⓓ	181	Ⓐ Ⓑ Ⓒ Ⓓ	191	Ⓐ Ⓑ Ⓒ Ⓓ
		152	Ⓐ Ⓑ Ⓒ Ⓓ	162	Ⓐ Ⓑ Ⓒ Ⓓ	172	Ⓐ Ⓑ Ⓒ Ⓓ	182	Ⓐ Ⓑ Ⓒ Ⓓ	192	Ⓐ Ⓑ Ⓒ Ⓓ
		153	Ⓐ Ⓑ Ⓒ Ⓓ	163	Ⓐ Ⓑ Ⓒ Ⓓ	173	Ⓐ Ⓑ Ⓒ Ⓓ	183	Ⓐ Ⓑ Ⓒ Ⓓ	193	Ⓐ Ⓑ Ⓒ Ⓓ
		154	Ⓐ Ⓑ Ⓒ Ⓓ	164	Ⓐ Ⓑ Ⓒ Ⓓ	174	Ⓐ Ⓑ Ⓒ Ⓓ	184	Ⓐ Ⓑ Ⓒ Ⓓ	194	Ⓐ Ⓑ Ⓒ Ⓓ
		155	Ⓐ Ⓑ Ⓒ Ⓓ	165	Ⓐ Ⓑ Ⓒ Ⓓ	175	Ⓐ Ⓑ Ⓒ Ⓓ	185	Ⓐ Ⓑ Ⓒ Ⓓ	195	Ⓐ Ⓑ Ⓒ Ⓓ
		156	Ⓐ Ⓑ Ⓒ Ⓓ	166	Ⓐ Ⓑ Ⓒ Ⓓ	176	Ⓐ Ⓑ Ⓒ Ⓓ	186	Ⓐ Ⓑ Ⓒ Ⓓ	196	Ⓐ Ⓑ Ⓒ Ⓓ
147	Ⓐ Ⓑ Ⓒ Ⓓ	157	Ⓐ Ⓑ Ⓒ Ⓓ	167	Ⓐ Ⓑ Ⓒ Ⓓ	177	Ⓐ Ⓑ Ⓒ Ⓓ	187	Ⓐ Ⓑ Ⓒ Ⓓ	197	Ⓐ Ⓑ Ⓒ Ⓓ
148	Ⓐ Ⓑ Ⓒ Ⓓ	158	Ⓐ Ⓑ Ⓒ Ⓓ	168	Ⓐ Ⓑ Ⓒ Ⓓ	178	Ⓐ Ⓑ Ⓒ Ⓓ	188	Ⓐ Ⓑ Ⓒ Ⓓ	198	Ⓐ Ⓑ Ⓒ Ⓓ
149	Ⓐ Ⓑ Ⓒ Ⓓ	159	Ⓐ Ⓑ Ⓒ Ⓓ	169	Ⓐ Ⓑ Ⓒ Ⓓ	179	Ⓐ Ⓑ Ⓒ Ⓓ	189	Ⓐ Ⓑ Ⓒ Ⓓ	199	Ⓐ Ⓑ Ⓒ Ⓓ
150	Ⓐ Ⓑ Ⓒ Ⓓ	160	Ⓐ Ⓑ Ⓒ Ⓓ	170	Ⓐ Ⓑ Ⓒ Ⓓ	180	Ⓐ Ⓑ Ⓒ Ⓓ	190	Ⓐ Ⓑ Ⓒ Ⓓ	200	Ⓐ Ⓑ Ⓒ Ⓓ

5回目

Part 7

No.	ANSWER A B C D	No.	ANSWER A B C D	No.	ANSWER A B C D	No.	ANSWER A B C D	No.	ANSWER A B C D
		151	Ⓐ Ⓑ Ⓒ Ⓓ	161	Ⓐ Ⓑ Ⓒ Ⓓ	171	Ⓐ Ⓑ Ⓒ Ⓓ	181	Ⓐ Ⓑ Ⓒ Ⓓ	191	Ⓐ Ⓑ Ⓒ Ⓓ
		152	Ⓐ Ⓑ Ⓒ Ⓓ	162	Ⓐ Ⓑ Ⓒ Ⓓ	172	Ⓐ Ⓑ Ⓒ Ⓓ	182	Ⓐ Ⓑ Ⓒ Ⓓ	192	Ⓐ Ⓑ Ⓒ Ⓓ
		153	Ⓐ Ⓑ Ⓒ Ⓓ	163	Ⓐ Ⓑ Ⓒ Ⓓ	173	Ⓐ Ⓑ Ⓒ Ⓓ	183	Ⓐ Ⓑ Ⓒ Ⓓ	193	Ⓐ Ⓑ Ⓒ Ⓓ
		154	Ⓐ Ⓑ Ⓒ Ⓓ	164	Ⓐ Ⓑ Ⓒ Ⓓ	174	Ⓐ Ⓑ Ⓒ Ⓓ	184	Ⓐ Ⓑ Ⓒ Ⓓ	194	Ⓐ Ⓑ Ⓒ Ⓓ
		155	Ⓐ Ⓑ Ⓒ Ⓓ	165	Ⓐ Ⓑ Ⓒ Ⓓ	175	Ⓐ Ⓑ Ⓒ Ⓓ	185	Ⓐ Ⓑ Ⓒ Ⓓ	195	Ⓐ Ⓑ Ⓒ Ⓓ
		156	Ⓐ Ⓑ Ⓒ Ⓓ	166	Ⓐ Ⓑ Ⓒ Ⓓ	176	Ⓐ Ⓑ Ⓒ Ⓓ	186	Ⓐ Ⓑ Ⓒ Ⓓ	196	Ⓐ Ⓑ Ⓒ Ⓓ
147	Ⓐ Ⓑ Ⓒ Ⓓ	157	Ⓐ Ⓑ Ⓒ Ⓓ	167	Ⓐ Ⓑ Ⓒ Ⓓ	177	Ⓐ Ⓑ Ⓒ Ⓓ	187	Ⓐ Ⓑ Ⓒ Ⓓ	197	Ⓐ Ⓑ Ⓒ Ⓓ
148	Ⓐ Ⓑ Ⓒ Ⓓ	158	Ⓐ Ⓑ Ⓒ Ⓓ	168	Ⓐ Ⓑ Ⓒ Ⓓ	178	Ⓐ Ⓑ Ⓒ Ⓓ	188	Ⓐ Ⓑ Ⓒ Ⓓ	198	Ⓐ Ⓑ Ⓒ Ⓓ
149	Ⓐ Ⓑ Ⓒ Ⓓ	159	Ⓐ Ⓑ Ⓒ Ⓓ	169	Ⓐ Ⓑ Ⓒ Ⓓ	179	Ⓐ Ⓑ Ⓒ Ⓓ	189	Ⓐ Ⓑ Ⓒ Ⓓ	199	Ⓐ Ⓑ Ⓒ Ⓓ
150	Ⓐ Ⓑ Ⓒ Ⓓ	160	Ⓐ Ⓑ Ⓒ Ⓓ	170	Ⓐ Ⓑ Ⓒ Ⓓ	180	Ⓐ Ⓑ Ⓒ Ⓓ	190	Ⓐ Ⓑ Ⓒ Ⓓ	200	Ⓐ Ⓑ Ⓒ Ⓓ

著者紹介

株式会社メディアビーコン（Media Beacon）

▶1999 年創業。語学教材に特化した教材制作会社。TOEIC、英検、TOEFL をはじめとする英語の資格試験から、子供英語、中学英語、高校英語、英会話、ビジネス英語まで、英語教材全般の制作を幅広く行う。特に TOEIC の教材制作には定評があり、『TOEIC® テスト新公式問題集 Vol. 5』の編集制作ほか、TOEIC 関連企画を多数担当している。出版物以外にも英語学習アプリ、英会話学校のコース設計から指導マニュアルの開発、大手進学塾の教材開発まで、多角的な教材制作が可能な数少ない制作会社。「語学の力で世界中の人々の幸せに貢献する」をモットーに、社員一同、学習者の笑顔を想いながら教材の研究開発を行っている。また、同時に TOEIC® L&R テストのスコアアップを目指す方のための指導も行っている。
著書に『TOEIC L&R TEST 990 点獲得 Part 5&6 難問模試』（ベレ出版）、『寝る前 5 分暗記ブック TOEIC テスト単語＆フレーズ』、『寝る前 5 分暗記ブック TOEIC テスト英文法』、『寝る前 5 分暗記ブック 英会話フレーズ集 < 基礎編 >』、『寝る前 5 分暗記ブック 英会話フレーズ集 < 海外旅行編 >』、『寝る前 5 分暗記ブック 英会話フレーズ集 < 接客編 >』、『寝る前 5 分暗記ブック 英会話フレーズ集 <おもてなし編 >』（以上、学研プラス）、がある。
YouTube「ビーコン イングリッシュ チャンネル」にて TOEIC 学習者のために役立つ情報を配信中。
メディアビーコンの公式ラインにて、TOEIC テストのスコアアップに役立つ情報を発信中。

● ── ナレーション　　　　　　Chris Koprowski
● ── カバー・本文デザイン　　竹内 雄二
● ── DTP　　　　　　　　　　清水 康広（WAVE）／三松堂株式会社
● ── 校正、ネイティブチェック　仲 慶次／株式会社オレンジバード

［音声DL付］TOEIC® L&R TEST 990点獲得 最強Part 7模試

| 2020 年 1 月 31 日 | 初版発行 |
| 2024 年 6 月 24 日 | 第 8 刷発行 |

著者	メディアビーコン
発行者	内田 真介
発行・発売	ベレ出版
	〒162-0832　東京都新宿区岩戸町12 レベッカビル
	TEL.03-5225-4790 FAX.03-5225-4795
	ホームページ　https://www.beret.co.jp/
印刷	三松堂株式会社
製本	根本製本株式会社

ISBN 978-4-86064-596-0 C2082　　　　　　　　　編集担当　綿引ゆか

Part 7 模試
60日間プログラム

ベレ出版

TEST 1

TEST1 (Day 1〜13) の学習の進め方

下の表を参照して、Day ごとに指定した問題を制限時間以内で解いてください。
解き終わったら、学習日と解答時間を記入しましょう。

Day1 学習日 /	TEST1 シングルパッセージ 2 題 Q147-148, Q149-150 1/5 回目 制限時間 4 分 解答時間 分		**Day8** 学習日 /	TEST1 トリプルパッセージ 1 題 Q186-190 1/5 回目 制限時間 5 分 解答時間 分
Day2 学習日 /	TEST1 シングルパッセージ 2 題 Q151-152, Q153-154 1/5 回目 制限時間 4 分 解答時間 分		**Day9** 学習日 /	TEST1 トリプルパッセージ 1 題 Q191-195 1/5 回目 制限時間 5 分 解答時間 分
Day3 学習日 /	TEST1 シングルパッセージ 2 題 Q155-157, Q158-160 1/5 回目 制限時間 6 分 解答時間 分		**Day10** 学習日 /	TEST1 トリプルパッセージ 1 題 Q196-200 1/5 回目 制限時間 5 分 解答時間 分
Day4 学習日 /	TEST1 シングルパッセージ 2 題 Q161-163, Q164-167 1/5 回目 制限時間 7 分 解答時間 分		**Day11** 学習日 /	TEST1 全シングルパッセージ Q147-175 2/5 回目 制限時間 29 分 解答時間 分
Day5 学習日 /	TEST1 シングルパッセージ 2 題 Q168-171, Q172-175 1/5 回目 制限時間 8 分 解答時間 分		**Day12** 学習日 /	TEST1 全マルチプルパッセージ Q176-200 2/5 回目 制限時間 25 分 解答時間 分
Day6 学習日 /	TEST1 ダブルパッセージ 1 題 Q176-180 1/5 回目 制限時間 5 分 解答時間 分		**Day13** 学習日 /	TEST1 全問 Q147-200 3/5 回目 制限時間 54 分 解答時間 分
Day7 学習日 /	TEST1 ダブルパッセージ 1 題 Q181-185 1/5 回目 制限時間 5 分 解答時間 分			

TEST1 の 4 回目は Day53 で、5 回目は Day57 で取り組みます。
詳細は別冊 96 ページをご覧ください。

Questions 147-148 refer to the following e-mail.

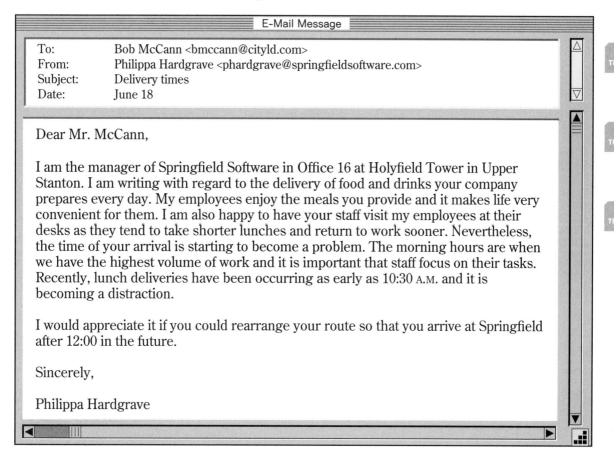

E-Mail Message

To: Bob McCann <bmccann@cityld.com>
From: Philippa Hardgrave <phardgrave@springfieldsoftware.com>
Subject: Delivery times
Date: June 18

Dear Mr. McCann,

I am the manager of Springfield Software in Office 16 at Holyfield Tower in Upper Stanton. I am writing with regard to the delivery of food and drinks your company prepares every day. My employees enjoy the meals you provide and it makes life very convenient for them. I am also happy to have your staff visit my employees at their desks as they tend to take shorter lunches and return to work sooner. Nevertheless, the time of your arrival is starting to become a problem. The morning hours are when we have the highest volume of work and it is important that staff focus on their tasks. Recently, lunch deliveries have been occurring as early as 10:30 A.M. and it is becoming a distraction.

I would appreciate it if you could rearrange your route so that you arrive at Springfield after 12:00 in the future.

Sincerely,

Philippa Hardgrave

147. Who most likely is Mr. McCann?

(A) The owner of a food company
(B) A convenience store manager
(C) A research assistant
(D) A local politician

148. What is the purpose of the e-mail?

(A) To ask for improvements to a product
(B) To explain the reason for a delay
(C) To offer to help with a project
(D) To ask for later delivery

GO ON TO THE NEXT PAGE

Questions 149-150 refer to the following text-message chain.

HARRY BUTLER (7:50 P.M.)
I'm still in New York now. My flight was canceled due to the inclement weather.

TINA KAPOOR (7:51 P.M.)
Don't you have a meeting tomorrow with Dean Pharmaceutical?

HARRY BUTLER (7:53 P.M.)
Yes, at 3 P.M. I'm trying to book the earliest flight for tomorrow, but I might not be able to make it.

TINA KAPOOR (7:55 P.M.)
It might work. There should be an early morning flight which can bring you here on time.

HARRY BUTLER (8:05 P.M.)
You're right. They got me a seat for tomorrow morning. I'll be arriving at the office around noon.

TINA KAPOOR (8:07 P.M.)
Great. You can have some time to prepare for the meeting then.

149. What problem does Mr. Butler mention?

(A) Some seats were overbooked.
(B) A flight was called off.
(C) A colleague will arrive late.
(D) Some furniture has been damaged.

150. At 7:55 P.M. why does Ms. Kapoor write, "It might work"?

(A) She believes that Mr. Butler can get a job.
(B) She likes the painting of Mr. Butler.
(C) She thinks Mr. Butler can arrive on time.
(D) She wants Mr. Butler to take over her duties.

Questions 151-152 refer to the following notice.

Branson Soap Factory Tours

On May 19, the Goldberg Cultural Revival Society is hosting a tour of the Branson Soap Factory. The soap factory, which was once among the most famous in the country, has been vacant for more than 50 years. It is one of many local businesses that failed when the temptation of cheap imported goods attracted customers away. The Goldberg Cultural Revival Society is looking to purchase the building and restart the soap factory. The money raised from the tour will be used to fund our various cultural awareness projects and attract new members.

People or businesses interested in becoming a partner in the revived Branson Soap Company can contact our corporate operations manager at 555-8392.

---

151. What is a purpose of the event?

(A) To display the factory for investors
(B) To attract employees to a local business
(C) To raise money for an organization
(D) To teach people traditional production methods

152. What is indicated about the event organizers?

(A) They are members of the Goldberg City Council.
(B) They specialize in importing goods.
(C) They will provide refreshments for participants.
(D) They are attempting to buy an abandoned factory.

GO ON TO THE NEXT PAGE

Help Wanted

Van Hausen Repair and Maintenance specializes in providing affordable maintenance work on various equipment after the manufacturer's warranty has expired. We fix all range of items including refrigerators, air-conditioners, and office equipment. We currently have an opening in our photocopier division. Experience working as a technician for one of the major manufacturers and an electrician's certificate are a must. Working hours are 9:00 A.M. to 5:00 P.M. Monday through Friday. You may also be required to carry out emergency repairs on either Saturday or Sunday from time to time. In such cases, a generous overtime rate will be provided as compensation. To apply, visit our Web site at www.vanhausenrandm.com and follow the links.

153. What is indicated about the position?

(A) Some contribution to volunteer activities is required.
(B) Extra payment is offered for weekend work.
(C) Employees must own a full set of tools.
(D) Training will be offered in the evenings.

154. What equipment will the new technician be hired to maintain?

(A) Cameras
(B) Air-conditioners
(C) Photocopiers
(D) Elevators

DEVONSHIRE (November 21) — Toby Wood, the president of Wood Education, has announced that the Wood School of Business on Whelan Street will be moving to a larger building on Frampton Avenue. This is a result of the business being acquired by Kirkland University, which also owns the building on Frampton Avenue. Mr. Wood will continue in his position as president until he retires next month. The Wood family has run the Wood School of Business for almost 60 years and this is the first time a non-family member will take control.

In an interview, Mr. Wood stated that he believed the school was in good hands and hoped that the stronger association with the university would ensure the school's future prosperity. A letter explaining the decision and how it would affect students was sent out to all concerned last week. The move is scheduled to take place in time for the start of the new school year in February.

155. Where would the article most likely appear?

(A) In an academic journal
(B) In a local newspaper
(C) In a job-offering magazine
(D) In an online catalog

156. According to the article, what will likely happen in December?

(A) A school will move to a new location.
(B) A new course will be offered at a university.
(C) An executive will leave a business.
(D) An award will be given to a business owner.

157. What is indicated about students of Wood School of Business?

(A) They have already been informed of the news.
(B) They will receive a discount on their tuition fees.
(C) They will be able to take part in university courses.
(D) They were invited to vote on the decision.

GO ON TO THE NEXT PAGE

The Halliburton Corporate Fitness Center Has Reopened!

Until it closed last month, many employees were taking advantage of the corporate gym. Unfortunately, the running costs had made it unfeasible for the company to continue. However, due to popular demand, the gym has reopened this week with one small change. The gym is now also available for employees of other tenants in the building. They will be charged membership fees depending on their frequency of use. The gym is still free for Halliburton staff, but this means that you will need to swipe your employee card to gain entry from now on.

To make the fitness center accessible to other users, we have had to relocate it. It can now be found in Office 3 on the building's first floor. We have arranged for Jim Cavalier, a local health expert, to visit the gym once a week to provide free consultations to users. If you would like to make an appointment, please check the schedule posted on the wall near the entrance. Users will be assisted on a first-come-first-served basis. Mr. Cavalier is the owner of Althex Fitness and Health on Rosemary Street, East Bronson. He is widely respected in sporting circles so we hope you make good use of this opportunity.

158. What is a purpose of the notice?

(A) To promote a local business
(B) To suggest a fitness program
(C) To announce the distribution of employee cards
(D) To explain a change in policy

159. What is indicated about the fitness center?

(A) It is in a new location.
(B) It was shut down due to a lack of interest.
(C) It has been designed by Jim Cavalier.
(D) It offers subsidized rates to employees.

160. What is true about Mr. Cavalier?

(A) He has joined the staff of Halliburton.
(B) He is a professional athlete.
(C) He is replacing another expert.
(D) He is self-employed.

Questions 161-163 refer to the following information from a Web page.

Langley Office Furniture
TEL: 734-555-9492 E-mail: cservice@langleyof.com

Langley Office Furniture offers substantial discounts to businesses registered as customers. — [1] — . It is easy to register and the discounts become available immediately. Simply fill out the online application by clicking the link below.

CLICK HERE

By registering, you will not only be eligible for discounts at our online store but also at our regular stores in any of the five capital cities we serve. Furthermore, all purchases will be covered by a two-year warranty on top of the manufacturers' one-year warranty. — [2] — . Business clients may also take advantage of our special customer support line any time, day or night.

If you contact customer support by e-mail, be sure to mention the order number in the subject line of your e-mail. — [3] — . This enables us to provide a response in the shortest possible time. — [4] — . It may take up to three days if this information is not provided.

---

161. What is the purpose of the information?

(A) To express appreciation to loyal customers
(B) To attract new customers to a business
(C) To explain the process for requesting a product return
(D) To announce a change to a product lineup

162. What is NOT mentioned about Langley Office Furniture?

(A) It manufactures its own brand of furniture.
(B) It has offices in multiple cities.
(C) It offers extended warranties.
(D) It provides 24-hour customer support.

163. In which of the positions marked [1], [2], [3], and [4] does the following sentence best belong?

"Our system ensures that it is automatically sent to the relevant support worker."

(A) [1]
(B) [2]
(C) [3]
(D) [4]

To:	Fred Yates <fyates@veritasmotors.com>
From:	Roberta Wilson <rwilson@scarboroughbc.com>
Date:	May 6
Subject:	Scarborough Business Center
Attachment:	📎 pamphlet

Dear Mr. Yates,

Thank you for your e-mail of May 5. Attached you will find a pamphlet for our new meeting spaces at 34 Fielding Street. I understand your company is considering reserving one of our meeting rooms every Sunday for an indefinite period. This is not something we have done in the past. Nevertheless, I am very interested in discussing the possibility with you when you visit our current facility at 234 Grundy Street, Chicago, on May 9. I would be happy to pick you up from the station so please let me know your arrival time.

I have taken the liberty of reserving the room you mentioned for the next six months starting on May 14. As we have not received a formal request from you, there will be no charge if you choose not to use the room. I am open to discussing discounts and we can be flexible with some of our conditions of use in consideration of this long-term agreement. Nevertheless, I hope you will keep in mind that Scarborough Business Center is already one of the most reasonably priced providers of meeting space in Chicago.

Sincerely,

Roberta Wilson
Scarborough Business Center

---

164. What is included with the e-mail?

(A) A brochure
(B) A receipt
(C) A travel itinerary
(D) A reservation confirmation

165. When will Mr. Yates meet with Ms. Wilson?

(A) On May 3
(B) On May 6
(C) On May 9
(D) On May 14

166. What is NOT implied about Scarborough Business Center?

(A) It offers meeting rooms for corporate clients.
(B) It is relocating soon.
(C) It is open in the evenings.
(D) It charges cancellation fees.

167. What most likely is Ms. Wilson's job?

(A) Training officer
(B) Salesperson
(C) Analyst
(D) Event planner

Questions 168-171 refer to the following text-message chain.

Col Stephens[3:30 P.M.]:
I've just received a request to help with a move tomorrow. I'm sorry about the last minute notification, but who's in?

Hank Rogers[3:31 P.M.]:
Is it a corporate job or a domestic job?

Meredith Harper[3:33 P.M.]:
I'm afraid, I'm committed elsewhere tomorrow.

Col Stephens[3:33 P.M.]:
I understand, Meredith. It's domestic, I'm afraid. That means there will be a lot of boxes.

Daphne Phisher[3:35 P.M.]:
I'm afraid Frank Wallace and I are busy tomorrow. We have to go to Boston to buy a new van.

Hank Rogers[3:37 P.M.]:
You just replaced your van a few months ago.

Daphne Phisher[3:46 P.M.]:
Don't get me started. We've been paying for repairs ever since we got it.

Col Stephens[3:49 P.M.]:
Sorry to hear that. I hope you have better luck with the new one.

Daphne Phisher[3:51 P.M.]:
Thanks, Col. Me, too.

Hank Rogers[3:54 P.M.]:
It looks like it's you and me, Col.

Col Stephens[3:57 P.M.]:
OK. I'll send you an e-mail with the start time and the client's address.

168. Where do the writers most likely work?

(A) At car dealerships
(B) At an airline
(C) At moving companies
(D) At a cleaning service

169. Why is Frank Wallace going to Boston?

(A) To give a presentation
(B) To meet with a client
(C) To visit some family members
(D) To purchase a vehicle

170. At 3:46 P.M., what does Ms. Phisher mean when she says, "Don't get me started"?

(A) She will make her own way to a work location.
(B) She has had a lot of expenses recently.
(C) She would like to take a rest.
(D) She is not interested in a new product.

171. Who will assist Mr. Stephens tomorrow?

(A) Ms. Phisher
(B) Mr. Rogers
(C) Mr. Wallace
(D) Ms. Harper

GO ON TO THE NEXT PAGE

Hobart, September 12—Mike Sylva only intended to stay in Hobart for three months after his company transferred him there 15 years ago. Today, he is still here and he is now the owner of one of the city's most successful cafés. — [1] — . This is a far cry from what he could have imagined when he first arrived to help open a veterinary hospital for a large national chain.

— [2] — . Twenty years earlier, while he was still in veterinary school, Sylva met fellow student and musician, Il Sok Kim. His friendship with Il Sok led to his appreciation of music and eventually resulted in him learning to play the guitar and joining a band. The pair lost contact when Il Sok quit school to follow his musical ambitions.

— [3] — . The two immediately rekindled their friendship. Il Sok's laidback lifestyle appealed to Sylva, who had put his career before anything else. They started playing together again and by the time Sylva was scheduled to return to the company's head office in Sydney, they had formed a band.

Sylva elected to stay in Hobart and work at the veterinarian clinic, but he soon found that that was taking too much of his time. — [4] — . He used all of his savings to buy the café and started to run the business. He has completely revamped the menu and updated the interior. At night, he serves amazing meals with top class musical entertainment by local performers and his best friend, Il Sok. The restaurant is called Treble Clef and it is open from 7:00 A.M. to 10:00 P.M. every day except Tuesday.

172. What is the main purpose of the article?

(A) To profile a local business person
(B) To promote a new veterinary clinic
(C) To explain the benefits of living in Hobart
(D) To introduce a popular new pastime

173. Who is Il Sok Kim?

(A) A veterinarian
(B) A promoter
(C) A restaurant owner
(D) A musical performer

174. Why did Mr. Sylva leave his job?

(A) It did not allow him enough freedom.
(B) It was not paid well enough.
(C) It was in a very secluded region.
(D) It did not make use of his qualifications.

175. In which of the positions marked [1], [2], [3], and [4] does the following sentence best belong?

"So, it felt like fate when Sylva visited the café next to the newly opened veterinary clinic to find his old friend serving drinks and chatting with patrons."

(A) [1]
(B) [2]
(C) [3]
(D) [4]

Questions 176-180 refer to the following e-mail and article.

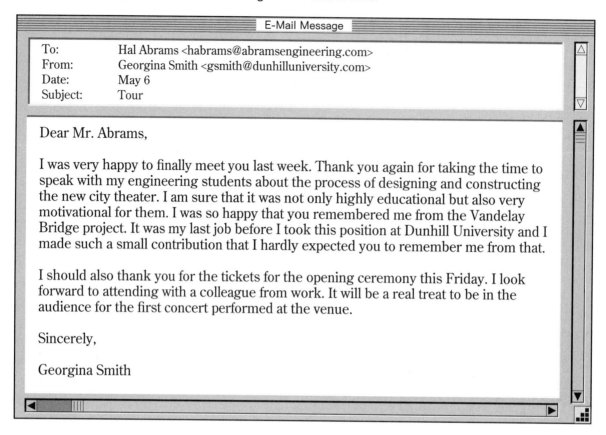

E-Mail Message

To: Hal Abrams <habrams@abramsengineering.com>
From: Georgina Smith <gsmith@dunhilluniversity.com>
Date: May 6
Subject: Tour

Dear Mr. Abrams,

I was very happy to finally meet you last week. Thank you again for taking the time to speak with my engineering students about the process of designing and constructing the new city theater. I am sure that it was not only highly educational but also very motivational for them. I was so happy that you remembered me from the Vandelay Bridge project. It was my last job before I took this position at Dunhill University and I made such a small contribution that I hardly expected you to remember me from that.

I should also thank you for the tickets for the opening ceremony this Friday. I look forward to attending with a colleague from work. It will be a real treat to be in the audience for the first concert performed at the venue.

Sincerely,

Georgina Smith

Bronsonville Theater Opening Soon

By Greta Holmes

May 7—The new Bronsonville Theater is a marvel of engineering. The amazing egg-shaped building is certainly eye-catching, but that is not all it has going for it. It promises the best acoustic features of any major indoor performance space in the world, on paper at least. We won't know if it measures up to expectations until it opens on May 8.

The chief engineer on the project, Hal Abrams, took over from Jon Gregory, who had to leave the project due to scheduling issues brought on by construction delays. Abrams came directly from the famous Vandelay Bridge project he was in charge of in Amsterdam. Under his excellent leadership, the construction got back on schedule and the construction company has even qualified for an early completion bonus.

176. What is the purpose of the e-mail?

(A) To express gratitude for a past event
(B) To alert employees about a policy change
(C) To request assistance with a project
(D) To remind customers to submit orders

177. What is suggested about Ms. Smith and Mr. Abrams?

(A) They studied together at university.
(B) They will present an award at a banquet.
(C) They are employed by the same company.
(D) They both worked on a project in Amsterdam.

178. When most likely will Ms. Smith next visit the Bronsonville Theater?

(A) On May 6
(B) On May 7
(C) On May 8
(D) On May 9

179. What is NOT indicated about the Bronsonville Theater?

(A) It has a very striking appearance.
(B) The city council paid for the construction.
(C) Its chief engineer changed during the project.
(D) The construction company received an additional payment.

180. In the article, the phrase "on paper" in paragraph 1, line 7 is closest in meaning to

(A) in print
(B) as shown
(C) in theory
(D) for now

GO ON TO THE NEXT PAGE

17 March

Sean Monroe
123 Halifax Road,
London,

Dear Mr. Monroe,

Thank you for agreeing to write a segment for the *London Culinary Journal*. I am sure our readers will be excited to read an article by you especially considering your recent experiences working for Camden House in Sunbury. As your article will be under 1,500 words, we will only be able to use a two-page spread. Typically, we try to fill the page with 60 percent text and 40 percent graphical content. If you have some pictures you would like us to use or have a specific request for our photographer, please let me know as soon as possible.

The title for the article is to be *Summer in Sunbury*. You can submit the completed manuscript to us using the upload link on the Web site. For security purposes, it is important that you do not send any content for publication to us by e-mail.

Depending on the relevance of the article, we may print it in one of our other publications. If for example, the recipe has historical significance, we may feature it in *Historian Monthly*. Should such a republication occur, you will receive £750 per instance on top of the previously agreed sum of £750. You will be given an opportunity to turn down such offers before publication. Please fill out the enclosed publishing contract and send it back using the self-addressed envelope. Also, I need you to e-mail me your banking particulars as soon as possible so that I can arrange the advance payment of the originally commissioned article as we agreed by the end of the month.

Sincerely,

Tina Day

Tina Day
Editor — Coot Publishing

To:	Sean Monroe <smonroe@bluejay.com>
From:	Tina Day <tday@cootpublishing.com>
Date:	27 July
Subject:	Article

Dear Mr. Monroe,

I am happy to inform you that this month, we will be providing you payment of a total of £750 for the use of *Summer in Sunbury*. Payment will be made on the 15th of next month. Due to the popularity of the article, we would like to commission you to write a new article for our October-December issue. We would like to tentatively title it *Winter in Sunbury*. However, you may suggest a different topic and title if you have something else in mind. Please let me know if you would like to renegotiate your payment. Otherwise, we will assume the same arrangements are satisfactory.

Sincerely,

Tina Day
Editor — Coot Publishing

181. What is the purpose of the letter?

(A) To suggest a location for a meeting
(B) To confirm the details of an assignment
(C) To request attendance at a conference
(D) To announce the adoption of a new policy

182. What is indicated about Coot Publishing?

(A) It has offices in several capital cities.
(B) It provides translations of articles online.
(C) It specializes in articles about Sunbury.
(D) It publishes magazines in various genres.

183. What does Ms. Day ask Mr. Monroe to send by e-mail?

(A) His bank account details
(B) Information about Camden House
(C) Photographs of his work
(D) His employment history

184. What is suggested about Mr. Monroe's article?

(A) It was used in multiple publications.
(B) Its publication was delayed.
(C) It has been reviewed in a newspaper.
(D) Its length was over the agreed number of words.

185. According to the e-mail, why might Mr. Monroe contact Ms. Day?

(A) To thank her for paying him a commission
(B) To ask for higher compensation
(C) To introduce another writer
(D) To offer advice on a publication date

GO ON TO THE NEXT PAGE

Customer name: Robert Paulson
Account number: U7384834
Date: June 7

Galvonesta Online Shopping

Quantity	Description	Price
1	GHT Cordless drill	$143.00
1	GHT Stepladder (180cm)	$87.00
1	GHT Disk saw	$210.00
1	Brianbuilt Wire cutters	$54.00
	Subtotal:	$494.00
	Galvonesta Members' Discount (5%):	$24.70
	Delivery:	$0.00
	Amount paid:	**$469.30**

You may access this receipt at any time by checking the archived orders under the account tab of Galvonesta Online Shopping. Items to be returned must be in their original packaging and they must be returned with all of their parts intact. Customer support can provide return mailing labels which enable customers to return items without paying for postage.

To:	Robert Paulson <rpaulson@firecrab.com>
From:	Marla Carter <macarter@galvonesta.com>
Date:	June 12
Subject:	Returned goods
Attachment:	📎 form

Dear Mr. Paulson,

I am sorry to learn one of the items you ordered was not entirely satisfactory. Please use the attached form to submit a return request. Once that has been received by us, we will refund the $87 purchase price. When we receive the product back, we will investigate the problem and contact the manufacturer to ensure that it does not happen again.

In case you require a replacement, please allow me to recommend the Faraday 500. It is a fine alternative to the GHT model and very similarly priced. You will see that it has excellent reviews and a 36-month warranty.

Sincerely,

Marla Carter

To:	Marla Carter <macarter@galvonesta.com>
From:	Robert Paulson <rpaulson@firecrab.com>
Date:	June 13
Subject:	RE: Returned goods

Dear Ms. Carter,

Thank you for processing my refund so quickly. It was much faster and simpler than I had imagined. As I am purchasing these items for work, it is necessary for me to view the updated receipt. Please advise me on how to do that.

Sincerely,

Robert Paulson

186. What is indicated about Galvonesta?

(A) It ships some purchases free of charge.
(B) It purchases goods from local manufacturers.
(C) It advertises its services on the radio.
(D) It only sells GHT brand products.

187. What is suggested about Mr. Paulson?

(A) He has purchased goods online before.
(B) He was introduced to Galvonesta by a colleague.
(C) He requires an express shipment.
(D) He is a registered customer of Galvonesta.

188. Which item was Mr. Paulson dissatisfied with?

(A) Cordless drill
(B) Stepladder
(C) Disk saw
(D) Wire cutters

189. In the first e-mail, the word "fine" in paragraph 2, line 2 is closest in meaning to

(A) excellent
(B) delicate
(C) penalty
(D) responsible

190. What will Ms. Carter most likely advise Mr. Paulson to do?

(A) Write a product review
(B) Read some operating instructions
(C) Access the Web site
(D) Attend a workshop

https://www.airholidayz.com ▶

AirHolidayz

AirHolidayz is your one-stop online shop for transportation, accommodations, and entertainment all around the world.

In June of this year, we are launching our new mobile phone services, which will allow you to connect to the Internet from the moment your plane arrives. In order to use your existing phone, simply pick up your choice of Wi-Fi router or sim card from our desk at the airport in any major capital city. Alternatively, you may also purchase a disposable smartphone at a very reasonable price.

We are offering 20 percent off on all hotel rooms booked through AirHolidayz between June 1 and August 25. If you introduce a friend, who then uses the service before or during the special offer period, you can get a further 10 percent off.

To:	Davida Travis <dtravis@sheffieldconstruction.com>
From:	Hank Jeffries <hjeffries@camdenbuildingsupplies.com>
Date:	June 19
Subject:	Trip
Attachment:	📎 JeffriesTS

Dear Davida,

I was just looking online for some things for us to do while we are in Brisbane next month. We have a couple of evenings free and as both of us are unfamiliar with the region, I thought it might be a good idea to arrange something in advance. Today, I found a Web site called AirHolidayz and I used them for all of my reservations including my flights and accommodation.

Anyway, there is a huge list of interesting things to do in their entertainment section. Please take a look, and let me know if there is anything you would like to check out. I will make the reservations and put it on my travel allowance. I believe that Camden Building Supplies is paying for your travel expenses so please send me the receipts when you have made a reservation. I will see that you are reimbursed by the end of the week. If you would like to take the same flights as me, you can check them by looking at the attached itinerary.

Sincerely,

Hank Jeffries
Sales Manager — Camden Building Supplies

To:	Hank Jeffries <hjeffries@camdenbuildingsupplies.com>
From:	Davida Travis <dtravis@sheffieldconstruction.com>
Date:	June 19
Subject:	RE: Trip

Dear Hank,

Thank you for contacting me about the trip. It had slipped my mind. I plan to register with AirHolidayz and make all of the arrangements through them. However, I was unable to read the document you sent me. Would you mind sending it again in another format?

Sincerely,

Davida Travis
Project Manager — Sheffield Construction

191. What is indicated about AirHolidayz?

(A) It does not have any offices in other countries.
(B) It offers discount airfares.
(C) It can provide international reservations.
(D) It has merged with a telephone manufacturer.

192. What is NOT a service offered by AirHolidayz?

(A) Tickets for events
(B) Transportation arrangements
(C) Communications
(D) Travel insurance

193. What is probably true about Mr. Jeffries?
(A) He is an employee of Sheffield Construction.
(B) He received a discount on his lodgings.
(C) He made Ms. Travis' travel arrangements for her.
(D) He has been to Brisbane in the past.

194. In the first e-mail, the word "see" in paragraph 2, line 5 is closest in meaning to

(A) ensure
(B) view
(C) attend
(D) conclude

195. What does Ms. Travis ask Mr. Jeffries to send?

(A) His contact details
(B) A discount coupon
(C) A project update
(D) His schedule

GO ON TO THE NEXT PAGE

Choose Spark Advertising for your next promotion!

Spark Advertising is an award-winning firm with more than 40 years in the business. We handle all types of promotion and advertising from store openings to community festivals, but our main area of expertise is courses for professional development.

Visit our special Web site at www.sparkadvertising.promotion.com to learn more about our offerings. There, you will find a portfolio of some of our most important work, our mission statement, a timeline showing the main events in our corporate history, and a helpful list of phone numbers and extensions so that you can get in touch with the customer service agents in the department most relevant to your needs.

In order to attract new clients, this month we are offering an all-inclusive package with one month of radio and Internet advertising and all associated production and design work for just $4,000. That is a saving of over $2,500.

To: Mel Waterhouse
From: Dourine Cleminson
Subject: Campaign
Date: December 17

Dear Mel,

Just so you know, I have arranged to have Spark Advertising handle our promotional campaign this year. It will cost us only $4,000, which is far cheaper than what Donaldson Associates has been charging. I would like you to attend a meeting with me and one of their representatives this Friday afternoon.

I have reserved Conference Room 3 from 3:00 P.M. She is coming all the way from Salisbury to meet with us. I would like some assistance evaluating her proposal, so please invite one or two of your department members who have been involved in advertising our products over the last two years.

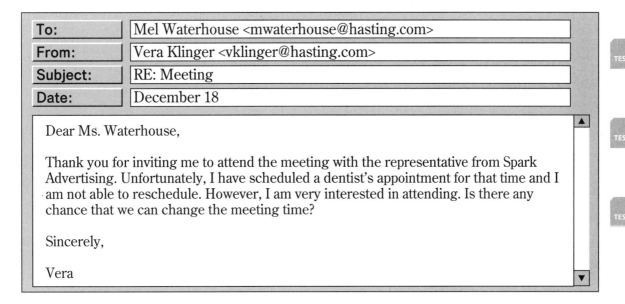

To:	Mel Waterhouse <mwaterhouse@hasting.com>
From:	Vera Klinger <vklinger@hasting.com>
Subject:	RE: Meeting
Date:	December 18

Dear Ms. Waterhouse,

Thank you for inviting me to attend the meeting with the representative from Spark Advertising. Unfortunately, I have scheduled a dentist's appointment for that time and I am not able to reschedule. However, I am very interested in attending. Is there any chance that we can change the meeting time?

Sincerely,

Vera

196. According to the advertisement, what kind of promotion does Spark Advertising specialize in?

(A) Store openings
(B) Education
(C) Community events
(D) Theater

197. What is NOT featured on the Spark Advertising special Web site?

(A) Directions to the company's offices
(B) Samples of work from previous projects
(C) Contact details for company representatives
(D) Information about Spark Advertising's past

198. What is probably true about Ms. Cleminson's organization?

(A) It has renewed its contract with Donaldson Associates.
(B) It is based in Salisbury.
(C) It has not used Spark Advertising before.
(D) It has won a business award.

199. What is implied about Ms. Klinger?

(A) She has recently transferred to Hastings College.
(B) She attended a conference in Salisbury.
(C) She is familiar with the work of Donaldson Associates.
(D) She introduced Spark Advertising to Ms. Waterhouse.

200. In the e-mail, the word "chance" in paragraph 1, line 4 is closest in meaning to

(A) risk
(B) speculation
(C) accident
(D) possibility

TEST 2

TEST2 (Day14〜26) の学習の進め方

下の表を参照して、Day ごとに指定した問題を制限時間以内で解いてください。
解き終わったら、学習日と解答時間を記入しましょう。

Day14	TEST2 シングルパッセージ 2 題 Q147-148, Q149-150　1/5 回目
学習日 ／	制限時間　4 分　解答時間　　　　　分

Day15	TEST2 シングルパッセージ 2 題 Q151-152, Q153-154　1/5 回目
学習日 ／	制限時間　4 分　解答時間　　　　　分

Day16	TEST2 シングルパッセージ 2 題 Q155-157, Q158-160　1/5 回目
学習日 ／	制限時間　6 分　解答時間　　　　　分

Day17	TEST2 シングルパッセージ 2 題 Q161-163, Q164-167　1/5 回目
学習日 ／	制限時間　7 分　解答時間　　　　　分

Day18	TEST2 シングルパッセージ 2 題 Q168-171, Q172-175　1/5 回目
学習日 ／	制限時間　8 分　解答時間　　　　　分

Day19	TEST2 ダブルパッセージ 1 題 Q176-180　1/5 回目
学習日 ／	制限時間　5 分　解答時間　　　　　分

Day20	TEST2 ダブルパッセージ 1 題 Q181-185　1/5 回目
学習日 ／	制限時間　5 分　解答時間　　　　　分

Day21	TEST2 トリプルパッセージ 1 題 Q186-190　1/5 回目
学習日 ／	制限時間　5 分　解答時間　　　　　分

Day22	TEST2 トリプルパッセージ 1 題 Q191-195　1/5 回目
学習日 ／	制限時間　5 分　解答時間　　　　　分

Day23	TEST2 トリプルパッセージ 1 題 Q196-200　1/5 回目
学習日 ／	制限時間　5 分　解答時間　　　　　分

Day24	TEST2 全シングルパッセージ Q147-175　2/5 回目
学習日 ／	制限時間　29 分　解答時間　　　　　分

Day25	TEST2 全マルチプルパッセージ Q176-200　2/5 回目
学習日 ／	制限時間　25 分　解答時間　　　　　分

Day26	TEST2 全問 Q147-200　3/5 回目
学習日 ／	制限時間　54 分　解答時間　　　　　分

TEST2 の 4 回目は Day54 で、5 回目は Day58 で取り組みます。
詳細は別冊 96 ページをご覧ください。

Questions 147-148 refer to the following notice.

NOTICE

**The counter area must be kept clear
for service technicians to use at any time.**

- Please do not store delivered items, personal items, or tools on the workbench.

- Due to the sensitive nature of the equipment used in this section, you must not eat or drink here at any time.

- If you need to use the area for any purpose other than the maintenance or repair of merchandise, please contact the chief of the service department, Alex Steele.

147. For whom is the notice most likely intended?

(A) Employees
(B) Customers
(C) Business owners
(D) Job applicants

148. According to the notice, what activity is forbidden in the area?

(A) Use of electronic equipment
(B) Preparation for meetings
(C) Taking breaks from work
(D) Consumption of beverages

GO ON TO THE NEXT PAGE

Questions 149-150 refer to the following text-message chain.

TIM CLEM (4:20 P.M.)
That delivery of food for the party you ordered still hasn't arrived. What time was it due again?

ANDREA ORTA (4:21 P.M.)
About 20 minutes ago. I'll give them a call and find out what's going on.

ANDREA ORTA (4:25 P.M.)
They said someone's on the way. We'll just have to wait. I'll gather everyone in the conference room and we can start the party. Would you mind waiting at reception?

TIM CLEM (4:27 P.M.)
I don't mind, but what for?

ANDREA ORTA (4:28 P.M.)
We have to pay the delivery driver in cash.

TIM CLEM (4:30 P.M.)
I can hear the doorbell in the conference room.
I don't think there's any need to wait in reception.

ANDREA ORTA (4:31 P.M.)
OK, then. Let's get the party started. It's time.

---

149. Why does Mr. Clem start the text-message chain?

(A) To announce the start of a party
(B) To inquire about a delivery time
(C) To request money to pay for some food
(D) To ask about a menu item

150. At 4:30 P.M., why does Mr. Clem write, "I can hear the doorbell in the conference room"?

(A) He believes that their doorbell is in working order.
(B) He thinks that the volume is set too high.
(C) He would prefer not to wait at reception.
(D) He is letting Ms. Orta know a delivery has arrived.

Expand your business
the safe way with Carter, Inc.

Carter, Inc. provides skilled, short-term employees to businesses of any size to overcome seasonal staffing shortcomings or tentatively fill positions as they expand. Register your business online and immediately get access to our easy-to-use request system. You can easily indicate the required qualifications, set the duration of the contract, and indicate working hours. In most cases, you can expect a reply within hours. Carter, Inc. ensures that it has the top people for any position by providing in-house training to every candidate. We offer courses in secretarial skills, construction work, customer service and even cooking and hospitality. That is why Carter, Inc. is the place most businesses turn to for personnel when time is of the essence.

Carter, Inc.

---

151. What is being advertised?

(A) A business consultancy
(B) Employment opportunities
(C) A temporary staffing agency
(D) Communications software

152. What is indicated about Carter, Inc.?

(A) It has an agreement with a local vocational college.
(B) It can provide customer assistance 24 hours a day.
(C) It allows users to search its online database.
(D) It offers employees opportunities to improve their skills.

GO ON TO THE NEXT PAGE

Flanders Kitchenware
Montgomery Shopping Mall
362 Holden Rd., Seattle, WA 98019
(206) 555-8394

June 1

Mr. Hans Ferdinand
63 Hannover Avenue, Apt. 7
Seattle, WA 98018

Dear Mr. Ferdinand,

Flanders Kitchenware is proud to have you among its clientele. In the past, you mentioned our store on your very popular radio cooking program on Radio 4JK. While we have never paid for your endorsements, we have benefited greatly from the publicity your show brings us. In fact, since your show was syndicated, we have been welcoming more and more clientele from outside Seattle.

For the last month, the store has been closed so that some expansion and a complete renovation could be carried out. I am writing to announce that the store will be reopening on June 14. We will be holding a celebration, which includes cooking demonstrations, giveaways, and special discounts for registered customers.

We would be honored if you could visit Flanders Kitchenware on that date. If you would like to broadcast the show from the store, you would be welcome to make use of any or all of our amenities as well as have the complete cooperation of our six highly capable staff members.

If you are interested, you may contact me at skildare@flanderskitchenware.com.

Sincerely,

Steve Kildare

Steve Kildare
Manager

153. What is a purpose of the letter?

(A) To confirm a broadcast schedule
(B) To announce a special event
(C) To explain membership rules
(D) To offer payment for advertising

154. Who most likely is Mr. Ferdinand?

(A) The manager of a store
(B) An engineer of a radio station
(C) A local celebrity
(D) The owner of a construction company

Questions 155-157 refer to the following schedule.

Raymond City
12th Annual Rhythm and Blues Festival
Sunday, September 21

10:00 A.M.–12:00 NOON.	**Blues concert with performances by the Glendale High School Band as well as a number of excellent local amateur performers.** Tickets are free, but it is necessary to register in advance on the Web site. Gather in the Greenwood Park Center Auditorium.
11:00 A.M.–12:00 NOON.	**A guitar lesson with Val Borland.** All are welcome! Just bring a guitar to the main tent at the entrance of Greenwood Park.
11:45 A.M.–1:00 P.M.	Enjoy lunch served from stalls operated by local restaurants. The stalls will be located on the pathway along the Raymond River. Delicious food at competitive prices.
12:00 NOON.–2:00 P.M.	**An open-air concert by The Blues Cats.** This wonderful band will take a break from their national tour to lend their support to the Raymond City Rhythm and Blues Festival.
2:00 P.M.–3:30 P.M.	**Battle of the Bands.** 20 acts from in and around Raymond City will vie for the top prize and a possible recording contract with TVW Record Company. Sign up on the day. Registration forms are available from the main tent at the venue.

All events will be held at Greenwood Park on Orlando Street.
For more information, visit the festival Web site at www.raymondcrabfest.com.

155. According to the schedule, what will be sold at the festival?

(A) Concert tickets
(B) Meals
(C) Guitar lessons
(D) Albums

156. When will the outdoor event start?

(A) At 10:00 A.M.
(B) At 11:00 A.M.
(C) At 12:00 NOON.
(D) At 2:00 P.M.

157. Where can people obtain a registration form for the competition?

(A) At the outdoor stage
(B) From the Web site
(C) At the park entrance
(D) On the river path

GO ON TO THE NEXT PAGE

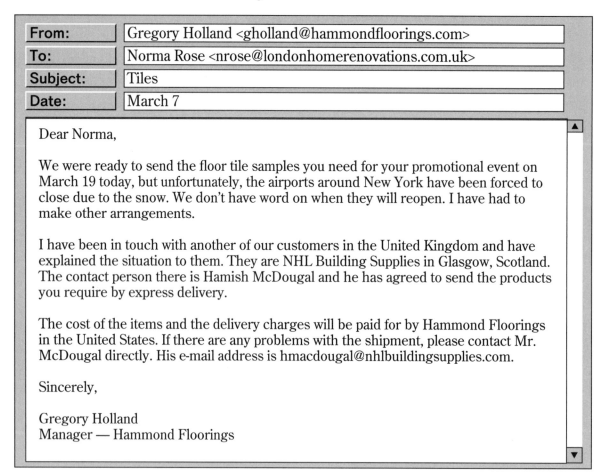

From:	Gregory Holland <gholland@hammondfloorings.com>
To:	Norma Rose <nrose@londonhomerenovations.com.uk>
Subject:	Tiles
Date:	March 7

Dear Norma,

We were ready to send the floor tile samples you need for your promotional event on March 19 today, but unfortunately, the airports around New York have been forced to close due to the snow. We don't have word on when they will reopen. I have had to make other arrangements.

I have been in touch with another of our customers in the United Kingdom and have explained the situation to them. They are NHL Building Supplies in Glasgow, Scotland. The contact person there is Hamish McDougal and he has agreed to send the products you require by express delivery.

The cost of the items and the delivery charges will be paid for by Hammond Floorings in the United States. If there are any problems with the shipment, please contact Mr. McDougal directly. His e-mail address is hmacdougal@nhlbuildingsupplies.com.

Sincerely,

Gregory Holland
Manager — Hammond Floorings

158. What is the purpose of the e-mail?

(A) To apologize for a shipping error
(B) To offer an alternative product
(C) To request an update on an order
(D) To explain a change in plans

159. What has Mr. McDougal agreed to do?

(A) Invoice Mr. Holland's company
(B) Represent Hammond Floorings in the United Kingdom
(C) Attend a product demonstration in London
(D) Publish product details on his company's Web site

160. What does Mr. Holland instruct Ms. Rose to do?

(A) Order through NHL Building Supplies in the future
(B) Send a refund request to Hammond Floorings
(C) Return any damaged products to the manufacturer
(D) Contact Mr. McDougal with any delivery issues

Questions 161-163 refer to the following article.

Woodhill (January 16)—The Richmond Art Gallery has reopened in a new location. It is now on the corner of Walton and Norbert Streets in the building which once housed the Camden Theater. — [1] — . For more than 100 years, the Richmond Art Gallery has housed artwork from the best of our local artists as well as the great European masters.

On February 17 the gallery will host a series of paintings by Henrietta Chang. The most famous of these is her depiction of the popular city mayor, Paula Shore. — [2] — . Ms. Shore worked to diversify the city's economy so that it relied not just on manufacturing but also on culture and tourism. This shift has measurably improved the lives of our citizens. — [3] — .

The paintings on show include works spanning Ms. Chang's whole career — a period of some 60 years. Admission to the main gallery is free. However, tickets to see Ms. Chang's works cost $10. They can be purchased online at www.richmondag.com or at the ticket booth on the first floor. — [4] — . The gallery's opening hours are from 9:30 A.M. to 6:00 P.M. Monday to Friday and from 10:00 A.M. to 7:00 P.M. on Saturday and Sunday.

161. What is announced in the article?

(A) The commencement of a new exhibition
(B) Plans to relocate an art gallery
(C) The closure of a popular theater
(D) The retirement of a politician

162. Who is Paula Shore?

(A) A model for a character in a novel
(B) An actress in a theatrical company
(C) A popular local artist
(D) The subject of a portrait

163. In which of the positions marked [1], [2], [3], and [4] does the following sentence best belong?

"These much larger and ornate premises lend the gallery the air of grandness it truly deserves."

(A) [1]
(B) [2]
(C) [3]
(D) [4]

GO ON TO THE NEXT PAGE

Clarkson Associates is a partnership between highly regarded business professionals each with a record of success as employees in the private sector and as advisors to a diverse range of businesses. We offer tailored advice from our most suited partners to our highly valued clients. At our initial consultation, we review your company's business plan and financial statements in detail to assess our ability to bring about a positive change in your organization. Based on that assessment, we assign a specialist with the experience and expertise you need moving forward.

In a recent article in *Business Brain* magazine, Clarkson Associates was acknowledged as the most sought after and demonstrably successful business consultancy in Australia. The article assessed our performance guiding fledgling businesses, our knowledge of recruitment strategies, and our familiarity with the rules of trade with Australia's largest trading partners.

Between March 23 and April 14, Clarkson Associates will be interviewing prospective clients. If you are interested in speaking with our team and discovering whether or not you are a match for our services, please contact our new client hotline at 02-555-3432. During the process, you will need to send representatives to our main office in central Melbourne. Please be advised that in some cases, it is necessary for prospective clients to come in for follow-up meetings on short notice.

CLARKSON ASSOCIATES

164. What is a purpose of the information?

(A) To describe a company's customer service principles

(B) To encourage people to apply for jobs at Clarkson Associates

(C) To explain regulations that apply to private businesses in Australia

(D) To report on the financial forecast for a business sector

165. What is true about Clarkson Associates?

(A) It has offices in several countries.

(B) It was founded by a property developer.

(C) It was mentioned in a magazine article.

(D) It is looking to hire more staff members.

166. What is NOT a service offered by Clarkson Associates?

(A) Advice for new businesses

(B) Introductions to financial lenders

(C) Assistance in finding suitable employees

(D) Provision of information about international business

167. What is mentioned about prospective clients?

(A) They can receive an initial consultation for free.

(B) They should call Clarkson Associates about interviews.

(C) They can attend the Clarkson Associates office of their choice.

(D) They should analyze their financial statements.

Questions 168-171 refer to the following online chat discussion.

Red Morris[3:30 P.M.]:
Thanks for welcoming me to the Fairfield Chamber of Commerce. I'd like to have some advice from other members. I need to hire a cleaning service for our new offices. Can anyone recommend a reliable company?
Steph Jordan[3:31 P.M.]:
We use a company called Duma Clean. They've been good for us.
George Day[3:31 P.M.]:
They're great, but they specialize in the food and beverage industry. It suits to the business Steph has, but I don't think that's what Red is looking for.
Red Morris[3:33 P.M.]:
Yes. I need a company with a track record with large institutions. The college has 20 classrooms so it will be a big contract.
Coleen Vale[3:35 P.M.]:
Red, my company is experienced with that kind of work. Would you mind if we submitted a proposal?
George Day[3:35 P.M.]:
Red, I can vouch for Coleen's firm. We've used Beaumont Cleaning for more than 15 years and they've always given us great service at competitive rates.
Red Morris[3:40 P.M.]:
I would like to meet with you to discuss the contract, Coleen. Do you have time to come and look at the college tomorrow?
Coleen Vale[3:49 P.M.]:
I' ll be out of town tomorrow to meet one of my clients, but I can send one of our sales representatives around if that's OK with you.
Red Morris[3:54 P.M.]:
That'll be fine. I'm free between 2 P.M. and 3 P.M.
Coleen Vale[3:56 P.M.]:
OK. I'll call you in a few minutes to sort out the details.

168. Who are the writers?

(A) Employees of a laundry service
(B) Real estate agents
(C) Members of a business association
(D) College students

169. What kind of business does Ms. Jordan most likely work for?

(A) A dry cleaning service
(B) A financial institution
(C) An online store
(D) A restaurant

170. What will Ms. Vale most likely do tomorrow?

(A) She will meet with Mr. Morris.
(B) She will attend a meeting.
(C) She will interview a job applicant.
(D) She will recommend a course to some employees.

171. At 3:54 P.M., what does Mr. Morris mean when he writes, "That'll be fine"?

(A) He can welcome Ms. Vale in the afternoon.
(B) He is happy to meet Ms. Vale's colleague.
(C) He finds Ms. Vale's rates acceptable.
(D) He expects the weather to clear up.

Nasser Aims for Mutually Assured Prosperity by Brandon Harps

Cambridge (19 November) — The Cambridge-based online bookstore Nasser was recently the subject of a documentary film which explored the company's unusual internal structure and policies with regard to profit sharing.

At the time of the company's foundation, the president instituted an unusual rule which stated that no employee may earn more than five times the wage of the lowest paid full-time employee in the business. This rule ensures that upper management may only enjoy the fruits of the company's success if they share the rewards with those lower down the chain.

— [1] — . Publishers wishing to sell books through the online service pay a commission of only five percent to the company, which is the lowest sales commission charged by any online bookstore in the country. — [2] — . Nasser is able to do this because of the incredible efficiency it is able to achieve in its warehouses and the entire supply chain. This is something only possible where every employee benefits directly from the company's profitability.

The film, directed by Claude Rossi, was shown on Channel 7 last Friday, 12 November and since then, Nasser's sales have increased by some 12 percent. It seems that the community wants to reward the company for its progressive attitude toward profit. — [3] — .

The company does not have sales or offer discounts. — [4] — . However, it does allow publishers to distribute free online content to generate interest in their products. This usually takes the form of downloadable eBooks or audio versions of underperforming titles. It appears this is one of the reasons for the business' incredible success and it is something that competitors are starting to imitate.

172. What is the article mainly about?

(A) The dangers associated with running an online business

(B) Strategies employed by a publisher to train employees

(C) The career of a successful documentary filmmaker

(D) A company president's goal of distributing wealth fairly

173. What is indicated about Nasser?

(A) It is the country's longest-running online bookstore.

(B) It prefers to hire graduates straight out of university.

(C) It strives to reduce wastefulness in its processes.

(D) It commissioned Claude Rossi to make its documentary.

174. According to the article, why did Nasser experience an increase in sales?

(A) It enjoyed some positive publicity.

(B) It launched a new service.

(C) It received an award from the government.

(D) It ran a seasonal sale.

175. In which of the positions marked [1], [2], [3], and [4] does the following sentence best belong?

"This ideal is not only applied to employees but also suppliers."

(A) [1]

(B) [2]

(C) [3]

(D) [4]

GO ON TO THE NEXT PAGE

NetNex Internet Service
373 Bruce Street, Boise ID 83702

Ms. Trisha Colbert
165 Rio Bravo Drive, Apt. 201
West Boise, ID 83642
Account Number: 8423-4390-43

October 26

Dear Ms. Colbert:

You are currently signed up for our NetNex Lite plan, which is the cheapest plan we offer. It allows you to use up to one gigabyte of data each month at the very low monthly rate of $10. Data used in excess of that amount will be charged at a rate of 10 cents per megabyte. NetNex Internet Service is obliged to contact you by e-mail if your usage exceeds the amount included in your monthly plan. On October 20, your usage came to a total of 1.2 gigabytes.

Since that date, you have used almost 500 megabytes of data. That comes to a total of $50 to date. If you were to upgrade to the NetNex Basic plan, you could use three gigabytes of data for just $20 per month. I strongly recommend this plan if you expect to continue using a larger amount of data. We would be willing to retroactively implement this new plan so that your fee for this month would be reduced from a total of $65 to just $20. You can do this by logging onto the Web site and filling in a plan upgrade form.

Rhod Davies

Rhod Davies
Customer Service Manager

NetNex Internet Service	Monthly Statement
Ms. Trisha Colbert	November
165 Rio Bravo Drive, Apt. 201	Account Number: 8423-4390-43
West Boise, ID 83642	Service Plan: NetNex Basic plan
Service for the period: November 1 through November 30	Total Charges: $32.50
This amount will be deducted from your bank account automatically on December 10. If you see any discrepancies in this bill and your actual usage, please contact the customer service division at 986-555-2343 by December 31.	

176. Why was the letter sent to Ms. Colbert?

(A) To advise that she switch to another plan
(B) To inform her about an upcoming sale
(C) To announce a change to the service agreement
(D) To request that she update her bank account information

177. What is implied about NetNex Internet Services?

(A) It recently changed its name.
(B) It offers special rates to customers who switch from another provider.
(C) It has multiple offices in the Boise area.
(D) It recently sent Ms. Colbert an e-mail.

178. What should Ms. Colbert do if she wishes to accept Mr. Davies' offer?

(A) Call the customer service section
(B) Complete an online application
(C) Reply to an e-mail from NetNex Internet Service
(D) Agree to pay a processing fee

179. What does the monthly statement imply about Ms. Colbert?

(A) She has not paid her previous month's charges.
(B) She rejected Mr. Davies' offer.
(C) She has used more than three gigabytes of data.
(D) She has changed her home address.

180. According to the monthly statement, why might Ms. Colbert call the customer service division?

(A) To revert to her original plan
(B) To request weekly billing
(C) To discuss an error in her bill
(D) To cancel her Internet service

GO ON TO THE NEXT PAGE

Surefire Car Rental

| FAQ | RESERVATIONS | DIRECTIONS | HOME |

Are discount rates available?

We offer a discount of 10 percent to business travelers.

In order to qualify as a business traveler, it is necessary to make the booking under your company's name. The company must register as a customer with Surefire Car Rental in advance.

Can I pick up my vehicle from the airport?

Surefire Car Rental does not have an office in the airport itself. However, we offer a free shuttle bus ride to our offices, which are all located within five minutes of the airport. Simply call our customer service line as soon as you have your luggage and request a pickup from the front of the arrivals terminal.

What is included with my rental?

The rental rates we list cover only the car itself. You must refill the car with fuel when you return it. Failure to do so will result in a minimum refilling fee of £50. If you would like to use navigation systems or child seats, please request them when you make your reservation. There is an additional charge of £15 and £20 respectively. The rate covers the full rental period no matter how long or short.

E-Mail Message

From:	Dale Waters <dwaters@novashark.com>
To:	Customer Service <cs@surefirecr.com>
Date:	23 March
Subject:	Rental receipt

To Whom It May Concern,

I recently hired a car through Surefire Car Rental for a business trip I took to Belgium. I have lost the receipt I received from Surefire Car Rental so I am using my credit card statement to seek reimbursement from my company. Looking at the statement, I see a £15 charge that I cannot explain. Would you mind sending me a copy of the receipt by e-mail so that I can justify this expense to my company?

I was extremely happy with the reservation and car pickup process. Nevertheless, I would like to highlight one area of disappointment. Frankly, the car was older and in worse condition than I had anticipated looking at the description and photographs on the Web site. As I was happy with every other aspect of this transaction, I hope that future rental vehicles will be in better shape.

Sincerely,

Dale Waters
Nova Shark Water Pumps

181. According to the Web page, who is eligible for a discount?

(A) People who are registered customers of Surefire Car Rental
(B) People whose reservations are made under company names
(C) People who have used Surefire Car Rental in the past
(D) People whose rental period is longer than 10 days

182. When should people arrange transportation from the airport?

(A) When they make a reservation
(B) When they learn their arrival time
(C) When their plane arrives
(D) When they have retrieved their luggage

183. What is implied about Surefire Car Rental?

(A) Its cars are supposed to be returned with a full tank of fuel.
(B) Its cars come with free extras.
(C) It offers a wide variety of makes and models.
(D) It provides 24-hour customer support.

184. What is most likely true about Mr. Waters?

(A) He requested a navigation system with his rental.
(B) He failed to refill the car with fuel before returning it.
(C) He traveled to Belgium for personal reasons.
(D) He has rented from Surefire Car Rental before.

185. What does Mr. Waters mention about the car he rented?

(A) It was returned to a rental agency in Belgium.
(B) It did not live up to his expectations.
(C) It had excellent fuel economy.
(D) It was more expensive than his travel budget allowed for.

GO ON TO THE NEXT PAGE

Join the Gladwell Humane Society

By becoming a member of the Gladwell Humane Society, you can help support a large number of worthwhile local causes both financially and through activities run by the society. As a member of the society, you can take advantage of many benefits provided by like-minded local businesses and even the local government. These benefits include discounts on goods and services and free tickets to many events. Of course, these benefits are only available to current members and it is necessary to devote a certain number of hours each month to maintain your membership.

Membership Levels:

Gold — For members who contribute over 12 hours of service a week. Benefits include all silver level benefits as well as a State Museum and Art Gallery membership, 10 percent off on all purchases at participating stores, including Greenmart and South Hampton Shopping Center.

Silver — For members who contribute over six hours of service a week. Benefits include all bronze level benefits as well as free use of public swimming pools and gyms. Five percent off on all purchases at participating stores, including Greenmart and South Hampton Shopping Center.

Bronze — For members who contribute over three hours of service a week. Benefits include free registration in the Annual Gladwell Fun Run and a three percent discount on council taxes.

Standard — For members who contribute to at least one event a year. You will receive a monthly newsletter which provides information about upcoming volunteer opportunities and social events.

To learn more about the club, please contact the president, Red Pearlman, at rpearlman@gladwellhumanesociety.org.

GHS The Gladwell Humane Society

Ms. Henrietta Wright
783 Hillview Terrace
Bradman, WA
98004

July 7

Dear Ms. Wright,

Please find enclosed your new membership card. I hope you will take full advantage of all the benefits it offers. You certainly deserve them. I have gotten the Art Gallery membership using mine and it has given me many hours of pleasure. I hope that you will do the same. I would be very happy if you would join me in attending an exhibition of Mr. Greg Holland's work there on July 30. I have made an arrangement with the museum curator for a private tour before the exhibition officially opens.

I have enclosed the monthly newsletter with this letter. You will notice that our next meeting is scheduled for July 27. I would like you to give a five- to ten-minute inspirational talk to the other members.

Sincerely,

Red Pearlman

Red Pearlman

To:	Red Pearlman <rpearlman@gladwellhumanesociety.org>
From:	Henrietta Wright <hwright@gladwellhumanesociety.org>
Date:	July 9
Subject:	Thank you

Dear Mr. Pearlman,

Thank you so much for your letter of July 7. I get great joy from my work with the Gladwell Humane Society. Now that my working life is over, I hope to dedicate even more time to our local community. I am grateful to you and the Gladwell Humane Society for helping me do that.

Unfortunately, I am unable to attend the next scheduled meeting of GHS as I will be away visiting family. However, I would be honored to accompany you to the Art Gallery to see Mr. Holland's exhibition. Please let me know what time and where you would like to meet.

Regards,

Henrietta Wright

---

186. What is suggested about the Gladwell Humane Society?

(A) It offers entitlements to members according to their service time.
(B) It has received an achievement award from the city council.
(C) It is run by a privately-owned financial institution.
(D) It was founded by a popular politician.

187. What is NOT a benefit of membership in the Gladwell Humane Society?

(A) Entry to government-run fitness centers
(B) Discounts from local retail stores
(C) A reduction of local government taxes
(D) One free ticket to movie theaters a month

188. What level of membership has Ms. Wright most likely received?

(A) Gold
(B) Silver
(C) Bronze
(D) Standard

189. What is suggested about Ms. Wright?

(A) She has retired from her job.
(B) She is a founding member of GHS.
(C) She will hire an inspirational speaker.
(D) She has introduced other people to GHS.

190. When will Ms. Wright and Mr. Pearlman most likely meet next?

(A) On July 7
(B) On July 9
(C) On July 27
(D) On July 30

GO ON TO THE NEXT PAGE

Questions 191-195 refer to the following Web page, e-mail, and ticket.

https://www.TravelProX.com ▼

Welcome to TravelProX

TravelProX is unlike most other travel Web sites in that it derives its profit from membership dues rather than taking a commission from hotels and airlines when you buy your tickets. This means that the businesses who sell through us can afford to offer you better rates. Our membership fee is only $20 per year, which means that you will easily offset the cost of membership with your first booking of a hotel, flight or tour from our huge selection.

For those of you looking for a holiday with no specific destination in mind, we have a weekly specials page where you can choose from hundreds of package deals at heavily discounted prices. For extra adventurous people, we have the mystery tour option. For the low price of $100, you can book an overnight holiday in a foreign country. The destination, transport there and back and accommodation will be chosen randomly by our reservations software. You could end up almost anywhere in the world. Naturally, certain conditions apply. You must be able to travel in as little as 24 hours' notice. You must be able to commit to a trip taking as long as five days in total. There can be no changes to the itinerary once it has been issued.

E-Mail Message

To: Simon Chang <schang@princelax.com>
From: Customer Service <cs@travelprox.com>
Date: September 21
Subject: Your booking

Dear Mr. Chang,

Thank you for booking your trip through TravelProX. Please check the following details and make sure that they are completely accurate. If they are, please click the link marked "confirm" at the bottom of this e-mail. You will be returned to the Web site, where you can finalize your purchase.

Hotel: Rasmussen's Lodge, 123 Frank Drive, West Thornberry
Date of arrival: October 4
Date of departure: October 6
Room: Standard with buffet breakfast (Single occupancy)
Price: $220.00

Your search history on TravelProX indicates that you have shown an interest in playing golf. Unfortunately, there are no courses near the hotel you have chosen. Before you finalize your purchase, you may wish to consider the Beaumont Hotel. Rooms are available at the same price as the ones you have reserved, and there is a golf course within walking distance. Otherwise, you may confirm the trip as it appears above.

CONFIRM

Please print out this voucher and show it to the hotel staff at check-in.

Reservation Number: MU7482383
Reservation Type: Accommodation only
Guest Name: Simon Chang
Hotel: Beaumont Hotel
Check-in: Friday, October 4
Check out: Sunday, October 6
Room Type: Standard
Breakfast: Included (Buffet in Stylez Restaurant on the first floor.)

191. What is the purpose of the Web page?

(A) To explain ways that people can make money from home
(B) To suggest positions for job seekers to apply for
(C) To describe the benefits of an online service
(D) To recommend a specific travel destination

192. What is NOT a condition of the mystery tour?

(A) There is a fixed price.
(B) Only international destinations are available.
(C) The return date is not negotiable.
(D) All travel must be taken alone.

193. What is indicated about Mr. Chang?

(A) He reserved his transportation with TravelProX.
(B) He took out a membership in TravelProX.
(C) He has advertised his business with TravelProX.
(D) He was previously employed at TravelProX.

194. In the e-mail, the word "returned" in paragraph 1, line 3 is closest in meaning to

(A) sent back
(B) responded
(C) replaced
(D) looked over

195. What is most likely true about Mr. Chang's trip?

(A) He took advantage of the mystery tour option.
(B) He will travel with some family members.
(C) He will receive a reimbursement from his company.
(D) He intends to play golf during his stay.

GO ON TO THE NEXT PAGE

To:	Claire Thompson <cthompson@thompsonco.com>
From:	Blair Goldman <bgoldman@thompsonco.com>
Date:	November 6
Subject:	Stirling Advertising Agency

Dear Ms. Thompson,

You asked me to send a review of the performance of Stirling Advertising Agency. My personal opinion is that they are simply repeating different variations of the same kind of advertising they did for us in the first year. The success we experienced then was because of the originality and the high quality of the advertisements. It seems that the new advertisements are less and less successful because the company has already used up all of its best ideas. Stirling Advertising has been requesting a bigger budget each year and despite this, sales of our confectionaries are more and more discouraging. The returns on our investment in advertising have been decreasing. It is a big problem as we only produce confectionary and we've given the whole contract to one agency. In short, I believe it is time for us to replace Stirling Advertising Agency or at least offer part of the contract to another company.

Sincerely,

Blair Goldman
Chief of Sales — Thompson Co.

To:	Blair Goldman <bgoldman@thompsonco.com>
From:	Claire Thompson <cthompson@thompsonco.com>
Date:	November 6
Subject:	RE: Stirling Advertising Agency

Thank you for your insightful review of Stirling Advertising's performance. It cannot be denied that sales have declined since we started using Stirling. However, I am not sure that this is a failing on Stirling Advertising's part. I think we should discuss the matter with our own product development department and get their opinions. I will put Stirling Advertising Agency on notice that their performance is under review and pressure them to produce a more successful campaign this year.

Claire Thompson
President — Thompson Co.

Pineapple Water
A treat to beat the summer heat!

This new sports beverage comes from Thompson Co. and has all the essential salts and minerals you need to stay active through the summer.
Don't let the heat slow you down.
Stay fit, stay active, stay hydrated!

196. According to the first e-mail, what did Ms. Thompson request Mr. Goldman to do?

(A) Provide some updated sales statistics
(B) Do an evaluation of a service
(C) Announce a company's decision
(D) Offer assistance with a project

197. What is stated about Stirling Advertising Agency?

(A) It has been employed by Ms. Thompson's company for several years.
(B) It has had its budget reduced since last year.
(C) It has gradually been having greater and greater success.
(D) It has contracts with several other companies.

198. What do Mr. Goldman and Ms. Thompson agree about?

(A) Stirling Advertising Agency's responsibility for sales
(B) A prediction for the company's future profits
(C) The company's current sales performance
(D) The marketing strategy for a product

199. In the second e-mail, the word "under" in paragraph 1, line 5 is closest in meaning to

(A) covered by
(B) secondary to
(C) subject to
(D) available for

200. What is most likely true about Thompson Co.?

(A) It is no longer using Stirling Advertising Agency.
(B) It has stopped producing some of its products.
(C) It has reduced its product development department.
(D) It is experimenting with a new product type.

TEST 3

TEST3 (Day27〜39) の学習の進め方

下の表を参照して、Day ごとに指定した問題を制限時間以内で解いてください。

解き終わったら、学習日と解答時間を記入しましょう。

Day27 TEST3 シングルパッセージ 2 題			Day34 TEST3 トリプルパッセージ 1 題		

Day27	TEST3 シングルパッセージ 2 題 Q147-148, Q149-150 1/5 回目		**Day34**	TEST3 トリプルパッセージ 1 題 Q186-190 1/5 回目	
学習日 /	制限時間　4 分　解答時間　　　分		学習日 /	制限時間　5 分　解答時間　　　分	
Day28	TEST3 シングルパッセージ 2 題 Q151-152, Q153-154 1/5 回目		**Day35**	TEST3 トリプルパッセージ 1 題 Q191-195 1/5 回目	
学習日 /	制限時間　4 分　解答時間　　　分		学習日 /	制限時間　5 分　解答時間　　　分	
Day29	TEST3 シングルパッセージ 2 題 Q155-157, Q158-160 1/5 回目		**Day36**	TEST3 トリプルパッセージ 1 題 Q196-200 1/5 回目	
学習日 /	制限時間　6 分　解答時間　　　分		学習日 /	制限時間　5 分　解答時間　　　分	
Day30	TEST3 シングルパッセージ 2 題 Q161-163, Q164-167 1/5 回目		**Day37**	TEST3 全シングルパッセージ Q147-175 2/5 回目	
学習日 /	制限時間　7 分　解答時間　　　分		学習日 /	制限時間　29 分　解答時間　　　分	
Day31	TEST3 シングルパッセージ 2 題 Q168-171, Q172-175 1/5 回目		**Day38**	TEST3 全マルチプルパッセージ Q176-200 2/5 回目	
学習日 /	制限時間　8 分　解答時間　　　分		学習日 /	制限時間　25 分　解答時間　　　分	
Day32	TEST3 ダブルパッセージ 1 題 Q176-180 1/5 回目		**Day39**	TEST3 全問 Q147-200 3/5 回目	
学習日 /	制限時間　5 分　解答時間　　　分		学習日 /	制限時間　54 分　解答時間　　　分	
Day33	TEST3 ダブルパッセージ 1 題 Q181-185 1/5 回目				
学習日 /	制限時間　5 分　解答時間　　　分				

TEST3 の 4 回目は Day55 で、5 回目は Day59 で取り組みます。
詳細は別冊 96 ページをご覧ください。

Questions 147-148 refer to the following advertisement.

Wesson A to B

Our highly-trained employees will ensure that your prized possessions make it to their destination in one piece. Whether you are relocating your apartment down the street or a fully furnished house across the country, Wesson A to B is the clever choice.

We offer:

Free same-day price estimates

24-hour service

Furniture assembly and disassembly at both ends

Comprehensive insurance for your belongings

Call a customer service representative at 555-4782 to make an appointment.
Payment can be made by credit card or bank transfer.
www.wessonatob.com

147. What is being advertised?

(A) A moving company
(B) A travel agency
(C) A shuttle bus service
(D) A local competition

148. What is indicated about the company?

(A) It is looking to update its equipment.
(B) It has recently expanded.
(C) It has been nominated for an award.
(D) It can provide its service in the evenings.

Questions 149-150 refer to the following text-message chain.

BRENDA CARTER 3:51 P.M.
Vladimir, are you busy this evening?

VLADIMIR DRAGO 3:53 P.M.
I don't have any jobs, but I was looking forward to going home.

BRENDA CARTER 3:53 P.M.
I have a delivery job for you. It's a big one at short notice so we can offer you higher rates than usual.

VLADIMIR DRAGO 3:54 P.M.
What's the job?

BRENDA CARTER 3:59 P.M.
We need you to deliver some building materials to an address on Tambourine Mountain by 8:00 P.M.

VLADIMIR DRAGO 4:02 P.M.
Can I take them home with me and deliver them first thing in the morning?

BRENDA CARTER 4:03 P.M.
We can't have that, I'm afraid. Our insurance doesn't allow that kind of thing.

VLADIMIR DRAGO 4:20 P.M.
I'll be there at 5:00 P.M. It'll take me a while to get back to the shipping center at this time of day.

149. What is the purpose of the text-message chain?

(A) To request a refund
(B) To arrange a delivery
(C) To explain a new policy
(D) To offer some advice

150. At 4:03 P.M., what does Brenda mean when she writes, "We can't have that"?

(A) Some equipment is no longer in production.
(B) A reservation has already been accepted.
(C) They do not have permission for an action.
(D) A device has been reserved by another group.

Questions 151-152 refer to the following letter.

Harmony Textiles
563 Dawson Creek Road,
Stanford, QLD 4563

June 19

Dear Ms. Kline,

Thank you for contacting me about launching your new enterprise in China. While I am deeply honored that Mr. Holmes recommended me, I regret that I may not be the best person for the job. I have never worked in the textile business before and have no contacts in the industry.

I have an acquaintance by the name of Roger Lim, who is much more suited to the role. Please contact him at rlim@limconsultancy.com.

I am sorry that I am unable to assist you with this project and hope that you will contact me again if something more suited to my skillset comes along.

Sincerely,

Trevor Wang

Trevor Wang

151. What is implied about Ms. Kline?

(A) She is currently living in China.
(B) She is employed by Mr. Holmes.
(C) She plans to open a new business.
(D) She is looking to hire a secretary.

152. Why is Mr. Wang unable to assist Ms. Kline?

(A) He has too much on his schedule.
(B) He has committed to help a competitor.
(C) He does not take international contracts.
(D) He lacks appropriate experience.

GO ON TO THE NEXT PAGE

Questions 153-154 refer to the following postcard.

Snaptech

Dear Valued Customer:

Snaptech prides itself on its excellent product quality and customer service, so it pains us to admit that a product recall is necessary for one of our recently released products. Purchasers of the U766X mini projector are being asked to return their devices to have the battery replaced. The turnaround should take no more than two weeks. We understand that two weeks is too long to be without this important device for some people. By way of compensation, we are offering a price reduction of 20 percent on your next purchase of a Snaptech device. Simply show this postcard to the clerk when you make your purchase. Please keep in mind that this discount is only available from official retailers of Snaptech products.

Sincerely,

Dale Shepheard
CEO — Snaptech

153. What are customers asked to do?

(A) Download a users' manual
(B) Return a product
(C) Send in a warranty form
(D) Register as customers

154. What compensation is offered?

(A) A full refund of the purchase price
(B) A product upgrade
(C) A discount on a future purchase
(D) A written apology

Questions 155-157 refer to the following advertisement.

Would you like to improve your confidence in the kitchen?
If so, you need to attend a session with a qualified chef.

Saul White, a highly respected chef who has worked in five-star hotels around the world, is giving an introductory cooking class at the Vandelay Convention Center.

Chef White's appearance fees and the rent on the hall have been covered by the Regent Cooking School so anyone is welcome to attend for free. We simply ask that you register in advance as seats are limited. To register you must contact the Regent Cooking School enrollments office directly. You can do so by calling 555-7432, sending an e-mail to enrollments@regentcs.com, or by sending a text message with your name to 030-555-5150.

An Afternoon with Chef Saul White
Brought to you by
Regent Cooking School

---

155. What is being advertised?

(A) A documentary
(B) A seminar
(C) An online service
(D) A recipe book

156. What is indicated about Saul White?

(A) He will be paid for his appearance.
(B) He has appeared at Vandelay Convention Center before.
(C) He is a full-time employee of Regent Cooking School.
(D) He has recently published a book.

157. What registration method is NOT mentioned?

(A) Sending a text-message
(B) Calling a cooking school
(C) Writing an e-mail
(D) Sending a fax

GO ON TO THE NEXT PAGE

Holyfield Museum of Modern Art
56 Harborview Road, Sydney, NSW 2003, Australia

Ms. Yoko White
45 Giordano Court
Sydney, NSW 2012

May 2

Dear Ms. White,

As a member of the Holyfield Museum of Modern Art Society (HMMAS), you will be eager to know the status of our plans to add an additional wing to the museum. I am happy to inform you that the work is complete and that we will be opening our first exhibition in the space on Friday, July 17. The exhibition is called *Art in Nature* and it features photographs of plants and animals taken with a special zoom lens. The exhibition features works by Neil Davis, Bob Chang, Helen Unaday, as well as three other photographers.

As a platinum member, you are entitled to attend a special pre-opening event on the evening of Thursday, July 16. I strongly encourage you to attend as the preview audience who will not be restricted from approaching the artworks, and none of them will be shielded by the glass barriers we put up for the public exhibition. Furthermore, the museum's head guide will be taking visitors around each of the works explaining them and their place within the context of the exhibition. This will be led by Ms. Dotty Smith, who has been with the museum for more than 20 years.

Tickets for the general public to see *Art in Nature* will be available online or from the museum box office. The exhibition will be on display for only two weeks so please be sure not to miss this brief opportunity to see some very exciting artworks.

Sincerely,

Rose McTavish

Rose McTavish
Museum Curator

158. Why was the letter written?

(A) To request payment of membership dues
(B) To announce the release of a new product
(C) To thank a visitor for writing a review
(D) To provide a situation update

159. What is NOT mentioned about *Art in Nature*?

(A) It will be touring several countries.
(B) A preview will be shown to certain people.
(C) It is a collaborative exhibition.
(D) The artworks will be shown temporarily.

160. Who is Dotty Smith?

(A) A television personality
(B) A member of HMMAS
(C) A nature photographer
(D) A tour guide

Questions 161-163 refer to the following notice.

Important Notice

Every day, certain rides at the park are closed for maintenance. You will be pleased to learn that today, all of our most popular rides are available for you to enjoy. — [1] — . These include the Whizzer, Gold Rush Roller Coaster, and The Mighty Drop. — [2] — . However, Wild Water and Radical Race will be shut while workers conduct an inspection and mechanical upkeep. Work on the latter will not be finished early enough for visitors to ride it before closing time. We regret any inconvenience this causes.

You can get information about which rides are scheduled for maintenance by looking at the Web site at www.lunaland.com. — [3] — . Visitors who have purchased their one-day tickets online may ask for a refund before entering the park if the ride they intended to enjoy is unavailable. Naturally, this does not apply to season or lifetime pass holders. — [4] — .

Management

161. For whom is the notice most likely intended?

(A) Amusement park guests
(B) Maintenance workers
(C) Bus drivers
(D) Ticket sellers

162. According to the notice, what attraction is NOT available today?

(A) The Whizzer
(B) Gold Rush Roller Coaster
(C) Wild Water
(D) Radical Race

163. In which of the positions marked [1], [2], [3], and [4] does the following sentence best belong?

"Therefore we encourage you to check the status of your favorite attractions before leaving home."

(A) [1]
(B) [2]
(C) [3]
(D) [4]

Questions 164-167 refer to the following article.

Papua New Guinea Awards Young Entrepreneur at Gala Event

The Port Moresby Chamber of Commerce last night awarded a young entrepreneur from Porebada for his contribution to the local community and our local economy. Reece Carmody's company, Luscious Balms has been making skin cream from several plant species native to the area. After a series of fortunate incidents, the creams caught the attention of several international news and current affairs programs, which ran positive stories making Luscious Balms a highly sought-after brand. The production requirements have forced Carmody to expand his operations three times in the last two years and employ more than 200 additional staff. He is now the region's largest employer and that is what earned him the Businessperson-of-the-Year award this year.

The company now has factories in Port Moresby and Hula as well as the most recently opened plant in Kokoda. It was there that the awards ceremony was held as a joint celebration of the plant's opening and Mr. Carmody's achievements for the community. During his acceptance speech, Mr. Carmody talked about his plans for the future, expressing his belief that the company needed to expand into other product lines.

While he would not go into detail, he did mention that he was negotiating the purchase of an abandoned food processing plant in central Port Moresby. He said that he believed that people around the world would soon be enjoying delicacies from the forests of Papua New Guinea.

164. Why was Reece Carmody given an award?

(A) He has provided many jobs in Papua New Guinea.
(B) He donated money to support the local community.
(C) He encouraged businesses to join the chamber of commerce.
(D) He won a design competition.

165. Who is Reece Carmody?

(A) An importer of products from Papua New Guinea
(B) The owner of a manufacturing plant
(C) The chairperson of the chamber of commerce
(D) An expert in farming processes

166. Where was the award presented?

(A) In Port Moresby
(B) In Porebada
(C) In Kokoda
(D) In Hula

167. What is indicated about Luscious Balms?

(A) It will change ownership soon.
(B) It will diversify its product range.
(C) It has received government support.
(D) It is opening its own retail stores.

Questions 168-171 refer to the following online chat discussion.

Colin Sorenson [3:30 P.M.]:
It's getting close to summer and a lot of people are going to start placing orders soon. Perhaps we should offer a discount to people who order early.

Harry Rollins [3:31 P.M.]:
I agree. That way we can space out the work over the busy season a bit better.

Lisa Wang [3:31 P.M.]:
Perhaps we should put an advertisement in this month's issue of House and Garden. A lot of new home builders read that magazine and they'll be thinking of swimming with their families over summer.

Colin Sorenson [3:33 P.M.]:
Sounds good, Lisa. Can you call them and find out about the cost of placing a full-page advertisement?

Lisa Wang [3:35 P.M.]:
Sure thing.

Donna Petrov [3:38 P.M.]:
Instead of offering a discount, how about offering free upgrades? A deluxe filter or an automated cleaning system might appeal to busy people who don't have time for cleaning.

Harry Rollins [3:42 P.M.]:
That's an idea! Otherwise, we could offer a free set of a parasol and two chairs to set by the water.

Colin Sorenson[3:45 P.M.]:
These are all good ideas. Let's get together on Tuesday morning to discuss it before we make any decisions.

Donna Petrov [3:46 P.M.]:
I know Harry and Lisa are free. I've got to visit a client in Melville. How's Wednesday?

Colin Sorenson [3:49 P.M.]:
I'm sure that'll be fine. They'll be around until Thursday.

---

168. Where do the writers most likely work?

(A) At an advertising agency
(B) At a magazine publisher
(C) At a pool building company
(D) At a house cleaning company

169. What is Ms. Wang asked to do?

(A) Calculate the cost of production
(B) Purchase a copy of a magazine
(C) Attend a marketing conference
(D) Check the price of advertising

170. At 3:42 P.M., what does Mr. Rollins mean when he writes, "That's an idea"?

(A) He doubts a plan will work.
(B) He likes the suggestion.
(C) He has heard the idea before.
(D) He needs more time to consider.

171. When will the writers most likely meet?

(A) On Tuesday
(B) On Wednesday
(C) On Thursday
(D) On Friday

GO ON TO THE NEXT PAGE

To:	Kent Walsh <kwalsh@freemontfarms.com>
From:	Stephanie Carter <scarter@verhovenproductions.com>
Date:	September 9
Subject:	123 Field's Road

Dear Mr. Walsh,

My name is Stephanie Carter and I am a producer for the video production company, Verhoven Productions. I got your e-mail address from the sign in front of your property at 123 Field's Road. We are looking for locations to shoot a drama about the lives of some early 20th Century New England dairy farmers and one of our location scouts discovered your farm while driving through the area. — [1] — . She took some photographs from the road and I believe it will be a perfect setting. I would like to ask whether or not you would object to our using the farm as a location for the drama.

— [2] — . A few members of the production team and I are currently staying in the Grand Hotel in Bangor while we make preparations for filming. You can contact me at this e-mail address or by telephone at 090-555-8323. We would like to confirm the production locations by Friday, September 15 as we will be returning to Philadelphia on September 16. Therefore, I would be most appreciative if you could contact us as soon as possible.

I have brought the director and a production designer with me on this trip. — [3] — . We would be happy to visit you at your farm or get together in one of the meeting spaces in the hotel.

The production is likely to take around three weeks from mid-February to early March. We would like to use your barns for our interior and exterior shots. We can schedule production for mornings or afternoons depending on your work schedule. — [4] — . If you are not able to accommodate our request, we would appreciate an introduction to any of your neighbors who might be interested in cooperating with the production.

Sincerely,

Stephanie Carter
Verhoven Productions

172. Who most likely is Mr. Walsh?

(A) A dairy farmer
(B) An experienced filmmaker
(C) A real estate agent
(D) A movie director

173. What is NOT suggested about Ms. Carter?

(A) She has visited Mr. Walsh's property.
(B) She is an employee of Verhoven Productions.
(C) She works for a company in Philadelphia.
(D) She will return to Bangor in February.

174. What is Mr. Walsh asked to do?

(A) Visit Verhoven Productions' studios
(B) Supply some photographs of his land
(C) Allow a movie crew to use his property
(D) Reserve a meeting space at the Grand Hotel

175. In which of the positions marked [1], [2], [3], and [4] does the following sentence best belong?

"If there are any questions you would like to ask them, please let me know."

(A) [1]
(B) [2]
(C) [3]
(D) [4]

| Customer name: Freda Dali
Account number: 7834939
Date: December 3 | **NutriSpark** |

Quantity	Description	Price
1	BBN Facial Cleanser 250ml	$56.00
3	Coconut Oil Body Cream 500ml	$36.00
2	Dr. Swan's Body Wash	$30.00
1	Wood pin hairbrush	$54.00
	Subtotal:	$176.00
	NutriSpark Frequent Shopper's Discount (5%):	$8.80
	Delivery:	$0.00
	Amount paid:	**$167.20**

Thank you for choosing to shop at the NutriSpark Online Shopping. Purchases totaling more than $100 automatically qualify for free delivery within the United States.

Please take the time to write a review of the products after trying them out. Consistent and informative contributors to the reviews section are often rewarded with discounts or even free items from manufacturers.

To:	Freda Dali <fdali@novabird.com>
From:	Brendan Philips <bphilips@ysc.com>
Date:	December 21
Subject:	Thank you

Dear Ms. Dali,

Yakkleman Skin Care has signed a deal with NutriSpark Online Shopping making them the only retailer with access to our products. In return for making this exclusive commitment to NutriSpark, Yakkleman has been afforded assistance with its marketing efforts. Your name and contact details were provided to us in accordance with the NutriSpark member's agreement.

We would like to send you some free product samples in return for an honest review to be posted on the NutriSpark Web site. To ensure that shoppers get completely honest and reliable information, your reviews will be attributed to a username unknown to Yakkleman Skin Care. Reviews will be monitored by NutriSpark Online Shopping to ensure quality. You are under no obligation to write positive reviews of the free products you receive.

If you are interested in taking part, please click the following link and register as a trusted reviewer with NutriSpark Online Shopping. You may then nominate Yakkleman Skin Care as a candidate for product reviews.

Trusted Reviewer Registration Page

Sincerely,

Brendan Philips
Yakkleman — Marketing Division

176. What is probably true about NutriSpark?

(A) It specializes in health and beauty products.
(B) It recently changed ownership.
(C) It does not accept payment by credit card.
(D) It promises same day delivery.

177. How did Ms. Dali qualify for free delivery?

(A) By living outside the United States
(B) By becoming a NutriSpark frequent shopper
(C) By ordering during the month of December
(D) By spending more than a certain amount

178. What is indicated about Yakkleman Skin Care?

(A) It has supplied products to Ms. Dali in the past.
(B) It has merged with NutriSpark Online Shopping.
(C) Its products are only available from NutriSpark.
(D) Its customers are automatically entered into a competition.

179. What is implied about Ms. Dali?

(A) She is an employee of NutriSpark Online Shopping.
(B) She has written reviews of products she purchased.
(C) She purchased a Yakkleman Skin Care product.
(D) She will pay a visit to the Yakkleman Skin Care headquarters.

180. How is Ms. Dali directed to take up an offer?

(A) By sending an e-mail
(B) By purchasing a product
(C) By accessing a Web page
(D) By completing a survey

Bremerton Sun

| Home | Advertising | Subscriptions | Archives | Jobs | Contact |

Grand Design Architecture has the following positions available:

Structural Engineer
Our New Jersey office has a vacancy for a structural engineer. The position requires you to be available to both clients and the in-house architects to consult on the structural strength and sustainability of building designs. The successful applicant must have some experience in housing construction.

Marketing Manager
There is an opportunity for an experienced marketing manager at our Boston office. The role requires you to come up with innovative and effective strategies to attract new clients to the firm. Applicants must have a solid understanding of architecture and the building industry. The position is suited to someone with experience as a real estate agent, particularly in houses and apartments. You will regularly be required to attend marketing events on Saturdays and Sundays so you must be flexible when it comes to taking time off.

Preliminary interviews for both positions will be carried out using video conferencing software. However, the final interview will take place at our head office in Springfield.

March 23
Dear Ms. Kim,

I am very interested in working for Grand Design Architecture. In fact, the home I grew up in was designed by Grand Design Architecture and indeed that is what inspired me to study engineering in college. I studied engineering and architecture at Valiance University in Manchester. After graduating, I took a job working as a building inspector for the state government, where I learned a great deal about efficient home design. I think my education and experience make me highly suited to the structural engineer position.

Please find my résumé enclosed.

Sincerely,

Brad Durden

Brad Durden

181. What is a requirement for both of the positions?

(A) A background in residential property
(B) The possession of a driver's license
(C) Certification to use specialized equipment
(D) Experience in management

182. What is suggested about Grand Design Architecture?

(A) It generates publicity through television advertising.
(B) It was founded by a team of architects.
(C) It specializes in creating unusual buildings.
(D) It carries out promotional activities on weekends.

183. In the letter, the word "deal" in paragraph 1, line 5 is closest in meaning to

(A) arrangement
(B) amount
(C) selection
(D) distribution

184. In his letter, what does Mr. Durden communicate to Ms. Kim?

(A) The motivation for his career choice
(B) The reason for his leaving his current position
(C) The kind of salary he expects to receive
(D) The date of an appointment

185. Where would Mr. Durden prefer to work?

(A) In Springfield
(B) In Boston
(C) In New Jersey
(D) In Manchester

GO ON TO THE NEXT PAGE

Rasmussen Science Fiction Writers' Guild
Conditions of Membership

The Rasmussen Science Fiction Writers' Guild is based in Chicago, Illinois. It is an organization created by like-minded writers for the purpose of sharing story ideas, supporting and fostering new talent and providing career advice to people who make their living from creative writing specifically in the science fiction genre.

Applicants for membership in the Rasmussen Science Fiction Writers' Guild (RSFWG) must satisfy the following conditions for consideration.

Applicants must :
- have had a science fiction story published in one of the magazines listed on the RSFWG Web site at www.rasmussensfwg.org/acceptedmagazines and have had a novel or short story published by one of the publishers listed with the North American Publishing Association www.napa.com.
- make the major portion of their personal income from the publication and sale of fictional works.
- live in the United States of America.
- be over the age of 21.
- be contactable by both e-mail and telephone.

Applications will be reviewed by the chairperson of the guild, Mr. Lee Davies and the members of the steering committee.

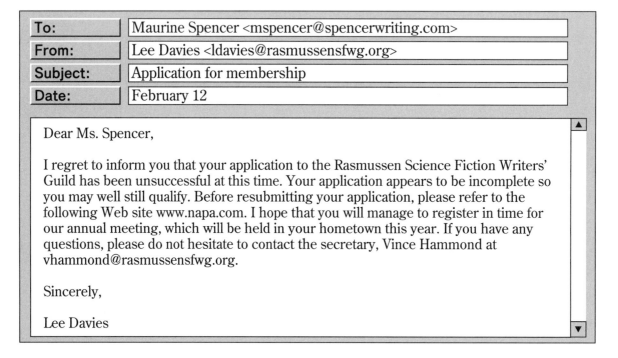

To:	Maurine Spencer <mspencer@spencerwriting.com>
From:	Lee Davies <ldavies@rasmussensfwg.org>
Subject:	Application for membership
Date:	February 12

Dear Ms. Spencer,

I regret to inform you that your application to the Rasmussen Science Fiction Writers' Guild has been unsuccessful at this time. Your application appears to be incomplete so you may well still qualify. Before resubmitting your application, please refer to the following Web site www.napa.com. I hope that you will manage to register in time for our annual meeting, which will be held in your hometown this year. If you have any questions, please do not hesitate to contact the secretary, Vince Hammond at vhammond@rasmussensfwg.org.

Sincerely,

Lee Davies

Annual Meeting of the Rasmussen Science Fiction Writers' Guild In Boulder, Colorado

This year's annual gathering of the Rasmussen Science Fiction Writers' Guild will be held at the Hillview Inn in Boulder, Colorado. The event takes place over two days — April 23 and 24.

There will be presentations from some industry professionals as well as networking opportunities for writers.

In addition, several major literary agents will have booths where members can discuss subjects such as writing contracts, publicity, and industry standards. Register in advance by calling the organizing committee at 773-555-9078.

186. What is NOT an objective of the Rasmussen Science Fiction Writers' Guild?

(A) Encouraging inexperienced writers
(B) Conducting survey research for publishing
(C) Exchanging thoughts about story writing
(D) Suggesting ways to succeed professionally

187. From whom did Ms. Spencer receive an e-mail?

(A) The president of an association
(B) The secretary of a guild
(C) An editor from a publishing company
(D) A retired science fiction writer

188. Why most likely was Ms. Spencer's application unsuccessful?

(A) Her age has not reached the minimum requirement.
(B) She has not read the guild's code of conduct.
(C) She is employed full time in another profession.
(D) She did not provide information on her previous publications.

189. What is implied about Ms. Spencer?

(A) She is from Boulder, Colorado.
(B) She will give a presentation at the annual meeting.
(C) She is planning on visiting Chicago.
(D) She was admitted into RSFWG.

190. How should interested people register for the annual meeting?

(A) By e-mail
(B) By telephone
(C) By letter
(D) By text message

GO ON TO THE NEXT PAGE

Introducing the Resoluxe line of video projectors!

Resoluxe H78	Resoluxe Y65
Designed for the home cinema, this projector is an excellent balance of quality, function, and value for money. The H78 won this year's home cinema design award at the Paris Technology Expo. $730	The Y65 has the brightest lamp of the entire Resoluxe range. This projector can be used in well-lit rooms or even outdoors. Picture resolution is also second to none. This is truly the choice of professionals. $3,500
Resoluxe X45	**Resoluxe T67**
A perfect choice for classrooms and conference centers. This projector can automatically detect a whiteboard or blackboard and adjust its colors and light intensity to match. $2,040	This tiny portable projector is perfect for projecting photographs or advertisements in dimly lit spaces. $198

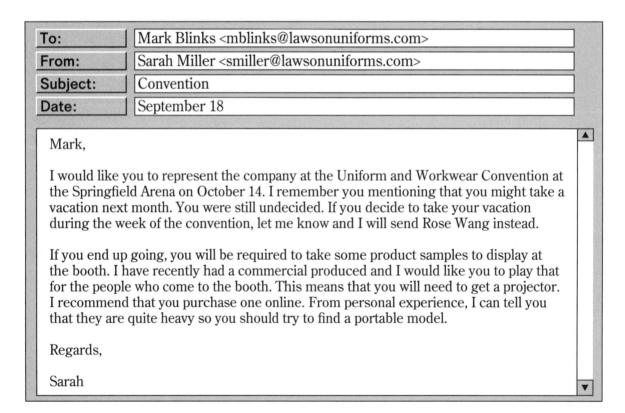

To:	Mark Blinks <mblinks@lawsonuniforms.com>
From:	Sarah Miller <smiller@lawsonuniforms.com>
Subject:	Convention
Date:	September 18

Mark,

I would like you to represent the company at the Uniform and Workwear Convention at the Springfield Arena on October 14. I remember you mentioning that you might take a vacation next month. You were still undecided. If you decide to take your vacation during the week of the convention, let me know and I will send Rose Wang instead.

If you end up going, you will be required to take some product samples to display at the booth. I have recently had a commercial produced and I would like you to play that for the people who come to the booth. This means that you will need to get a projector. I recommend that you purchase one online. From personal experience, I can tell you that they are quite heavy so you should try to find a portable model.

Regards,

Sarah

Product Reviews

Reviewer: Rose Wang (Corporate Customer) Date: October 14
Rating: ★★★★☆

We needed a projector to display presentation slides at a convention booth. I was very impressed with the speed of delivery. I ordered the projector on October 12 and it arrived on October 13, which was in time for the event on October 14. I did not read the advertisement carefully enough. The room I was in was far too bright for the projector to work effectively. In a more suitable venue, I am sure that the projector would have performed adequately. Based on the quality of this item, I will probably purchase more Resoluxe products in the future.

191. What is implied about the Resoluxe Y65?

(A) It comes with a 12-month warranty.
(B) It has received an award for its design.
(C) It has the highest image quality available.
(D) It is the company's best-selling model.

192. Which projector did Lawson Uniforms most likely buy?

(A) Resoluxe H78
(B) Resoluxe Y65
(C) Resoluxe X45
(D) Resoluxe T67

193. What has Sarah Miller recently done?

(A) Tested several Resoluxe products
(B) Commissioned a promotional video
(C) Visited a convention venue
(D) Written a spending report

194. What is implied about Mr. Blinks?

(A) He took a vacation in October.
(B) He forgot to take the projector.
(C) He agreed to replace Ms. Wang.
(D) He recommended Resoluxe brand.

195. In the review, the phrase, "Based on" in paragraph 1, line 6 is closest in meaning to

(A) Located in
(B) Conditioned for
(C) Founded on
(D) Judging from

Welcome to the
Boatman's Arms Hotel.

The management and staff hope you have a great time during your stay and would be more than happy to assist in any way they can. If you need anything, please do not hesitate to contact the concierge desk on Ext. 772.

To celebrate our 50th anniversary, a complimentary nightly concert is being held in the hotel's main ballroom each evening. Entertainment will include well-known singers and comedians such as Holly Fields and Reg Sumner. On Saturday, May 29 and Sunday, May 30, a golf tournament is being held on the Royal Wings Golf Course attached to the hotel. There are still some spots available for hotel guests so please contact the Golf Clubhouse on Ext. 623 to register. There is $5,000 in prize money up for grabs and you can register for the price of a standard round of 18 holes.

Sincerely,

Ying Pin Lo

Ying Pin Lo
Manager

June 1

To whom it may concern:
I am writing to commend the staff of the Boatman's Arms who made my stay in Charleston such a pleasure. I was originally planning to stay there from May 28 to 29 to purchase some land for a new business I am launching. Unfortunately, the negotiations fell through, and I was feeling rather disappointed. My interactions with the staff there were cheerful and put me in a more positive state of mind, and I decided to stay one more night to attend the event in the hotel's facility. I hardly expected to walk away from the trip thousands of dollars better off, but thanks to the auspicious timing of my visit, I ended up making money. By chance, I met a local business person in the lobby and spent both evenings discussing other potential locations for my business.

Considering the excellent service and wonderful experiences I had at the Boatman's Arms Hotel, I can assure you that I intend to stay there whenever I am back in Charleston.

Sincerely,

Matthew Klinger

Matthew Klinger
MishMash Home Decor

To:	Matthew Klinger <mklinger@mishmash.com>
From:	Rhonda Montgomery <rmontgomery@charlestoncoc.com>
Subject:	Our meeting
Date:	June 2

Dear Mr. Klinger,

As I mentioned during our impromptu meeting on the evening of May 29, I am a member of the Charleston Chamber of Commerce, and as such, I am involved in supporting new businesses moving into the area. Having spoken with a number of other members, I have learned of a few properties you may be interested in. None of them have been listed with real estate agents yet. So, you will have to negotiate directly with the owners. I would be glad to help facilitate that communication if you so wish.

We discussed meeting again on June 5 so that I could take you around the properties. I will pick you up at your hotel in the morning so please let me know where you will be staying. It is not the busy season so I am sure you will be able to find vacancies at most hotels.

Let me know if you need to change our arrangements.

Sincerely,

Rhonda Montgomery
Chairperson — Charleston Chamber of Commerce

196. For whom is the card intended?

(A) A health inspector
(B) A hotel patron
(C) A customer service trainee
(D) A financial advisor

197. What is being offered for free?

(A) Admission to a performance
(B) Entry into a golf competition
(C) Tours of Charleston
(D) Club membership

198. What is implied about Mr. Klinger?

(A) He attended one of the nightly concerts.
(B) He was able to negotiate a price reduction.
(C) He took part in the sporting competition.
(D) He has joined a frequent guest program

199. In the e-mail, the word "supporting" in paragraph 1, line 2 is closest in meaning to

(A) approving
(B) enduring
(C) encouraging
(D) affording

200. What is probably true about June 4?

(A) There will be a meeting of the Charleston Chamber of Commerce.
(B) Ms. Montgomery will introduce Mr. Klinger to a real estate agent.
(C) A special event will be held in the town of Charleston.
(D) Mr. Klinger will stay at the Boatman's Arms Hotel.

TEST 4

TEST4（Day40〜52）の学習の進め方

下の表を参照して、Day ごとに指定した問題を制限時間以内で解いてください。
解き終わったら、学習日と解答時間を記入しましょう。

Day40 学習日 /	TEST4 シングルパッセージ 2 題 Q147-148, Q149-150　1/5 回目 制限時間　4 分　解答時間　　　　　分	**Day47** 学習日 /	TEST4 トリプルパッセージ 1 題 Q186-190　1/5 回目 制限時間　5 分　解答時間　　　　　分
Day41 学習日 /	TEST4 シングルパッセージ 2 題 Q151-152, Q153-154　1/5 回目 制限時間　4 分　解答時間　　　　　分	**Day48** 学習日 /	TEST4 トリプルパッセージ 1 題 Q191-195　1/5 回目 制限時間　5 分　解答時間　　　　　分
Day42 学習日 /	TEST4 シングルパッセージ 2 題 Q155-157, Q158-160　1/5 回目 制限時間　6 分　解答時間　　　　　分	**Day49** 学習日 /	TEST4 トリプルパッセージ 1 題 Q196-200　1/5 回目 制限時間　5 分　解答時間　　　　　分
Day43 学習日 /	TEST4 シングルパッセージ 2 題 Q161-163, Q164-167　1/5 回目 制限時間　7 分　解答時間　　　　　分	**Day50** 学習日 /	TEST4 全シングルパッセージ Q147-175　2/5 回目 制限時間　29 分　解答時間　　　　　分
Day44 学習日 /	TEST4 シングルパッセージ 2 題 Q168-171, Q172-175　1/5 回目 制限時間　8 分　解答時間　　　　　分	**Day51** 学習日 /	TEST4 全マルチプルパッセージ Q176-200　2/5 回目 制限時間　25 分　解答時間　　　　　分
Day45 学習日 /	TEST4 ダブルパッセージ 1 題 Q176-180　1/5 回目 制限時間　5 分　解答時間　　　　　分	**Day52** 学習日 /	TEST4 全問 Q147-200　3/5 回目 制限時間　54 分　解答時間　　　　　分
Day46 学習日 /	TEST3 ダブルパッセージ 1 題 Q181-185　1/5 回目 制限時間　5 分　解答時間　　　　　分		

TEST4 の 4 回目は Day56 で、5 回目は Day60 で取り組みます。
詳細は別冊 96 ページをご覧ください。

Important Notice

HBM Fitness Club on Sutter Street prides itself on the quality of its equipment, the cleanliness of the facilities, and its ability to stay open 24-hours a day. Twice a year, however, we need to close between the hours of 12:00 midnight and 6:00 A.M. for upgrades to the amenities and maintenance work to be carried out on the security system. The next closure will occur on Saturday, October 27. The facilities will be available again from 6:00 A.M. on Sunday morning. We sincerely regret this disruption to your workout schedule. Please keep in mind, the HBM Fitness Club in Hampton will be available during these hours and that your membership entitles you to the use of that location as well.

147. For whom is the notice most likely intended?

(A) Gym members
(B) Vehicle owners
(C) Security personnel
(D) Event organizers

148. According to the notice, what will be unavailable on October 28?

(A) Network connections
(B) Membership information
(C) Public transportation
(D) 24-hour access

GO ON TO THE NEXT PAGE

JACK VOORHEES [8:50 A.M.]
I'm going to apply for a bigger budget for the landscaping project.

MARY WANG [8:51 A.M.]
I'm sure they'll just tell you to get estimates from more companies.

JACK VOORHEES [8:53 A.M.]
I know. The problem is that there are no other companies that can do the work by the December deadline.

MARY WANG [8:53 A.M.]
Did you try searching online?

JACK VOORHEES [8:54 A.M.]
That was the first place I looked. There is a company that I haven't called, but their reviews weren't very good.

MARY WANG [8:59 A.M.]
Best to steer clear, then. We don't want any complications or poor workmanship.

JACK VOORHEES [9:02 A.M.]
Right. I'll let you know how it goes. If they say "no," we'll have to save money by scrapping the plans for a fountain.

MARY WANG [9:03 A.M.]
I hope it doesn't come to that. I think one would look great there.

149. What is the text-message chain mostly about?

(A) An advertising campaign
(B) A project budget
(C) A news story
(D) A building relocation

150. At 9:03 A.M., what does Ms. Wang mean when she writes, "I hope it doesn't come to that"?

(A) She thinks that a fountain is affordable for the company.
(B) She cannot support Mr. Voorhees' request.
(C) She does not want to compromise on the plans.
(D) She would like to postpone a project.

Questions 151-152 refer to the following e-mail.

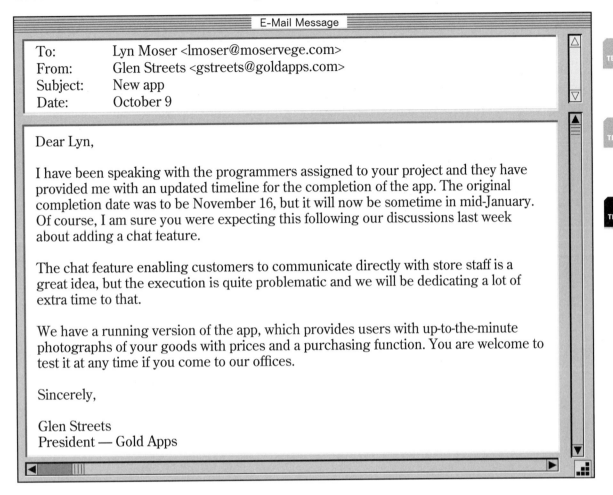

E-Mail Message

To: Lyn Moser <lmoser@moservege.com>
From: Glen Streets <gstreets@goldapps.com>
Subject: New app
Date: October 9

Dear Lyn,

I have been speaking with the programmers assigned to your project and they have provided me with an updated timeline for the completion of the app. The original completion date was to be November 16, but it will now be sometime in mid-January. Of course, I am sure you were expecting this following our discussions last week about adding a chat feature.

The chat feature enabling customers to communicate directly with store staff is a great idea, but the execution is quite problematic and we will be dedicating a lot of extra time to that.

We have a running version of the app, which provides users with up-to-the-minute photographs of your goods with prices and a purchasing function. You are welcome to test it at any time if you come to our offices.

Sincerely,

Glen Streets
President — Gold Apps

151. What is the purpose of the e-mail?

(A) To explain the cancellation of a project
(B) To request payment for some services
(C) To provide an updated project schedule
(D) To describe the process of creating an app

152. What has caused the delay in the development of the app?

(A) An unexpected software update
(B) Changes in government regulations
(C) Usage of copyrighted material
(D) An additional request from the client

GO ON TO THE NEXT PAGE

Volunteer at Porpoise Point!

Every year, groups of concerned citizens gather at the lighthouse on Porpoise Point to carry out a general cleanup of the area after the busy tourist season. We all benefit from the boost to the economy the tourists bring, and it is upon all of us to do our part to help return the environment to an acceptable condition after they leave. Porpoise Point is a protected environmental reserve so we must do our best to remove all trash and signs of human use where possible.

After the cleanup, popular local band Dukes of the Dunes will be providing a free concert. Furthermore, Harper's Steak and Seafood has promised a free hamburger and drink to every registered volunteer.

Learn more at www.porpoisepoint.gov/annualcleanup.

---

153. Why are volunteers needed?

(A) To guide tourists around Porpoise Point

(B) To remove trash from a protected area

(C) To help plan an outdoor concert

(D) To deliver refreshments at a sporting event

154. What is mentioned about Harper's Steak and Seafood?

(A) Its employees will all be volunteering.

(B) It is run inside the lighthouse.

(C) It will be providing free food for participants.

(D) Its menu was changed at the end of summer.

Get Fit Quick

The Dundee area has a wide variety of activities available for people looking for something to do after work or on the weekend. However, it has been mentioned in the past that when it comes to healthy endeavors the region is sorely lacking.

That is until now. Ben and Joe Harper have recently founded the Dundee Fitness and Fun Foundation (DFFF) to coordinate the activities of a number of local health and fitness enthusiasts and encourage more people to try out healthier lifestyles and activities. They did this in response to an observation that the only physical pastime popular in the area was ten pin bowling at Double P Lanes — something that while fun, has few health benefits.

The DFFF now publishes a monthly newsletter and helps coordinate more than 10 events a week. These include bushwalks, bicycle tours, indoor and outdoor climbing events as well as a number of sporting competitions for people of various ages. If you are interested in joining, contact Ben Harper at bh@dundeefff.org.

155. Where would the article most likely be found?

(A) In a business news magazine
(B) In an entertainment guide
(C) In an investment magazine
(D) In a museum newsletter

156. What is implied about Double P Lanes?

(A) It has a longer history than DFFF.
(B) It is sponsored by the local government.
(C) It is owned by Ben and Joe Harper.
(D) It is no longer open for business.

157. What kind of event is DFFF NOT associated with?

(A) Athletic contests
(B) Hiking
(C) Cooking classes
(D) Cycling trips

GO ON TO THE NEXT PAGE

Questions 158-160 refer to the following flyer.

The Wagon Train
The Authentic Taste of the West

The Wagon Train has been serving meals based on the recipes of the European settlers to America for more than 40 years. In order to serve more hungry Orlando residents than ever before, we have recently transferred to Shop 45 in the Bronson Hotel Building on Hounslow Road.

We still have the same hugely popular menu and rustic interior, which have made the restaurant a success since it was founded by Davida Coleman. Ms. Coleman has handed over the duties of head chef to her grandson and now spends most of her time planning her Saturday afternoon cooking class, which she runs in the restaurant's huge, modern kitchen. It is so large, in fact, that the restaurant can continue to operate while the class is in session. Indeed, that day of the week is the busiest for the restaurant as it hosts live performances from local musicians and usually remains open past midnight.

Make a reservation for your next night out by calling 732-555-4899.

158. What is a purpose of the flyer?

(A) To announce the launch of a new menu
(B) To encourage people to attend a special event
(C) To provide information about an investment opportunity
(D) To inform customers of a changed location for a business

159. What is stated about Ms. Coleman?

(A) She established The Wagon Train.
(B) She works as the head chef.
(C) She lives above the restaurant.
(D) She has appeared on television.

160. What is NOT indicated about Saturdays?

(A) Entertainment is provided for diners.
(B) Cooking classes are available.
(C) The restaurant operates until late.
(D) Discount meals are on offer.

https://www.blueflowos.com

BlueFlow Online Shopping

— [1] — . November 11 is the date of our yearly sale and items in every category will be sold at between 30 and 50 percent off.

Preorder now and save! All items being sold as part of the November 11 sale are marked with a purple star. — [2] — . Every year, most of the items sell out before the closing time. So that you don't miss out, we have made it possible to preorder.

By choosing the preorder option, you will be charged 10 percent now, and the balance will be charged automatically on November 11.

Please note that November 11 sale items will not be shipped until the sale is completed. — [3] — . Also, the 10-percent deposit cannot be refunded even if you choose not to go through with the purchase. — [4] — . Naturally, if you make the purchase and then find any defect in the product, you will receive a refund of the full purchase price.

161. Why should customers order before November 11?

(A) Their products are likely to be out of stock quickly.
(B) They can take advantage of even larger discounts.
(C) They will receive free shipping on their orders.
(D) They can receive a free bonus item.

162. What is indicated about the deposit?

(A) It will only be refunded if the product is flawed.
(B) It will be donated to a worthy cause.
(C) It will be used for future product development.
(D) It is a flat rate for all products.

163. In which of the positions marked [1], [2], [3], and [4] does the following sentence best belong?

"Therefore, if you need an item urgently, you should be careful not to select the preorder option."

(A) [1]
(B) [2]
(C) [3]
(D) [4]

Centenary Tower Office Suites
101 Ocean View Parade
Miami, FL 33132

March 23

Ms. Helen Carter
Fielding Accounting Agency
Post Office Box 1204
Miami, FL 33132

Dear Ms. Carter,

It is my sincere pleasure to welcome you and your staff to Centenary Tower Office Suites, Miami's most distinguished business address. I hope that you will take some time to make your employees aware of the building management authority's rules concerning the use of the facilities and conduct within the building and on its grounds.

The building has some amenities which are available for all tenants to use. To ensure that these shared assets are used fairly by all tenants, there are some guidelines which we must all follow.

Parking in the underground garage is limited to one car per tenant unless other arrangements are agreed to at the time of signing the lease. Any cars parked in spaces allocated to other tenants will be towed away at the owner's expense. The first-floor meeting room is available to each tenant for a total of 48 hours per year. There is a similar arrangement for use of the rooftop barbecue area and equipment on the 25th floor. It is necessary to make reservations for both online at www.centenarytoweros.com/amenres.

Building management is available between the hours of 9:00 A.M. and 5:00 P.M. Monday through Friday. Should you need assistance after hours, please call the emergency hotline at 555-9393. Please do not call this line to discuss matters regarding the lease or to discuss matters related to business.

Thank you for choosing Centenary Tower Office Suites. We hope your business will continue to prosper at its new address.

Sincerely,

Philip Gould

Philip Gould
Building Manager — Centenary Tower Office Suites

164. What is the purpose of the letter?

(A) To provide information to new tenants
(B) To inform a tenant about a renewal of the lease
(C) To ask for some financial advice
(D) To advertise office suites available for rental

165. What is indicated about Centenary Tower Office Suites?

(A) It is reasonably priced.
(B) It is very prestigious.
(C) It is located near a park.
(D) It has reached maximum occupancy.

166. What is NOT a part of the building's amenities?

(A) An underground parking garage
(B) A first-floor meeting room
(C) A spa and gym
(D) An open-air barbecue area

167. According to the letter, what should people avoid doing?

(A) Parking vehicles in the space in front of the building's front door
(B) Using the emergency line to discuss the rental agreement
(C) Inviting guests to tenant-only events
(D) Eating lunch in the building's lobby

Questions 168-171 refer to the following online chat discussion.

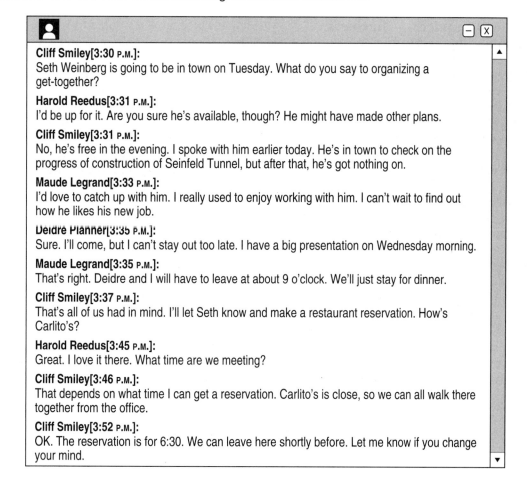

Cliff Smiley[3:30 P.M.]:
Seth Weinberg is going to be in town on Tuesday. What do you say to organizing a get-together?

Harold Reedus[3:31 P.M.]:
I'd be up for it. Are you sure he's available, though? He might have made other plans.

Cliff Smiley[3:31 P.M.]:
No, he's free in the evening. I spoke with him earlier today. He's in town to check on the progress of construction of Seinfeld Tunnel, but after that, he's got nothing on.

Maude Legrand[3:33 P.M.]:
I'd love to catch up with him. I really used to enjoy working with him. I can't wait to find out how he likes his new job.

Deidre Planner[3:35 P.M.]:
Sure. I'll come, but I can't stay out too late. I have a big presentation on Wednesday morning.

Maude Legrand[3:35 P.M.]:
That's right. Deidre and I will have to leave at about 9 o'clock. We'll just stay for dinner.

Cliff Smiley[3:37 P.M.]:
That's all of us had in mind. I'll let Seth know and make a restaurant reservation. How's Carlito's?

Harold Reedus[3:45 P.M.]:
Great. I love it there. What time are we meeting?

Cliff Smiley[3:46 P.M.]:
That depends on what time I can get a reservation. Carlito's is close, so we can all walk there together from the office.

Cliff Smiley[3:52 P.M.]:
OK. The reservation is for 6:30. We can leave here shortly before. Let me know if you change your mind.

168. Why did Mr. Smiley start the online chat?

(A) To introduce a new colleague
(B) To request an extension of a deadline
(C) To suggest a gathering
(D) To announce the signing of a contract

169. What is the purpose of Mr. Weinberg's trip?

(A) To take a vacation
(B) To inspect a construction project
(C) To purchase a property
(D) To interview a job applicant

170. Who most likely is Mr. Weinberg?

(A) A prospective client
(B) A potential supplier
(C) A financial consultant
(D) A previous co-worker

171. At 3:37 P.M., what does Mr. Smiley mean when he writes, "That's all of us had in mind"?

(A) All of the writers have to give a presentation on Wednesday.
(B) All of the writers were planning to leave after having dinner together.
(C) Some of the writers will meet Mr. Carlito before Tuesday.
(D) One of the writers will leave earlier than the others.

GO ON TO THE NEXT PAGE

Bradford Inquirer — Business Profile: Salinger Surfwear

Two years ago, Salinger Surfwear was nearly out of business. It had some loyal customers, but sales were far too low to sustain the company for more than a half year. As the situation became more and more apparent, several of the company's leaders left for more promising positions. These included chief designer, Carrie Heart, and head of marketing, Steve Pinochet. They were replaced by Dean Manos and Helen Frente respectively. — [1] — .

Neither Mr. Manos nor Ms. Frente had any experience in leading as both had graduated from university just one year earlier. — [2] — . Nevertheless, their energy, enthusiasm, courage, and newly acquired skills made them the perfect team to turn the company's fortunes around. Within four months, sales were at a 10-year high, and the company was having trouble filling the orders coming from both here and overseas.

The main reason for the success has been attributed to an idea that came from the new head of marketing. They sent junior employees out to film young surfers and skateboarders in the area. — [3] — . The videos included interviews and the participants were offered free clothes in return for their time. The videos were posted online and became an overnight hit, and the clothing, which had been newly designed by Mr. Manos, drew more and more attention as days and weeks passed. Slowly but surely, sales improved.

This week, the brand opened its first store at Atlantic Fair Shopping Center. — [4] — . Sales have been so high that the staff has been having trouble stocking the shelves with enough merchandise.

172. What is the purpose of the article?

(A) To explain how employee changes affected a company's earnings

(B) To describe a company's new clothing designs

(C) To report an expected change in a company's leadership

(D) To announce the launch of a new product line

173. What is true about Salinger Surfwear?

(A) It was founded by Carrie Heart.

(B) It sells its merchandise online.

(C) It has international customers.

(D) It has its merchandise produced locally.

174. Who suggested starting an online video channel?

(A) Helen Frente

(B) Carrie Heart

(C) Steve Pinochet

(D) Dean Manos

175. In which of the positions marked [1], [2], [3], and [4] does the following sentence best belong?

"According to its sales assistants, it has been a hectic few days."

(A) [1]

(B) [2]

(C) [3]

(D) [4]

GO ON TO THE NEXT PAGE

To:	Colin Freeman <cfreeman@hhmachinery.com>
From:	Rhonda Jones <rjones@hhmachinery.com>
Date:	September 27
Subject:	Update
Attachment:	🔗 VBIblank

Hi Colin,

At the end of last week, I was shown the revenue reports for the last six months. I was very pleased to find that your branch has beaten its previous best and has become HH Machinery Rental's most profitable location. I put this down to the efforts of you and your excellent staff. I have a couple of requests for the Verisdale branch. First, I would like you to accept a visit from the managers of some of the other branches. Please show them around and explain what you have been doing to achieve such excellent results.

Second, I understand that you are currently understocked on some kinds of machinery. I am planning to have surplus items transported from other offices around the state. It is also possible that you have some inventory that you do not need. If so, please let me know and I will consider distributing it to where it can do the most good. You can send me that information by filling in the required details in the attached spreadsheet.

Sincerely,

Rhonda Jones
General Manager — HH Machinery Rental

Inventory Tracking Form — HH Machinery Rental

Item	Quantity	Origin	Destination	Date of Arrival (Estimated)
Frontend loader	2	Stanthorpe	Verisdale	October 10
Cherry picker	1	Camden	Verisdale	October 12
Backhoe	1	Verisdale	Camden	October 19
Skid-steer loader	3	Camden	Stanthorpe	October 21

Unfortunately rental of power tools has been very limited across all of our locations. This is most likely because of the recent drop in the purchase price of such items as cheap imports have flooded the market. The products we have are excellent quality and the resale value is likely to be high. The company's entire inventory of these items will be sold to Brady's Used Machinery at the end of the year. All store managers will be instructed to send their entire stock to Brady's Used Machinery's head office in Brisbane by December 10.

176. What is one purpose of the e-mail?

(A) To commend employees
(B) To recommend a procedure
(C) To announce a new policy
(D) To suggest an advertising strategy

177. What is Mr. Freeman required to do?

(A) Reduce department spending
(B) Attend a weekend workshop
(C) Review a product design
(D) Share ideas with other branches

178. What is the attachment included with the e-mail?

(A) A product catalog
(B) A spreadsheet
(C) A photograph
(D) A revenue report

179. What is most likely true about the backhoe?

(A) It was in need of some repairs.
(B) It was purchased a long time ago.
(C) It is not needed by Mr. Freeman.
(D) It is not in working order.

180. What does the company intend to do with its power tools?

(A) Offer discount rental rates
(B) Advertise in an industry publication
(C) Sell them to a second-hand store
(D) Export them to another country

GO ON TO THE NEXT PAGE

Rosemont — On July 21 and 22, Rosemont will once again be hosting the Rosemont Country Music Festival. Every year since its inception some 40 years ago, the festival has grown. The first festival occupied only one stage and we hosted only five musical acts. This year we will have more than 100 artists performing on seven different stages. The main stage is, as it has always been, the one in Kingsmith Square on William Street. Workers have already begun assembling the stands for audience seating. This year, the city council has requested seating for more than 5,000 people. Acts that will be performing there include The Harry Wonder 5, The Heartbreakers, and Vavoom. So that we do not have a repeat of last year's unfortunate cancellations, a shelter is being erected over the stands and the stage itself.

Festival organizers have been encouraging local bands to enter a song contest as part of the festival. Traditionally, the contest has been held on the second day of the festival. Organizers say they will have to hold the event over two days if there are more entrants than last time. That may or may not happen, as last year saw a record number of entrants. The contest will be held at The Old Rosemont Hall on Sparrow Street. The event is sponsored by Radio 6TG, which will be supplying the $4,000 prize money for the winner.

To register for the competition, check the performance schedule, or find out anything more you need to know about the festival, visit the official Web site at www.rosemontcmf.org.

The Rosemont City Council Presents
The Annual Rosemont Country Music Festival
July 21 and 22

Enjoy the free performances at the main stage in Kingsmith Square from 11:00 A.M. to 7:00 P.M. on both days.

Register to take part in any one of 20 workshops by professional country music singers.

You can purchase tickets for performances at the other six stages from the usual ticket sellers. Ticket prices vary and specific information is only available from the respective promoters. Bands include Lumberjacks, Cloudplay, The Heartbreakers, and The Dudley Brothers.

The 21st Rosemont Residents' Song Competition is being held as part of the festival and this year the competition will be held over both days. Its results will be announced on July 22 on the main stage.

www.rosemontcmf.org.

181. What is indicated about the Rosemont Country Music Festival?

(A) Tickets are available online.
(B) It was first held at Kingsmith Square.
(C) It is expected to draw fewer people than before.
(D) Performers are all from the Rosemont area.

182. What is most likely true about last year's festival?

(A) Tickets were available from the Web site.
(B) It was held in another town.
(C) The preparations went over budget.
(D) There was some inclement weather.

183. According to the article, how can people get more information about the festival?

(A) By accessing the festival Web site
(B) By calling the organizers
(C) By subscribing to a newsletter
(D) By listening to a radio program

184. Which band will provide both free and ticketed performances?

(A) The Heartbreakers
(B) Lumberjacks
(C) The Harry Wonder 5
(D) Cloudplay

185. What is implied about the 21st Rosemont Residents' Song Competition?

(A) All performances will be given on the main stage.
(B) It has received a record number of applicants.
(C) Its venue was changed after the article was published.
(D) There is a registration fee for participants.

GO ON TO THE NEXT PAGE

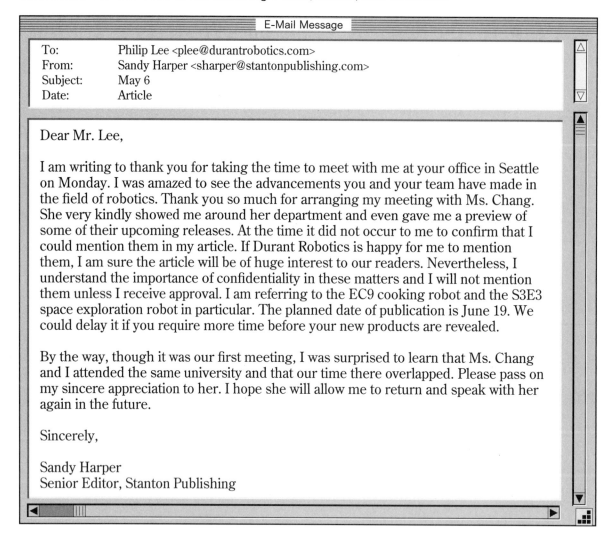

E-Mail Message

To: Philip Lee <plee@durantrobotics.com>
From: Sandy Harper <sharper@stantonpublishing.com>
Subject: May 6
Date: Article

Dear Mr. Lee,

I am writing to thank you for taking the time to meet with me at your office in Seattle on Monday. I was amazed to see the advancements you and your team have made in the field of robotics. Thank you so much for arranging my meeting with Ms. Chang. She very kindly showed me around her department and even gave me a preview of some of their upcoming releases. At the time it did not occur to me to confirm that I could mention them in my article. If Durant Robotics is happy for me to mention them, I am sure the article will be of huge interest to our readers. Nevertheless, I understand the importance of confidentiality in these matters and I will not mention them unless I receive approval. I am referring to the EC9 cooking robot and the S3E3 space exploration robot in particular. The planned date of publication is June 19. We could delay it if you require more time before your new products are revealed.

By the way, though it was our first meeting, I was surprised to learn that Ms. Chang and I attended the same university and that our time there overlapped. Please pass on my sincere appreciation to her. I hope she will allow me to return and speak with her again in the future.

Sincerely,

Sandy Harper
Senior Editor, Stanton Publishing

Durant Robotics Opens New Facility

By Sandy Harper
June 19

Durant Robotics is one of the most exciting companies in the robotics industry and their new facility in Bathurst is an architectural wonder. The head of design, Ms. Luisa Chang, is heading up a team of some of the world's most talented robotics engineers with a view to developing the next generation of robots, which will likely touch most of our daily lives. The facility employs some 300 people in its various departments including research, design, engineering, marketing, and production.

Durant Robotics' CEO, Philip Lee, stated that he expected the company to start mass producing robots for purchase by the general public within the two years. With this goal in mind, they are planning a new production facility in nearby Redmond. Work on that project should start early next year and they will be employing staff for the factory in late February.

From the desk of Luisa Chang

August

Sunday	Monday	Tuesday	Wednesday	Thursday	Friday	Saturday
12	13 Day off	14 2 P.M. Departmental meeting	15 Orientation for new staff members	16 EC9 Product Launch	17 Freemantle Robotics Conference	18 Meeting with Tim Rice at HTO

186. What is one purpose of the e-mail?

(A) To express gratitude for an introduction
(B) To announce the launch of a new publication
(C) To request an introduction to a supplier
(D) To congratulate a colleague on a promotion

187. What does Ms. Harper hope to do in the future?

(A) Take a position at Durant Robotics
(B) Bring forward the date of publication
(C) Purchase products from Durant Robotics
(D) Have another interview with Ms. Chang

188. What is suggested about Ms. Harper?

(A) She decided to delay the date of publication.
(B) She was asked not to write about certain technologies.
(C) She received assistance from her editor.
(D) She wrote the article as a freelance writer.

189. To whom did Ms. Harper send her e-mail?

(A) A company president
(B) A customer service officer
(C) A product designer
(D) A journalist

190. What will Ms. Chang do on August 16?

(A) Demonstrate a flying robot for a client
(B) Take a follow-up meeting with a journalist
(C) Introduce a cooking robot to the market
(D) Make a presentation at an industry convention

GO ON TO THE NEXT PAGE

Maxwell Adventures

We have an amazing holiday adventure package for the travelers looking for something new, and it's for as little as $600. This is amazing value for a week unlike anything you've ever experienced. Your first and last night will be enjoyed in Spandau Valley's only first-class hotel. The remaining five nights will be spent in the Canadian wilderness with a highly trained survival expert. You will learn to fish for salmon in a pristine mountain stream, build a camp in uninhabited forests, and climb mountains to take in breathtaking views of the Burroughs Range and beyond.

For an additional $130, you can purchase airfare from anywhere in Canada to Bania, which is only a short train journey to the beautiful Spandau Valley.

To learn more or to reserve a spot, check out the Maxwell Adventures Web site at www.maxwelladventures.com.

E-mail

From:	Clementine Day <cday@novastar.com>
To:	Jim Maxwell <jm@maxwelladventures.com>
Subject:	Spandau Valley
Date:	August 12

I would like to commend Maxwell Adventures for putting together this excellent package. They managed to get me an airplane ticket, even though I asked them to get it at the last minute. Moreover, the tour was excellent. If this is the standard for Maxwell Adventures, I would love to purchase another package for next year. Naturally, I would like to do something different from what I just did. Perhaps a river rafting tour would be an interesting option for your company to offer. I promise I will be among the first people to make a reservation should you decide to offer such a package.

I'm planning on advising some friends to take part so I was wondering if you have any special discount offers they could take advantage of.

Thanks,
Clementine Day

Reviews of Maxwell Adventures
Rating: ★★★★☆ Wonderful!
By: Clementine Day

I had a great time on this tour. Maxwell Adventures is a great little tour company run by some very professional and knowledgeable people. I recently took part in a rafting trip down the Dawson River and it was one of the most enjoyable experiences of my life. This is a new tour and I was invited to take part as a rehearsal for the guides and organizers. The only shortcoming was that the accommodation was not as nice as that of their other tour.

191. What is NOT mentioned as an attraction of the Spandau Valley?

(A) A pure river
(B) Luxury accommodation
(C) Traditional architecture
(D) Stunning scenery

192. What is one purpose of the e-mail?

(A) To commend a specific employee
(B) To reserve a seat on a vehicle
(C) To explain the reason for a delay
(D) To inquire about special prices

193. What is suggested about Ms. Day?

(A) She had taken part in the tour before.
(B) She paid a supplemental fee.
(C) She viewed the advertisement on television.
(D) She lives near the town of Bania.

194. In the advertisement, the word "spot" in paragraph 3, line 1 is closest in meaning to

(A) seat
(B) mark
(C) deal
(D) cause

195. What is most likely true about Maxwell Adventures?

(A) It has been mentioned in a television documentary.
(B) It employs people who speak different languages.
(C) It offers tours outside Canada.
(D) It adopted Ms. Day's idea.

GO ON TO THE NEXT PAGE

From:	Igor Popov <ipopov@goldburgassociates.com>
To:	Sally Winger <swinger@donaldadvertisinggroup.com>
Subject:	Sheffield Advertising Awards
Date:	March 13

Dear Ms. Winger,

It is my great pleasure to inform you that your company is one of those nominated for this year's Sheffield Advertising Awards. It is very important to the organizers that all nominees be in attendance at the ceremony. To remain in contention for a prize, a member of the staff of Donald Advertising must attend the event. While we would prefer it if a member of the team involved in the production attended, any member of the staff may accept the prize. In both cases, it is expected that award recipients will give a short acceptance speech. Please reply to this e-mail with the name of the person who will be attending the event by March 23. Otherwise, the nomination will be passed on to the creators of another of the qualifying advertisements.

Please visit the Sheffield Advertising Awards Web site at www.sheffieldaa.com to purchase tickets. Due to the modest size of the Hanson Convention Center, you are limited to two representatives for each nomination. Each ticket costs $120. The awards ceremony includes a number of speeches as well as entertainment from local artists. This year we will be entertained by local comedian, Jerry Wiseacre.

Best regards,
Igor Popov

Sheffield Advertising Awards Ceremony
Hanson Convention Center, June 12, 6:00 P.M.
(Tentative Schedule as of March 20)

Time	Presentation	Speaker (s)	Award Recipient
6:00	Dinner		N/A
7:00	Award for Greatest Sales Influence	Barry Day and Tina Sales	To be announced
7:15	Award for Best Use of Music	Valerie Chang	To be announced
7:30	Award for Best Special Effects	Jose Ramirez	To be announced
7:45	Entertainment — The Comedy of Holly Durant	Holly Durant	N/A
8:15	Award for Best Direction	Cloe Tanaka	To be announced
8:30	Keynote Speech: Truth in Advertising	Tim Clement, BTR Consultants	N/A

https://www.sheffieldaa.com/reservations

Sheffield Advertising Awards
— Reservations Page —

Name of Ticket Holder	Company	Preferred Table	Price
Sally Winger	Donald Advertising	Table B	$120.00
Ralph Xenedes	Donald Advertising	Table B	$120.00
Jill Forbes	Donald Advertising	Table B	$120.00
Tobe Salinger	Donald Advertising	Table B	$120.00
		TOTAL	$480.00

PURCHASE

196. What is a purpose of the e-mail?

(A) To request permission to host a ceremony
(B) To notify an award nominee
(C) To assign duties to an organizer
(D) To propose a change to competition guidelines

197. According to the e-mail, what is true about award recipients?

(A) They must prepare an acceptance message.
(B) They must be those who were directly involved in its production.
(C) They are chosen by the organizing committee.
(D) They can only be nominated in one category.

198. In the e-mail, the phrase "passed on" in paragraph 1, line 7 is closest in meaning to

(A) rejected
(B) affirmed
(C) transferred
(D) revealed

199. What is suggested about the awards ceremony?

(A) The audience was too large for the original venue.
(B) A number of nominations were changed.
(C) A change was made to the entertainment.
(D) An award was presented by the previous winner.

200. What is most likely true about Donald Advertising?

(A) It has won awards at the event in previous years.
(B) It was asked to organize next year's event.
(C) It is known for its use of special effects.
(D) It was nominated for multiple awards.

TEST1〜4（Day53〜60）の学習の進め方

下の表を参照して、Dayごとに指定した問題を制限時間以内で解いてください。
解き終わったら、学習日と解答時間を記入しましょう。

Day53	TEST1 全問
学習日 /	Q147-200 4/5 回目
	制限時間　54 分　解答時間　　　　　分

Day54	TEST2 全問
学習日 /	Q147-200 4/5 回目
	制限時間　54 分　解答時間　　　　　分

Day55	TEST3 全問
学習日 /	Q147-200 4/5 回目
	制限時間　54 分　解答時間　　　　　分

Day56	TEST4 全問
学習日 /	Q147-200 4/5 回目
	制限時間　54 分　解答時間　　　　　分

Day57	TEST1 全問
学習日 /	Q147-200 5/5 回目
	制限時間　54 分　解答時間　　　　　分

Day58	TEST2 全問
学習日 /	Q147-200 5/5 回目
	制限時間　54 分　解答時間　　　　　分

Day59	TEST3 全問
学習日 /	Q147-200 5/5 回目
	制限時間　54 分　解答時間　　　　　分

Day60	TEST4 全問
学習日 /	Q147-200 5/5 回目
	制限時間　54 分　解答時間　　　　　分

Day53 〜 60 は最後の総仕上げです。
Day60 まで終わると、すべてのテストを 5 回解いたことになります！

この冊子は取り外してご利用いただけます。